DR. CHRISTIAN HARFOUCHE

MIRACLES

DR. CHRISTIAN HARFOUCHE
MIRACLES

Foreword by
Dr. Morris Cerullo

Global Revival Distribution
Pensacola, Florida

Unless otherwise indicated, all scriptural references are from the *New King James Version* of the Bible.

Verses marked KJV are taken from the Holy Bible, *King James Version*, Cambridge, 1769.

Verses marked The Message are taken from *The Message*. Copyright © 1993, 1994, 1995, 1996, 2000, 2001, 2002. Used by permission of NavPress Publishing Group.

Verses marked NKJV are taken from the *New King James Version*. Copyright © 1982 by Thomas Nelson, Inc. Used by permission. All rights reserved.

Verses marked NLT are taken from the Holy Bible, *New Living Translation*, copyright © 1996. Used by permission of Tyndale House Publishers, Inc., Wheaton, Illinois 60189. All rights reserved.

Versus marked Wuest are taken from the The New Testament An Expanded Translation by Kenneth S. Wuest Copyright in 1961 by Wm. B. Eerdmans Publishing Company.

For emphasis, the author has placed selected words from Bible quotations in italics and/or parenthesis.

Miracles
ISBN 1-888966-70-X

Published by:
Global Revival Distribution
4317 N. Palafox St.
Pensacola, FL 32505
www.globalrevival.com

Cover & interior design and book production by:
M.E.D.I.A. Group
421 North Palafox Street, Pensacola, FL 32501
Cover illustration is protected by the 1976 United States Copyright Act.
Copyright © 2004 by M.E.D.I.A. Group, Inc

Copyright © 2005 Dr. Christian Harfouche. All rights reserved. Reproduction of text in whole or part without the express written consent by the author is not permitted and is unlawful according to the 1976 United States Copyright Act.
Printed in the United States of America

*"In an age of **"I'll believe it when I see it"**, Dr. Harfouche challenges every believer with his inspirational teaching on miracles backed with powerful demonstration of the Word. I encourage every one who wants to be used by God in a mighty way in these last days to pick up this book and apply its principles to your life."*

–**Dr. R.W. Schambach**
Schambach Ministries

"Dr. Harfouche is a proof producer, of the highest caliber. Always on the cutting edge, he is training a generation to perform signs and wonders for the Kingdom of God. Dr. Harfouche doesn't practice miracles… he sees them everyday of his life."

–**Dr. John Avanzini**
John Avanzini Ministries

"The miracle and prophetic ministry of Dr. Christian Harfouche has profoundly impacted our churches in South Africa. During the years of apartheid, his regular visits to the nation assisted believers in uniting as one family and, thereby, the destiny of our nation was affected. His ministry was instrumental in uniting us as a nation."

–**Pastor Neville McDonald**
Healing Word International

"I have known Dr. Harfouche for many years. His life and ministry are a Godly example to all of us. He has been in ministry over 25 years and is one of the finest teachers on faith and miracles that I have known. I know that his book will be a blessing to everyone who reads it and I would recommend it to anyone."

"Dr. Harfouche, Maggie and I want to thank you for your friendship over the years. In your over 25 years of ministry, you and Robin have truly demonstrated integrity, godliness and the love of God. Your teachings on faith and tithing are some of the best I have heard. It is a privilege and an honor to call you friends."

–**Dr. Norvel L. Hayes**
Norvel Hayes Ministries

"Rarely does intensity and joy exist happily together but when I think of Dr. Christian and Robin Harfouche their effervescent joy always comes together. I celebrate with them 25 years of miracles and ministry. May the next 25 years be just as intense and just a joyful."

–**Tommy Tenney**
GodChasers.Network

"The Key to the miracle ministry of my dear friend Dr. Christian Harfouche, is that for 25 years He has always pointed people to the healer - our precious savior Jesus. In a day and age when many draw people to themselves and lift up and exalt themselves. God uses Dr. Harfouche to teach practically and with a special anointing to see Jesus and raise up miracle workers for the 21st century. "

–**Dr. Rodney Howard-Browne**
Revival Ministries International

"Dr. Harfouche is an able minister of the Gospel of Jesus Christ, uniquely qualified to minister on the subject of miracles and healing. Keep going Doc... we need you".

–Pastor Randy Gilbert
Faith Landmark Ministries

"Congratulations on passing the 25 year mark for a fruitful and productive ministry. In the Bible, the number 25 is for the word grace - five times over. You have been gifted, enabled and graced for a signs and wonders ministry. Christian and Robin - In old Testament days, 25 years were spent in acquiring knowledge and learning. The next 25 years were spent in abundant fruit bearing. I predict according to Job 11:6 (NKJV), that your ministry will start doubling in results."

–Dr. Dick Mills
Dick Mills Ministries

We dedicate this book to our father in the faith, Dr. Lester Sumrall.

We thank God for the day when he laid his precious hands upon us... and prophesied that God would give us the Spirit of wisdom and understanding that He gave to Joshua... to lead the Children of Israel into the Promised Land.

I'll never forget when Dr. Lester Sumrall prayed that the Lord would impart to my wife and I... the same Spirit of faith that God had given him through the lineage of other great Generals of Faith.

Dr. Christian Harfouche

Drs. Christian and Robin Harfouche were ordained personally by Dr. Lester Sumrall

Dedication

*This book is dedicated
to the 400,000 Miracle Workers
and the Final Harvest of Souls.*

Contents

Foreword	*xvii*
Chapter 1	
TAUGHT BY GOD	1
Chapter 2	
SEE IT. SAY IT. DO IT.	25
Chapter 3	
GOD'S DIVINE ABILITY IS YOURS	43
Chapter 4	
KNOWING GOD	65
Chapter 5	
THE PRICE OF POWER	87
Chapter 6	
THE MYSTERY OF GODLINESS	109
Chapter 7	
THE TABERNACLE OF POWER	137

Chapter 8
    THE SUPPLY OF THE SPIRIT   *155*

Chapter 9
    THE WORDS OF THIS LIFE   *183*

Chapter 10
    HEARING GOD   *209*

Chapter 11
    YIELDING TO THE ANOINTING   *239*

Chapter 12
    POWER FOR THE HOUR   *259*

Chapter 13
    POSSESSING SUPERNATURAL POWER   *281*

Chapter 14
    THE POWER OF HIS GLORY   *313*

Chapter 15
    UNLEASH THE POWER OF FAITH   *335*

Chapter 16
    RELEASE YOUR FAITH   *363*

Foreword

It is my great joy to be able to write a foreword to Dr. Harfouche's *Miracles book*.

It is one thing to write about miracles - many writers can. But.....it is another to write with a pen in hand - when that hand has felt the power of miracles.

Christian Harfouche is truly one whom our Almighty God has chosen - chosen to anoint with the giftings of being able to manifest HIS miracles -

Under this mighty anointing, Christian inspires the reader to rise up - You can be mightily used by God to lay hands upon the sick, speak the Word, and experience, "These signs shall follow them that believe." Mark 16:17a

As Christian says, "You are the walking revelation of Jesus Christ!" If you ask anything in my Name, that will I do that the Father may be glorified in the Son.

—Dr. Morris Cerullo, President
Morris Cerullo World Evangelism

Chapter 1

Taught by God

The pages of history are filled with Old Testament Saints who yearned to fill your shoes!

> However, when He, the Spirit of truth, has come, *He will guide you into all truth...*
>
> John 16:13a

The Holy Spirit is your teacher. He is your educator – *your tutor in the things of God.* As your personal guide in this life, He is deeply committed to leading you into *all* Truth. The things He reveals to you are designed to change your life. They are designed to perfect you in the image of Christ and to grow you up in God from the inside out. As the Spirit of God leads you into all truth, the ability and the power of God will rise within you and shine powerfully through your life. You are the walking revelation of Jesus Christ! He lives in you and moves through you.

> **But the anointing which you have received from Him *abides in you*, and you do not need that anyone teach you; but as the same anointing teaches you concerning all things, and is true, and is not a lie, and just as it has taught you, *you will abide in Him.***
>
> **1 John 2:27**

You live in God and God lives in you. There is an *unction* from the Holy One that resides in you and leads you into a comprehensive understanding of divine truth. As a child of God, you have been anointed by the Lord to understand and to bear witness to Truth. Your spirit and the Holy Spirit in you will bear witness together to the things of God.

> **And He Himself gave some to be apostles, some prophets, some evangelists, and some pastors and teachers, for the equipping of the saints for the work of ministry, for the edifying of the body of Christ...**
>
> Eph 4:11-12

Jesus Christ is committed to perfecting His Body. As such, He has raised up men and women of God as five-fold ministry gifts—*as apostles, prophets, evangelists, pastors and teachers*. These ministry gifts have been given to build the Body of Christ and to perfect the Saints for the work of the ministry. Each of these five-fold ministry gifts has been given the supernatural ability to teach the Word of God to God's people.

> **But the anointing which you have received from Him abides in you, and *you do not need that anyone teach you...***
>
> 1 John 2:27a

If God has given the five-fold ministry to perfect His Saints, then what did the Apostle John mean when he wrote, "*...you do not need that anyone teach you?*" This great apostle wasn't campaigning for the end of the teaching ministry in the Church! He was simply instructing the born again child of God to remain *true* to Truth. You do no need to be taught by the skeptic, by the atheist or by the intellectual! You are led forth by the Spirit of Truth. You have a medium, an avenue of teaching, which comes *through the agency of the Holy Spirit.*

Training Your Spirit Man

It is written in the prophets, "And they shall all be taught by God."

John 6:45a

Whether you realize it or not, you are living in the most powerful dispensation of all time. It is during this hour that you have the privilege and the opportunity to be *personally taught* by the Holy Spirit. The pages of history are filled with Old Testament Saints who yearned to fill *your* shoes! They desired to hear the voice of God directly and to be led by His presence personally.

There was a day in human history when the average person wasn't taught by God. They didn't have access to His presence like you do now. Instead, they were taught by the letter of the law. This was their schoolmaster. This was their teacher. Without God on the *inside*, they had to be directed by the letter on the *outside*. Now that Jesus has been made available to every person, there is an unction, or an anointing, that is active on the inside of each and every believer. Instead of living by the law, you can be led by the anointing within.

The anointing within abides in you. It abides in your spirit. God has called you to live and move as a spiritual being. This isn't a passive experience. This is an active walk—a daily experience. Many times, Christians forget or perhaps fail to prioritize their spiritual growth. Instead of nurturing their spirit man through teaching and training in the Holy Ghost, they settle back into the easy chair of life—forgetting *whom* they are filled with. Many of us will train our intellect and our natural body for greatness, endurance and strength—but what about you spirit? As a matter of fact, you may have a head full of information, but do you walk in the power of revelation? These are questions that you need to ask yourself. Your spiritual growth is far too important to neglect!

The gifts of the Spirit are God-given endowments. They are divine packages that have been designed to promote you and to help you become all that Jesus has called you to be. Despite popular theology, Jesus did *not* come to Earth to become your example! That may be a shock to you, but religion has lied to the Church for far too long. Jesus did not come to be an example. He came to destroy the works of the devil! He came to pay your price in full so that you might have an experience called the new birth! When you step into this experience, Jesus is no longer your example. He is the new life that lives *in* you and *through* you!

> **Dear brothers and sisters, when I was with you I couldn't talk to you as I would to mature Christians. I had to talk as though you belonged to this world or as though you were infants in the Christian life.**
>
> **1 Corinthians 3:1 NLT**

Just because you're born again doesn't mean you're spiritual! The Apostle Paul told the seemingly "mature" Corinthian church that he had to teach them as if they were infants in Christ. In other words, they *should* have been mature, but because of neglect or indifference, they still needed the elementary teachings of Christ. You see, in order for Jesus to be big in you, you have to develop your spirit man.

So you want to operate in the miraculous? You desire to live in the realm of signs and wonders—that's great! That is *exactly* what God has called you to, but it's *not* an automatic experience. Just because you are born by the Spirit of God, doesn't mean that you are exempt from growing in God. Growing is a process. It's work! You have to nurture and exercise your spirit. If your spirit man is not developed—if you are not strong—you are going to live under the domination of the natural world. There are far too many children of God that are overridden by the natural dimension. If your desire is to see the miracles of God and the power of God manifested in your life, then you will have to train your spirit man to flow in that experience.

Place your hands on your spirit and say this:

> *I need to train my spirit man! I need to invest in, develop, and edify the spirit part of me. As I dedicate myself to this exercise, I will communicate and walk in harmony and fellowship with the Holy Ghost.*

Ignorance is Not Bliss

Now concerning spiritual *gifts*, brethren, I do not want you to be ignorant...

I Corinthians 12:1

The word *gifts* is italicized in the King James Version. A better rendering of this word in the original Greek is *spiritual matters, spiritual things*, or *spirituals*.

Paul was talking to *brethren*. He was talking to born again Saints, children of God. It is likely that these brethren were saved, baptized with water and filled with the Holy Ghost. In fact, we know that they were speaking in tongues fluently, so fluently that they all spoke at the same time! There was complete chaos in the Corinthian church! Not only did the Corinthians stand up in church and give messages in tongues at the same time, but there was no interpreter! They did not lack for spiritual gifts, but rather, Paul had to teach them how to utilize the gifts of God for the purpose of edifying someone else!

If Paul was telling brethren not to be ignorant about spiritual things, it is the logical conclusion that brethren *can* be ignorant about spiritual things. Many brethren are well acquainted with what's happening with Sister Bucket-Mouth and Brother Gossip. They may know what's happening in the natural realm, yet God wants His Church well acquainted with *spiritual matters*. There are even *leaders* in the Body of Christ that are ignorant about spiritual things! If the child of God is only acquainted with a natural education and has not been schooled in the Spirit, they will not be able to make a deposit into your spirit man. They may be able to feed your intellect, but they will not be able to produce mature Christians.

How do you become spiritual? How do you know if you are mature in God? A spiritually mature believer is *more interested* in ministering to others than in seeking ministry for themselves. This is not to say that you are no longer in need of a teacher or ministry. It simply means that your greatest priority is to help others. Instead of walking around as an introspective creature, you are looking out for your brethren. You are no longer a believer that thinks in desperation, *"Oh Lord, if I don't get ministered to, I may not last the whole day for Jesus!"* You have grown beyond that. If you are a spiritual person, you will be used by the Holy Spirit to edify someone else.

> **My people are destroyed for lack of knowledge.**
>
> Hosea 4:6

There are consequences to ignorance. It has never been God's will for man to be ignorant about spiritual things! If you are failing to see His power manifested in your life, then make a quality decision to pursue spiritual growth and to grow up in the Spirit. When you do, His power and His anointing will flood your life with spiritual deposits.

A Mandate from Jesus

> **Now, there are diversities of gifts, but the same Spirit. There are differences of administrations, but the same Lord. There are diversities of operations, but it is the same God which worketh all in all. But the manifestation of the Spirit is given to every man to profit withal.**
>
> 1 Corinthians 12:4-7 KJV

Like Paul, it is my desire to not only feed you the Word, impart information to you, and give you revelation, but I want to give you a *mandate* from Jesus. If you follow that mandate, you will develop your spirit man daily and begin to see Christ alive in your life.

Jesus Christ is still the miracle worker *today*! He is still a winner *today*! As a matter of fact, He's more of a winner on this side of the cross than He ever was on the other side! All power in Heaven and in Earth was given to Him when He rose from the dead!

As He is, so are we in this world.

1 John 4:17b KJV

We are as He is. Is this metaphorical? Is it allegorical? No, we are as He is when we are not ignorant about spiritual things! We are *not* as He is when we're ignorant about the Word of God. We are *not* as He is if we hear the Word and don't do it!

You can have a library full of books on prayer. You may be able to quote generals in the faith on the subject of prayer! However, if you don't pray, you are ignorant on the subject of prayer. You may lecture better than anyone else on prayer, but if you don't practice prayer, you're void of its benefits and impartations.

As He is resurrected…
As He is victorious…
As He is triumphant…
As He is rich…
As He is wise…

So are *we* in this present world!

For the kingdom of God is not in word but in power.

1 Corinthians 4:20

The Bible says that the Kingdom of God comes in power. It comes through the power of the Holy Ghost. Once the power of the Holy Ghost is operative in your life, then the things that pertain to Christ become evident and viable in your life.

One Gift—Nine Manifestations

Now there are *different kinds of spiritual gifts*,

> **but it is the same Holy Spirit who is the source of them all.**
>
> **1 Corinthians 12:4 NLT**

There are *different* distributions of spiritual gifts, but they originate from the *same* Spirit. This version of the Bible refers to it as *gifts*, but a better word is *manifestations*. A manifestation is an unveiling, a coming forth, a revelation, a display, or an exhibition of the Holy Spirit. This great unveiling will take place within you! The hidden Spirit who lives in you will come forth through you in manifestation. The world will see the proof of His indwelling and they will be drawn to the glory that emanates from within you.

> **Then Peter said to them, "Repent, and let every one of you be baptized in the name of Jesus Christ for the remission of sins; and you shall receive the gift of the Holy Spirit."**
>
> **Acts 2:38**

Technically, there is one gift—the gift of the Holy Spirit. However, there are nine ways the Holy Spirit manifests Himself in the life of a believer. Once you receive *the gift*, it's an all-inclusive package. When the Source Himself lives within you, you can be sure that you are well equipped with all of His assets!

There are some theologians who would say, *"Well, brother, we believe in the infilling of the Holy Spirit, but we don't believe everyone has the gift of tongues."* It's not that you receive the "gift of tongues" per se—*you actually receive the Holy Spirit*. His indwelling enables you to move and flow with God experientially.

> **For he who speaks in a tongue does not speak to men but to God, for no one understands him; however, in the spirit he speaks mysteries.... He who speaks in a tongue edifies himself...**
>
> **1 Corinthians 14:2, 4a**

When you pray in an unknown tongue, your spirit prays. You are edifying yourself and building yourself up on your most holy faith. We really don't have a "gift of tongues." We have the Holy Spirit who will reveal, or manifest, Himself through certain vessels in the form of diverse kinds of tongues. The Bible teaches that the one who gives a message in tongues should pray so that they might interpret their message as well.

We know that praying with other tongues is not a gift, but rather a sign because Jesus said, *"These signs shall follow them that believe"* (Mark 16:17, 18). He also said, *"In my name shall they cast out devils."* There is no gift of casting out devils! All believers are called to cast out devils! You are equipped to do so! Jesus also said, *"They shall lay hands on the sick, and they shall recover."* Did you know that there is no such gift as laying hands on the sick? It is a command – a mandate. It is the great commission! Every believer is called to lay hands on the sick and see them recover. *"They shall speak with new tongues."* Again, this experience belongs to every believer! It is simply the by-product of the indwelling.

> **Now there are diversities of gifts, but the same Spirit. And there are differences of administrations, but the same Lord. And there are diversities of operations, but it is the same God which worketh all in all. But the manifestation of the Spirit is given to every man to profit withal. For to one is given by the Spirit the word of wisdom; to another the word of knowledge by the same Spirit; To another faith by the same Spirit; to another the gifts of healing by the same Spirit; To another the working of miracles; to another prophecy; to another discerning of spirits; to another diverse kinds of tongues; to another the interpretation of tongues: But all these worketh that one and the self-same Spirit, dividing to every man severally as he will.**
>
> **1 Corinthians 12: 4-11 KJV**

The Bible is clear that there are diversities of manifestations but the same Spirit. In other words, the Holy Ghost will manifest Himself through different methods, but it's the *same* Holy Ghost.

You Have a Ministry!

"There are differences of administrations but the same Lord" (1 Corinthians 12:5). This means there are different distributions of various kinds of ministries!

Do *you* have a ministry?

"Ministry" doesn't just refer to the five-fold ministry. Every believer is a minister! A ministry is a *service*. It's the act of *ministering* to someone's need. Even if you're not an apostle, a prophet, an evangelist, a pastor, or a teacher—*you are a believer*. If you're a believer, then Jesus has called you to be a minister!

Jesus fulfilled the ministry of washing the feet of the disciples. He fulfilled the ministry of serving others. He fulfilled the ministry of being the burden bearer for others. There is a ministry in counseling. There is a ministry in comforting. There is a ministry in giving. It's so important to see this!

You are called to ministry. The very purpose of your existence it to let Jesus live *through* you! Whether He's living through you as the preacher or as the believer who prefers others above themselves, it makes no difference! It's still the same Jesus who is living through you. Paul said, *"For me to live is Christ"* (Philippians 1:21)! Like Paul, your life in Christ is ministry. Ministry is not just for the preacher in the pulpit, it's for every believer. There are *different* ministries—or services—but it's the *same* Lord. The same God called each of us. The same Jesus lives in every one of us. To be an effective minister, you must allow Jesus to minister in you and through you.

There are diversities of ministries and Jesus, filled with the Holy Ghost, fulfilled every one of them! For every *service* that God sanctioned, Jesus fulfilled it in His three and a half years of *ministry*. He was the best apostle that anyone could ever be. He was the best prophet that anyone could ever be. He was the best teacher, the best evangelist, the best pastor, the best rabbi, and the best friend that anyone could ever be. Jesus fulfilled His earthly ministry with complete and total perfection.

The Power in the Purpose

In Jesus' earthly ministry He did one thing that every one of us should learn from: He waited until the day He received the anointing. Wasn't Jesus the Son of God? Wasn't He the messenger from Heaven? He was and is all of these things, yet even *Jesus* waited until He received the anointing.

When God calls you, He gives you the Spirit to empower you to fulfill your purpose. It would be ignorant to have a purpose, but then to never learn about the power that backs it up. There is power in your life to fulfill your purpose!

Many Christians are frustrated in life. They are unfulfilled because they are not doing what they were created to do. These believers know that they need to be doing *something* for God. They may even desire to do great things for the Kingdom, but they ignore the power that was sent to equip them for their purpose. You need power to do what God has called you to do!

> **But *you shall receive power (or the anointing) when the Holy Spirit has come upon you*; and you shall be witnesses to Me in Jerusalem, and in all Judea and Samaria, and to the end of the earth."**
>
> **Acts 1:8**
> (parentheses added by author)

Do you want to learn how to be a witness? *"The manifestation of the Spirit is given to every man to profit withal"* (1 Corinthians 12:7). The word *manifestation* is only applicable when something unseen becomes visible. For example, someone could be possessed by a devil and no one may know about it. That same person could come to a church service and suddenly fall down under the power of God and start foaming at the mouth. At this point, everyone will see the manifestation of that spirit. A manifestation is something revealed.

Many Christians have the Holy Ghost *incognito*. He's undercover in their lives. He's undisclosed. It's not that He's absent, but the believer lacks the visible evidence of His life and power. Why is this?

The Holy Spirit living in *you* will never benefit *another* unless there is a manifestation of His presence in your life. The evidence of Heaven lives on the inside of you! You are filled with the fullness of God, but how will the world know it if they can't see it? In other words, if a person has the Holy Spirit, but never yields to Him, they are simply living carnal lives. A person like this cannot be an effective minister of the Gospel. God has no room to manifest Himself in them!

God won't take over your will. He won't drive you and He won't violate your free will. Only *you* have the key to release His power and influence in your life. You can lock the Lord away in your heart or you can yield to the outflow of His power and glory. The decision is yours.

The God-Kind of Faith

> **But the manifestation of the Spirit is given to every man to profit withal.**
>
> **1 Corinthians 12:7 KJV**

Every person is given spiritual gifts with the expectation that they will benefit another. A spiritual gift is for the common good.

> **For to one is given the word of wisdom through the Spirit, to another the word of knowledge through the same Spirit, to another *faith*...**
>
> **1 Corinthians 12:8, 9a**

There is a spiritual gift called *special* faith, or *great* faith. It's literally the "God kind of faith."

Some have said, *"I don't have the gift of faith. I can't believe God."* That's not true! If you're a believer, you can believe God *without a gift*. You're supernaturally equipped through your new nature to believe God. The act of believing God does not take a special manifestation of the Holy Spirit. It's your innate born again ability. Sometimes, however, a believer will require a special manifestation of the Spirit in order to step into *special* faith. This is the kind of faith that moves mountains! It's faith that is supernaturally turbo charged through a gift of the Holy Spirit.

If the Holy Spirit lives in you, then the manifold manifestation of His presence is available to provide you with the necessary spiritual equipment. However, if a child of God remains ignorant of the things of the Spirit, then they will not be able to partake of great faith or the fullness of His other gifts. The Holy Spirit indwells the believer so that He can supernaturally enable them to minister as the Christ-kind of person. It's not automatic, but it requires spiritual understanding and training. Ignorance will never move a mountain.

Do you believe that Jesus did what He did
by the power of the Holy Ghost?

Have you noticed that He never failed to see the
right gift manifested at the right time?

Do you wonder why He had the faith to raise the
dead when He needed it to raise the dead?

When He needed a word of knowledge, why did He
have a word of knowledge?

Jesus was informed. He was wise about spiritual things. Jesus was and is the most spiritual being the world has ever known. Some of you will subconsciously think, *"But He's God!"*

Then Jesus arrived from Nazareth, anointed by God with the Holy Spirit, ready for action. He went through the country helping people and healing everyone who was beaten down by the

Devil. He was able to do all this because God was with Him.

Acts 10:38 The Message

Jesus *emptied Himself* of his divine deity and became a man. The Bible says that He grew in favor with God and with man. *Jesus grew.* He grew as a man anointed by the Holy Ghost. As He grew, He increased in wisdom and stature. What method did Jesus use to grow spiritually? Jesus Christ—the Word Himself—studied the Word of God. He allowed the Spirit of God to teach Him and to build Him up as He prayed. Jesus developed sensitivity as a man to the things of the Spirit. In turn, He became the most spiritual person in the universe.

"But that was Jesus!"

"Most assuredly, I say to you, he who believes in Me, the works that I do he will do also; and *greater works* than these he will do, because I go to My Father."

John 14:12

How did Jesus do His works? He did them by the Holy Ghost. Jesus said that those who believe on Him will not only do the works that He did, but *greater works* than He did. He is saying, *"The person that believes on Me is not only going to receive the same Spirit I have, but he has the potential to grow up and become aware of spiritual things. He has the potential to grow in his familiarity with the Holy Spirit and work with Him in a way that will accomplish more on behalf of God than I did in three and a half years of ministry!"*

Basics in Spirit School

Jesus, the Head of the Church, is promising something *now*. Christians live and die waiting for the sweet *"by and by."* They die waiting to understand it better. The Spirit of God lives on the inside of you. You have the ability of Heaven within you. *Today*, you can access the full measure of that power.

> **And I will pray the Father, and He will give you *another Helper*, that He may *abide with you forever*—the Spirit of truth, whom the world cannot receive, because it neither sees Him nor knows Him; but you know Him, for *He dwells with you and will be in you.***
>
> John 14:16, 17

Jesus promised to give you another Helper. He promised to give you the Holy Spirit so that He may abide with you forever. Child of God, the moment you receive the Holy Spirit, your real education begins. The Holy Spirit comes alongside of you to help you, to teach you, and to lead you into truth. However, you can only be taught when you're willing to be taught. You can only be led when you're willing to be led.

I want to grow up in the things of the Spirit. I don't want to be a believer that is filled with knowledge, but is void of power. You can have a head full of knowledge and lack spiritual maturity. Knowledge is only power if it's infused with the power of the Holy Ghost. The Apostle Paul wrote of Saints that were always learning, but just never able to come to the knowledge of the truth. They had a form of godliness, but there was no power in it (2 Timothy 3:7, 5). Knowledge without revelation is powerless because power comes from the Holy Ghost.

How can a person be ever learning and never able to come to the knowledge of the truth? They're learning head knowledge. They can quote Scripture, but they're not putting their knowledge into practice. They're not employing the active power of the Word of God in their life. They are just a collector of an encyclopedia of facts. They're ever learning but never able to come to the knowledge of the truth.

The knowledge of the truth is an experiential knowledge. It's a revelation knowledge. It's a tangible experience. The Truth is the Lord Jesus Christ. Revelation knowledge of the truth produces Jesus in you or as Paul writes, *"Christ in you, the hope of glory"* (Colossians 1:27).

Paul boldly stated, *"For me to live is Christ"* (Philippians. 1:21). You too, can make this your life's confession. *To live is Christ.* Once you come to the knowledge of the truth, you *have* power. Revelation brings performance. You no longer have a form of godliness that denies the power. Instead, you have godliness living in you that manifests itself in an experiential understanding.

When you are filled with the Holy Ghost, you can come to an instantaneous knowledge of the truth. Recognize that you are a spiritual being called to follow your teacher—the Holy Ghost. Your Teacher will never leave you. He will lead you into godliness *with power*. As He leads you into that understanding and that experience, the manifestations of the Holy Ghost will be seen in your life. You are God's poster child for success!

> **The Spirit gives special faith to another, and to someone else He gives the power to heal the sick.**
>
> **1 Corinthians 12:9 NLT**

In the original Greek, "power to heal the sick" is literally "gifts of healings." Just as there are different kinds of diseases, there are different manifestations of healing.

> **He gives one person the power to perform miracles, and to another the ability to prophesy. He gives someone else the ability to know whether it is really the Spirit of God or another spirit that is speaking. Still another person is given the ability to speak in unknown languages, and another is given the ability to interpret what is being said.**
>
> **1 Corinthians 12:10 NLT**

Supernatural Gifts

But the *manifestation* of the Spirit is given to every man to profit withal.

1 Corinthians 12:7 KJV

Let's examine the word *manifestation*. I want you to notice that Paul didn't say, "the *indwelling* of the Spirit." Instead, he used the word *manifestation*. A manifestation is something revealed. It's something manifested. Yes, the indwelling of the Spirit *is* given to every man, but that *indwelling* is not enough! You may say, *"I've got the Holy Ghost living in me!"* Indeed you do, but if no proof of that indwelling is ever seen in you, then who will profit from it? In fact, if no one can visibly see that indwelling manifested in your life, then *you* are not even benefiting from that indwelling! If the indwelling of the Holy Ghost is benefiting you, your spirit will grow. When your spirit grows, you are ready to flow. When you're ready to flow, manifestations of the Holy Ghost will come forth through you. People will see them and will benefit from them.

There are three different categories of manifestations of the Spirit. Within each of those categories, there are three gifts. Again, it's the same Spirit, but there are three different manners by which He manifests Himself through His people. There are the *seeing* gifts, the *saying* gifts and the *doing* gifts. The seeing gifts *see* something. These are the revelation gifts—the word of wisdom, the word of knowledge, and discerning of spirits. The saying gifts, *say* something. These are the utterance gifts—prophecy, diverse kinds of tongues, and the interpretation of tongues. The doing gifts, *do* something. These are the power gifts—special faith, gifts of healing, and the working of miracles.

The Holy Spirit knows that His indwelling is not enough! Believe it or not, the Holy Spirit is smart. He's smart enough to know that some Christians are just going to have Him in their spirit but do nothing with Him. *"The manifestation of the Spirit is given to every man to profit withal."*

The Holy Spirit is saying to you: *"Listen! I want to visit you! I want to spiritually manifest Myself through you by an anointed, articulate, God-inspired prophecy; by tongues and interpretation; by a word of knowledge or a word of wisdom; by gifts of healings; by the working of miracles; by special faith; by the discerning of spirits. I want to manifest My knowledge, My power, and My ability through you so that others can bear witness to the fact that there is a divine force working in you. They will profit from it and they will be edified by it."*

What a privilege! The God of the universe has made Himself and all of His power subject to our cooperation and our obedience! Only you can allow God to express Himself in your life.

> **But all these *worketh* that one and the self-same Spirit, dividing to every man severally as He will.**
>
> **1 Corinthians 12:11 KJV**

All these *worketh*. The Holy Ghost never came into your life to remain stagnant. The gifts of God have never come into your spirit to lie dormant. God wants His gifts at work in you so that your life will cease to be natural and start operating supernaturally.

I want you to say, *"If there are no manifestations of the Spirit in my life, then there are no supernatural workings in my life."* You won't get taught *that* in most pulpits! Preachers will tell you, *"Just pray to the Lord! Just pray and the Lord will do it in His good time."* So many Christians live their whole lives ignorant of the things of the Spirit. They never put to work the gift of the Holy Spirit. Without those gifts working, they are simply unable to walk in the Christ-kind of results. These people will die, go to Heaven and find out that they ignored the most important Person—the one they needed for supernatural living! The Holy Ghost didn't come to just live in you. He came to *work* through you. He came to *manifest* through you.

> *...dividing to every man severally* **as He (the Holy Ghost) will...**
>
> **1 Corinthians 12:11b**
> (parentheses added by author)

It's the self-same Spirit—the same Holy Spirit—who will manifest Himself in several different ways. When you have the Holy Spirit, you have the potential for Him to manifest Himself through you in all of His nine manifestations. There is also the potential that He will never manifest Himself through you in even *one* of them. The Holy Ghost has a hard time getting some Christians to even pray in tongues, let alone flow in the manifestation of the gifts! You can have the Holy Spirit all of your life and fail to see His manifestations. On the other hand, you can have the Holy Spirit, and, at the very least, *several* of His manifestations will be evident in your life.

Naturally Supernatural

As I've observed people operate in the gifts of the Spirit or have watched videos of myself operate in the gifts, I've noticed that it is difficult in the natural to pinpoint which gift is in operation. For example, a minister may be prophesying, which the Bible says is for edification, exhortation, and comfort, and while they are flowing in that gift, there may be a word of knowledge given along with that prophecy.

Prophecy is a supernatural utterance in a known language. It is an inspired, God-breathed, power-packed, supernatural utterance. Most Christians think that it's just a bunch of words put together! The pure gift of prophecy, however, is not a manifestation of the flesh. It's not a manifestation of the intellect. It's not a manifestation of the theology or the vocabulary of the preacher. The pure gift of prophecy is a manifestation of the Holy Ghost in a known language. It's supernatural and it has the ability to edify, uplift and comfort the hearer.

A word of knowledge is a supernatural revelation about something that could not have been known with the natural intellect. In one of our miracle crusades, I had a word of knowledge about a woman who had been in an accident. I knew that she was sitting in that meeting and I knew that the Lord wanted to heal her. I also knew that she had experienced some things that had turned her off to the gifts of the Spirit. When I gave the word of knowledge, she came forward and God instantly healed her. Now in that instance, the word of knowledge opened the door for gifts of healing to flow into that woman's life. God used the word of knowledge to break through that barrier so that she would allow the Lord to heal her.

As you grow in the Spirit of God, you will begin to flow supernaturally. You will become *naturally supernatural*. You may even do something that seems to be the most natural thing for you to do. It's not until later that you recognize that it was a supernatural manifestation of the Holy Ghost! You were so tuned in with God that you were naturally supernatural. That's a great place to be! As you operate in this realm, there will be times that you won't even remember doing it at all. You may be witnessing or ministering to someone and *several different gifts* of the Spirit will come forth through you. It's possible that you won't even know it—you'll just think that you're on a roll! You can grow accustomed to the flow of the Spirit, but if you're sensitive, you will know what's going on.

In this life, you have two options. You can live *naturally* or you can live *supernaturally*. The choice is obvious, but it's ultimately yours to make. At best, the natural is frustrating. At worst, it's debilitating. As a believer, you will *never* be satisfied until you see the Christ-kind of results manifested in your life. You can't have Christ results and walk naturally. It's not possible. Only the Holy Ghost can make you supernatural.

A Daily Decision

Through the Holy Ghost, we've all been baptized
into the Body of Christ.

For by one Spirit we were all baptized into one body—whether Jews or Greeks, whether slaves

or free—and have all been made to drink into one Spirit.

1 Corinthians 12:13

How did the Holy Ghost do that?

You were baptized through the new birth. Jesus said, *"The water I give him shall be in him a well of everlasting water, springing up"* (John 4:14). Jesus is describing your salvation experience. You were born again by the Holy Ghost. At this point, your spirit was born of His Spirit. His Spirit immersed you into the Body of Christ. Immediately you became a member of the Body of the Lord through a miracle of the Holy Spirit. How did that happen? You just believed in your heart, confessed with your mouth, and you were saved. You were immersed into the Body of Jesus by the Holy Ghost.

It's amazing to me that you can be born by the Spirit and refuse to grow through the Spirit! The same Spirit that gives you the birth gives you the growth, if you let Him. The reason why it's harder to grow than it is to be born again is because praying the sinner's prayer is a one-time exercise. You put your faith to it, you do it, and it's done. Growing, however, is a daily decision. It takes a daily determination to yield to the Holy Ghost.

Make this decision: *"I'm going to take the natural man—the mind that has not been washed by the Word of God—out of the position of leadership. I'm going to put the spirit that was born by God in the driver's seat, in the forefront of my life. I'm going to invest in my spirit so that it will grow. As I yield to the Holy Ghost, God will bring light to my soul, change my mind, and bring me into agreement with His Word and His plan for my life."*

We have been baptized into one Body and made to *drink* into one Spirit. We have been made to drink of the Holy Ghost. Have you ever been really hot and tired—dehydrated? When you found water, it refreshed you and renewed your strength. To the spirit man, the Holy Ghost is that refreshing. He is the living water. You cannot allow your spirit man to go any length of time without yielding to that living water. It will refresh your spirit and revive you unto God. If you go without drinking His living water, you'll find that the old nature will rise up. Unbelief will rear its ugly head and discouragement will bear down upon you. Your flesh will wear you out. It's very hard for the Holy Ghost to manifest Himself through you if you're walking in the flesh.

The manifestations of the Spirit only work when you are in the Spirit. It does not work when you are in the flesh. Stepping into synch with the Spirit requires a faith decision. The Holy Ghost is likened unto water. You've been made to drink of the Holy Ghost. Do you want the peace that passes understanding? If you do, then you must make a decision to let go of the things that are pulling on you. You have to let go of the cares, of the worries and the fears. Through an act of faith, you have to let go and make the decision to drink of the living water.

God Wants to Use You!

> **If any man speak, let him speak as the oracles of God; if any man minister, let him do it as of the ability which God giveth, that God in all things may be glorified through Jesus Christ, to whom be praise and dominion for ever and ever. Amen.**
>
> **1 Peter 4:11 KJV**

What does it mean to speak as the oracle of God? To speak as the oracle of God is to allow divine utterance to flow through you. When you speak as God's mouthpiece, He may use your own vocabulary or you may hear yourself say words that you've never learned before! This utterance gift is only available if you are in the Spirit. You cannot speak as the oracle of God by saying, *"I think I will speak as the oracle of God now."* It doesn't work that way! If you've been walking and thinking in the natural, you won't be able to speak spiritual things. If you haven't given way to the Holy Spirit in your heart and in your mind, you won't be able to speak God-breathed words.

God will use you and your ability to manifest Him in the world. That's why we've heard the statement, *"God is a perfect God, using imperfect people."* I don't like to say it that way because we *are* perfect in His sight. God will pour His glory through you and limit Himself—to a certain extent—to *your expression* of His glory. It doesn't matter if you are profoundly articulate or if you speak simply. What matters is that the divine unction—the anointing, the life, and the power of the Holy Spirit—are backing up the words you speak. If you are flowing with that divine unction, then God will use you as an instrument to pour His power through. He will use you to change something, to influence someone, or to affect a region for Him. God wants to use you!

Give your mouth to God. Before you can flow in gifts of healing, the working of miracles, special faith, etc, you must give your mouth to the Lord. Before you give your mouth to the Lord, you must give your mind to the Lord.

Surely the Lord God will do nothing, but he revealeth his secret unto his servants the prophets.

Amos 3:7 KJV

How does He reveal the secret? *Revelation.*
How does He declare the secret? *Utterance.*
What happens after he has revealed and declared? *Power!*

The only way for you to see something in the Word of God is to meditate on the Word. God said that if you set your mind on Him, He will keep you in perfect peace. You can't speak as the oracle of God unless you have a revelation. You can't get a revelation unless you've meditated. When you meditate on God, you will get a revelation. Meditation brings revelation. When you have a revelation, you will open your mouth and speak as the oracle of God. You will flow with God! When you do these things, you will see the visible manifestation of the power of the Holy Spirit in your life.

Chapter 2

See It. Say It. Do It.

If your spirit is brimming with spiritual truth, then your mouth will flow with divine utterance.

And I beheld, and, lo, in the midst of the throne and of the four beasts, and in the midst of the elders, stood a Lamb as it had been slain, having seven horns and seven eyes, which are the seven Spirits of God sent forth into all the earth.

Revelation 5:6 KJV

The Lamb of God in the book of Revelation is described as having seven eyes and seven horns. The Bible says that these are the seven spirits of God. Technically speaking, there is no such thing as seven spirits. Seven, however, is the number of perfection. We know that there is *one* Spirit. Therefore, the seven eyes represent *all* knowledge. Jesus is omnipresent and omnipotent. He sees *everything*, is *everywhere* and is *all-powerful*.

When you received the baptism of the Holy Ghost, you received the Spirit of God who is everywhere, knows all, and can do everything. You received omnipotence, omniscience and omnipresence *through* Him! That means you don't have to be across town to know what's going on over there. If the Holy Ghost wants you to know about it, He can reveal it to you! He's not just in you; He is everywhere.

What is a word of knowledge? It's a little chip of the knowledge of God. *What is a word of wisdom?* It's a little chip of the all predictive, all foreseeing, and all foreknowing capability of God. What is the working of miracles or special faith? It is a little chip of the omnipotence of God. You have the Almighty living in you! You are filled with the fullness of God. What can stop you? Who can hold you back from

His fullness? The Lord would like to teach you how to allow Him to be *almighty* in manifested form. He wants to give you a little glimpse of how awesome He is in your life.

Glory in the Church

Unto him be glory in the Church by Christ Jesus throughout all ages, world without end. Amen.

Ephesians 3:21

If any man speak, let him speak as the oracles of God; if any man minister, let him do it as of the ability which God giveth, *that God in all things may be glorified through Jesus Christ*, to whom be praise and dominion for ever and ever. Amen.

1 Peter 4:11 KJV

Where does God get glory? *In the Church!*
How? *By Christ Jesus*!

You can only speak as the oracle of God when you realize that Christ is living in you. This realization is only possible through revelation knowledge. When you do speak by inspired utterance, it is Christ in you speaking—*in identity*—and the Holy Ghost flowing through you—*in ability*. So God gets glory through Christ Jesus *in the Church*! When God looks down and sees you operating in the pure gifts of the Spirit, He sees His Son living in you in identity and His Spirit manifesting through you in ability.

If any man speaks, let him do it as the mouthpiece of God. Jesus Christ is the mouthpiece of God. He is the Word. He created everything that is. The only reason that we can be the mouthpiece of God is that we have become members of the Body of Jesus Christ.

If any man minister, let him do it with the ability that God gives. How does God give ability? God gives ability through the Holy Ghost! In other words, Jesus calls you and the Holy Ghost equips you. When you allow the Holy Ghost to flow through you, it is Jesus living in you and the Holy Ghost empowering you. When the devil faces you, he's facing Christ! This is important for you to understand! Your revelation of this will determine the spiritual position you take.

To speak as the oracle of God, you have to *see* before you *say*. I have heard some sermons where it is quite evident that the preacher hasn't *seen* anything. You must see! You must have a revelation! When you get a hold of the mind of God about something, you will have something to say.

"Surely the Lord God will do nothing"—*That's power!*
"but he revealeth his secret"—*That's revelation!*
"to his servants the prophets"—*That's utterance!*

God said, *"I'm going to reveal it, they're going to declare it, and then I'm going to do it."* Most people stumble at that third step. They quit right before He does it! Why is this? People don't have a problem hearing it or seeing it. They don't even have a problem testifying about it. The minute they declare it, however, the devil moves in to stop it and then they quit before they see the manifestation.

Power Talk

It is the Spirit who gives life; the flesh profits nothing. The words that I speak to you are *spirit*, and they are *life*.

John 6:63

If you practice keeping your mind on spiritual things, then your spirit will be filled with spiritual truth. If your spirit is brimming with spiritual truth, then your mouth will flow with divine utterance. Divine utterance is anointed, prophetic speech. Jesus said that His words are Spirit and life. Do you believe that it's possible to talk out of the Spirit of God all of the time? Jesus did it. If Jesus did it, you can too. The Bible records only a miniscule amount of all that Jesus said. The Holy Ghost just brought out the highlights of His ministry on Earth! There are so many things that He said during His earthly ministry—that the world itself could not contain the books that would be written of Him!

> **But I say to you that for every idle word men may speak, they will give account of it in the day of judgment.**
>
> **Matthew 12:36**

The words of Christ were far from idle. If Jesus had spoken idle words, then He would have been guilty of sin. We know from the Word of God that Jesus was without sin and perfect in all His ways. So then, if Jesus wasn't guilty of idle talk, then how did He talk? For thirty-three and a half years, Jesus spoke *out of* the Spirit of God—which was *in* His Spirit! Jesus was a man anointed by the Holy Ghost. He spoke out of His human spirit, which was operating under the influence of the Holy Spirit. When your spirit is hooked into the Holy Spirit, it is easy to move from Biblical truth flowing through you into a place where specific Spirit revelation can come to you. It's hard to move into that place if you've been talking out of your mind and out of your flesh.

Get your spirit hooked into the Spirit of God. Wire your mouth into the Spirit of God. Tap into His divine frequency. If both your spirit *and* your mouth are wired to the Holy Spirit, then you will speak as the oracle of God. It's the natural outcome to a supernatural connection. You will *see* and then you will *speak* Truth. As you make the thoughts of God and the Word of God your priority, the Holy Ghost will give you the accuracy and the ability to minister with His power. First you see, then you say, then you will do.

Jesus said, *"Go, and in my name...."* When Jesus gave you His name, He gave you His identity. When Paul was praying for the Galatians, he prayed that Christ would be formed in them again (Galatians 4:19). The Bible also says that the new man is created after God in righteousness and true holiness (Ephesians 4:24). You have a new man in you that is created after Christ. As a matter of fact, you have been born again by His Spirit. He's the One living in you!

When the Bible says, *"Let him speak as the oracles of God,"* it's really saying: *"Start thinking like the mind of Christ so that the words of Christ will speak through you! Realize that you've been baptized into His new identity! You're a new member of the family of God! You're no longer a debtor to the flesh! You're a spiritual being with divine authority! When the enemy faces you, he's facing a member in the Body of Christ!"*

Child of God, this *is* the key! You cannot speak as the oracle of God unless you know that you have the legal right to do so!

Exercising Godliness

When I was born again and baptized in the Holy Spirit, I started going to Pentecostal and Full Gospel churches. In church, I watched people give messages in tongues. They would get overwhelmed by the Spirit and give a message in an unknown tongue. Not once, however, did I ever hear one of these people interpret their tongues. As I grew in the Lord and learned the Word, I found out why. The person giving the message in tongues did not have the faith to interpret the message!

Why would a person not have faith to interpret?

There's a rational responsibility—*a sober responsibility*—that comes with speaking on behalf of God. If you don't have the faith to do it, you won't hook your spirit into it. However, the same Holy Ghost that gives the message in tongues is well able to use your mouth to give the interpretation. The child of God can flow easily in both of these things. Giving a message in tongues without the interpretation is easier because it requires *no identification with the new identity*. A person doesn't have to feel like the mouthpiece of God—they just have to give the message and wait for somebody else to bear the responsibility of the interpretation!

It's worth repeating: Your growth in the gifts of the Spirit is dependent upon your ability to yield your mind and your tongue to the Holy Ghost. If you can't yield your tongue to the Holy Ghost, you're going to have a hard time yielding your body to the Holy Ghost!

If you have a hard time singing to the Lord or quoting the Word, then practice! Force yourself to say "Amen!" When you don't feel like it. Force yourself to shout when you don't feel like it. Train your spirit! The Bible calls it exercise.

> **For bodily exercise profiteth little; but godliness is profitable unto all things."**
>
> 1 Timothy 4:8a KJV

Exercise godliness!

Speaking From Another Realm

"If any man speak..." is not just a suggestion—it's a command! *"...Let him do it as the oracle of God."* The Apostle Peter knew this and walked in it. He realized that he was not walking just as *Peter*; he was walking as a new creation with Christ in him. He was an apostle, and he knew that it was Jesus doing the *"apostling"* through him. *"There are diversities of ministry but the same Lord."* He knew it was Jesus working through him. He wasn't saying, *"I wonder if God is with me?"* Peter knew that he was *one* with Jesus.

In the entire universe, there is only one Anointed One. That's what *Christ* means, *the Anointed One*. Did you know that *you* are anointed? You are anointed because the same Spirit that anointed the *Anointed One*, baptized you into the Body of the *Anointed One*! Where you walk, He goes! It's not just you going some place—it's the *Anointed One* going in you. Christ is the Anointed One and He lives in you. When you open your mouth to speak as the oracle of God, the Spirit within you will give you the ability.

Some Christians aren't anointed because they do not want to bear the responsibility of their identity in Christ. Peter knew that it was Jesus doing the *"apostling"* through him. His mind was stayed on the things of the Spirit and he was able to speak as the mouthpiece of God. This is how God gets glory through Christ Jesus. Christ Jesus is in Heaven at the right hand of the Father. When the Body of Christ on Earth flows in the gifts of the Spirit, speaks as the oracles of God and ministers with divine ability—it gives God glory *through Christ Jesus in the Church*. Jesus is not only in Heaven, He is still ministering on Earth today through His Body!

You don't have to struggle for a word because Jesus will speak in your life. When He's invited, revelation will come. When the Holy Ghost reveals something, utterance will come.

Who gives you the ability? *The Holy Ghost.*
Who gets the glory? *God.*
How? *By Christ Jesus!*

The Anointed One that is living and operating in you is giving God glory. Unto Him be glory in the Church by Christ Jesus!

> **Then the churches throughout all Judea, Galilee, and Samaria had peace and were edified. And walking in the fear of the Lord and in the comfort of the Holy Spirit, they were multiplied. Now it came to pass, as Peter went through all parts of the country, that he also came down to the saints who dwelt in Lydda. There he found a certain man named Aeneas, who had been bedridden eight years and was paralyzed. And Peter said to him, "Aeneas, Jesus the Christ heals you. Arise and make your bed." Then he arose immediately. So all who dwelt at Lydda and Sharon saw him and turned to the Lord.**
>
> **Acts 9:31-35**

The Bible says that Peter found a certain man named Aeneas who had been in bed for eight years. Where was God during those eight years? For eight long years that man was crippled, but Jesus Christ didn't make him whole until *Peter* found him! *"The manifestation of the Spirit is given to every man to profit withal."*

Almighty God was sitting on the throne. Jesus had already overcome the devil. The devil had been completely defeated for each of those eight years, yet Aeneas was *still* crippled. God needed a member in His Body to speak as His oracle. He needed a member in particular to rise up in boldness and claim the power of His identity that He had already supplied. He needed a vessel that was willing to allow *His power* and *His ability* to back up their ministry.

When Peter walked in, he said to Aeneas, *"Jesus is making you whole. I came in the name of Jesus! I came by the delegated authority of Jesus! Arise, and make your bed!"*

Now *that* is divine utterance! *"Arise, and make your bed!"* Is a divine command. You cannot command someone in that manner unless you're speaking from another realm. You cannot speak from another realm unless you identify with the Spirit of God. When you identify with the life of the one who has purchased you, you will live your life on a higher dimension.

Don't *Try* This at Home

Peter was operating in the *gift of faith*—the God-kind of faith. If he had been operating under the gift of working of miracles, it would have been different. He might have pulled Aeneas out of the bed. Gifts of healings would have been different still—he might have laid hands on him. The gift of faith, however, is the assurance that a circumstance is going to yield to you. In other words, the Holy Ghost rose up within Peter and reminded him of Jesus' words. He might have said, *"Have the God-kind of faith Peter! Whosoever shall say to Aeneas 'Get up, and make your bed!' And shall not doubt in his heart but shall believe that the things which he says will come to pass, He shall have whatsoever he says"* (See Mark 11:22-24)!

People have tried to do it and failed. People have tried it and said, "Mark 11:22-24 doesn't work—I've tried it!" Of course it didn't work! It didn't work because they *tried* it! It doesn't work for the *unanointed* one. It only works for the Anointed One. It works for the person who knows their identity in Christ. It works for those who know that Christ is living in them. It works for the person that hooks into the things of God until the power of a revelation sparks in their heart—and divine utterance flows from their lips. A person like that is used by God to speak His words.

You aren't going to give God glory by saying, *"Glory to God! He hasn't done a thing in my life for thirty years!"* The only way to give God glory is to minister with the ability that God provides. That will not happen automatically in the life of a believer. If it did, we wouldn't need to teach anyone! If this were the case, every one of us would be a spiritual giant, already doing what we're called to do. Remember, God does not want His Church ignorant about spiritual things!

"And all that dwelt at Lydda and Sharon saw him, and turned to the Lord" (Acts 9:38). They did not turn to Peter. They turned to Jesus! When you know who you are in Christ and you know your identity, then the Holy Spirit can give you a revelation. Peter spoke the revelation he received: *"Jesus Christ makes you whole!"* He spoke that revelation and the gift of faith rose up within him: *"Arise, and make thy bed."*

Do you know whose faith raised Aeneas? It was Peter's faith hooked into God's faith that healed the man. When he hooked into God's faith and told Aeneas to arise, the faith of God went into Aeneas. Aeneas then acted upon the faith he heard.

Could Aeneas have failed to rise from the palsy? Absolutely! Sometimes it's easier to move a mountain than it is to move a Christian! A mountain doesn't have a will. You can curse a fig tree and it won't talk back. It won't say, *"I've been bearing fruit faithfully for all these years! What do you mean nobody's going to eat fruit from me again?"* There are some believers that would put up a fit if you commanded them to get up! They would remark incredulously, *"I've been in bed eight years! What do you mean get up?"*

God can reveal something to you and give you *special faith* for it at the very moment you need it. However, when you're dealing with the will of another, there is more to the situation than the sovereignty of God. So many Christians throw away their confidence because they pray for someone and then fail to see them receive their healing. They may even see them die and then give up on the whole thing. The gifts of the Spirit are never given by God to violate the will of an individual. *They are given to profit withal.*

Who profited when Peter walked in on the situation? Everybody! Aeneas certainly profited! Those in the region who believed and turned to the Lord profited as well.

Knowing in Part—Yet Fully Known

> **For we know in part and we prophesy in part. But when that which is perfect has come, then that which is in part will be done away. When I was a child, I spoke as a child, I understood as a child, I thought as a child; but when I became a man, I put away childish things. For now we see in a mirror, dimly, but then face to face. Now I know in part, but then I shall know just as I also am known. And now abide faith, hope, love, these three; but the greatest of these is love.**
>
> **1 Corinthians 13:9-13**

The Bible says that we know in part and we prophesy in part. This is not referring to natural knowledge, but to spiritual knowledge. Many in the Church world use that verse to excuse ignorance. They may say, *"Well, we're going to understand it better in the by and by. We don't know why the Lord moves the way He does!"*

It's not referring to the knowledge of natural things *in part*. This is about knowing divine revelation *in part*. It's about speaking divine revelation *in part*. It's saying, *"Listen! God is all knowing, but while we're here on Earth, He's only going to give us a part of his all-knowing mind. God can utter things that are beyond our understanding and beyond the realm of our existence. So while we're here, we're only going to prophesy—to utter things—through divine inspiration."* Knowing comes before prophesying. Seeing comes before saying. Saying comes before doing. As believers we *see* and *know* in part.

The Church says, *"Oh yes! We don't know why people die sick!"* That's not what this Scripture is talking about. *"We just don't know why the Lord lets the devil beat up on some people."* That's not what this is talking about either! The Scripture is teaching us that we know the mind of God *in part*. We prophesy the mind of God *in part*. You wouldn't prophesy what you didn't know. You prophesy what you have received by divine revelation. It's an inspired, supernatural utterance given by the Spirit of God. He manifests Himself through you in a known language in order that He might use you to edify, exhort, and comfort the Body of Christ. The Body will benefit by what God is doing through you.

> **When I was a child, I spake as a child, I understood as a child, I thought as a child: but when I became a man, I put away childish things.**
>
> **1 Corinthians 13:11 KJV**

God gave us this *part knowing* and *part prophesying* to enable us to grow up and put away childish things. All you need is a part of the power of God, a part of the mind of God, and a part of the Word of God! That is all you need to grow. Yes, God *is* almighty, but you really don't need *all* of His power to be an overcomer in this life! He has already destroyed the enemy on your behalf. The power made available to you in your life is a part of the power of God. It's a chip off the block. When God told Paul, *"My grace is sufficient for thee,"* He was saying, *"Through the grace I gave you, you can receive from Me what you need to overcome"* (2 Corinthians 12:9).

> **For now we see through a glass, darkly; but then face to face: now I know in part; but then shall I know even as also I am known.**
>
> **1 Corinthians 13:12 KJV**

We see into the realm of the Spirit. We see into the realm of the Word. We see into the realm of God. We see, although it's through a glass darkly. We've taken this Scripture and made it negative, but it's actually very positive. God is simply saying, *"Listen. I'm going to let you look into Heaven, but you're going to have dark shades on. You won't be able to see into Heaven as well as you will see when you get there—because that which is perfect is not come yet."* In the here and now we can expect to look, to see, to know, and to prophesy in part.

Faith Works by Love

And now abide faith, hope, love, these three; but the greatest of these is love.

1 Corinthians 13:13

What is faith? Faith is the substance of things hoped for—the evidence of things not seen. Without faith it is impossible to please God (Hebrews 11:1, 6).

What is hope? Hope is what anchors your soul (Hebrews 6:19). Hope is what you set your eyes on and hook your faith into. Your faith in the *now* is the substance and tangible evidence of the thing you're hoping for.

Why is love greater than faith and hope? The Bible says that God gave us two commandments upon which the whole law hangs. One of those commandments is to love the Lord your God with all your heart (Mark 12:30). When you love God—you believe God. Faith works by love.

Somebody may say, *"Well, I believe the Lord! I just don't believe that He is going to do what He says He's going to do."* A person like this has not cultivated the love of God that is shed abroad in their heart by the Holy Ghost. They have not put that love in control of their spirit man. If they had done this, they would love God so much that they wouldn't dare entertain a doubt about His promises.

Why is love greater than faith? Without love, you can't really believe God. When you love the Lord, then you will believe what the Lord says.

Why is love greater than hope? When you believe the Lord, you will have the evidence of what you're hoping for. Without this hope, you cannot believe that you already have it. Faith works by love.

What does this have to do with the gifts of the Spirit? The Word of God exhorts us to prophesy according to the proportion of our faith (Romans 12:6). When a believer declares, *"Yea, yea!"* For about thirty minutes, you can tell what kind of faith they have! They have a "yea" faith and little more.

Faith requires the love of God. If you love someone, you will learn about them. You'll hang around them. When you love the Word, you'll spend time around the Word. You'll meditate on the Word. As you do, the Word will become alive to you. You will love God so much that you will believe Him—you will take Him at His word. As you take Him at His word, the faith that you have in God will hook into what the Word has promised. At that point, when you use your faith to prophesy according to the proportion of your faith, it will no longer be the *"Condensed Version"*—it will be the *"Amplified!"* You will have a lot to say in God! Your faith has grown because your love has grown.

The other commandment is to love your neighbor as yourself. The Bible says that faith without works is dead (James 2:20). If you tell a hungry person to *"Be filled,"* your faith is dead. There is no love fueling your faith. If there were, then your faith would be evident by your works. Love is the force behind faith. Without love, faith is inoperable. This is why love is *greater* than faith. Without love, the gifts of the Spirit can't freely operate.

I firmly believe that God gives people a grace period as they operate in the gifts of the Spirit. However, if they don't have love in their heart for others, they will eventually begin to operate by familiar spirits. The key to keeping your gift pure is to love people and to only speak the heart and mind of God about them. Love must become the guide that directs your words. We know that God is love. When God talks, *love flows*. He is the tangible expression of love. When the Lord speaks, His words are Spirit and life—brimming with the expression of His love. Allow God to speak His love through you.

I have a hard time listening to people operate in the gifts of the Spirit if they are without love. The gifts of the Spirit should never be used to hurt or wound a child of God! That is not what God is like! As a result of these abuses, there are many people that are fearful of these gifts. Once again, the gifts of the Spirit—or the manifestations—are given to every man to profit withal. Some people think that the gifts have been given to profit themselves! If a person begins to utilize the gifts of the Spirit to manipulate the lives of others, they are operating in *witchcraft*. Witchcraft is a work of the flesh. The Holy Ghost will not cooperate with that. *"And now abideth faith, hope, charity, these three; but the greatest of these is charity."*

God Breathed Boldness

> **For I am not ashamed of the gospel of Christ, for it is the power of God unto salvation to everyone that believeth; to the Jew first, and also to the Greek *(the heathen)*. For therein is the righteousness of God revealed from faith to faith; as it is written, the just shall live by faith.**
>
> **Romans 1:16-17 KJV**
> (parentheses added by author)

The Bible says, *"Let us therefore come boldly to the throne of grace"* (Hebrews 4:16). The word *boldly* means *with great plainness of speech*. It means *unashamedly* and *without hesitation*. There is only one way to come boldly to the throne of God. To do so, one must speak as the oracle of God. When He baptized us into the Body of His Son, He gave us the Spirit of His Son. In turn, we can cry, *"Abba Father."* *"We having the same Spirit of faith, according as it is written, I believed and therefore have I spoken"* (1 Corinthians 4:13). When the Spirit of Christ is in operation within you, you can come boldly to the throne and speak with supernatural, God-breathed utterance to God.

The Bible says that it's not possible to be a Christian and be without the Spirit of Christ. *"Now if any man has not the Spirit of Christ, he is none of his"* (Romans 8:9). Therefore, we *know* that we have the Spirit of Christ. It is not the residence of the Spirit, but the manifestation of the Spirit that will bring blessings, or profit.

One of the ways the Spirit manifests is through utterance. How are you going to pray to God with inspired utterance unless you receive divine revelation from God? You can't pray in this manner unless you have a revelation of the will of God on the subject. The Spirit of God gives you the *revelation* and the *inspiration* to come boldly to God without shame, without hesitation, and without fear. He gives you the ability to speak as His mouthpiece before Him.

You might be thinking, *"How could I speak to God as the oracle of God?"* Jesus prayed and Jesus *is* the Oracle of God. He prayed to the Father. The Bible says that we ought to pray to the Father in Jesus' name. This isn't about throwing in the name of Jesus at the end of a prayer! This is about *you* speaking to the Father, fully persuaded of the new identity that is in you through Christ. Lift up your voice with the Spirit of Christ and say, *"Abba Father."* When the Father looks at you, He sees Christ in you. He sees the Oracle of God.

Who then, is praying? The Anointed One is praying. It's an anointed prayer that you might obtain mercy and find grace to help in the time of need (Hebrews 4:16b).

The Bible says to *seek* the gifts. It says to desire all spiritual gifts, but to especially desire the gift of prophecy (1 Corinthians 14:1). Prophecy is a gift that is unselfish. Inspired utterance blesses others. Notice, the Bible did not say, *"Now, don't desire all of the gifts."* It just said, *"In the midst of the congregation, make sure that you're not messing around by just giving messages in tongues. If nobody knows what you're talking about, then nobody is going to be blessed but you."* You have to be mindful of others.

For I am not ashamed of the gospel of Christ.

Romans 1:16

The Gospel is the *good news*. It is Spirit and life in the mouth of a child of God who has a revelation of it. The good news *is* a fiery, anointed, life-imparting, Spirit-impacted life flow. I am not ashamed of it! It is the power, or the dunamis, of God unto salvation.

In order to speak the Gospel without shame and by inspired utterance, you must first receive a revelation of it. Secondly, you must yield your instrument, your vessel, your lips—*your mouth*—to the inspiration of the Holy Ghost. In turn, He will utter words through you that are intelligible and can be understood. As you preach, share and witness the Gospel, words of knowledge will flow out of your mouth.

Moving in Divine Inspiration

Everywhere I've preached, people tell me that I spoke directly to them during the sermon. Even when I preach to thousands, people will come up to me to say that I was speaking directly to them that day. They say, *"I know that I'm the only one here that needed to hear that sermon!"* When you come with divine utterance that is hooked into the ability that God gives, *you'll become His mouthpiece.*

When Jesus spoke with the woman at the well, He suddenly started saying things that He hadn't premeditated. They were coming out of His Spirit. The woman said, *"I perceive thou art a prophet."* The Bible says that God spoke in times past by the prophets and has now spoken to us by His Son. He still speaks to us by His Son and teaches us by His anointing. The same Lord is going to speak through you in *identity*. The same Spirit is going to bring the power through you in *ability*. *"Now the Lord is that Spirit; and where the Spirit of the Lord is, there is liberty"* (1 Corinthians 3:17 KJV).

The Gospel is the *utterance* or the *Word* of the Living God. I am not ashamed of God's words! I am not limited to the natural realm regarding those words. I will allow the Spirit of God to bring revelation to me so that I can rise to divine inspiration. When I do, I know that the very power of the living God is within those words.

There are the gifts that see something, say something and do something, but you cannot split up the Holy Spirit. When the Holy Spirit is living in you, then the eyes—or the revelations of God will begin to well up within your spirit. God will reveal something to His servant so that His servant can declare it. After His servant declares it, God can do it. The Lord will work with His servant to confirm the Word with signs following. The quickest way to flow in the power of God is to let God get a hold of your tongue!

People wonder all the time, *"What is my gift?"* If you stir it up, it will come out of you! Others say, *"I have the gift of discernment."* There is no such gift! There is a manifestation of the discerning of spirits. There are also certain things that are standard packaging with your new identity. Yes, a believer can discern. A believer discerns because Jesus discerned. He loved righteousness and hated iniquity. A believer has the ability to discern because Jesus is living in them.

What does he do when he discerns between good and evil, between righteousness and iniquity? *He chooses righteousness!* What does God do after that? *He anoints him with the oil of gladness!* If you will do the things pertinent to your *heavenly identity*, you will have the power pertinent to your *divine ability*.

Jesus has called us to be believers. A believer does what God says to do. The Bible says that God inhabits the praises of His people. A believer praises God. When do they praise God? *All the time!* How do they praise God? *Vocally!* You must *open your mouth* and praise God even when it sounds stupid. As you open your mouth in praises to God—you may feel stupid at first—but it won't last long because you will touch the realm where God inhabits your praises. At that point, you will be speaking as the oracle of God.

The quickest way to tap into the Holy Spirit's ability is to acknowledge your identity in Christ identity. Acknowledge *who* you are in Christ.

Lift your hands to the Lord and say this:

Father, I know that by my spirit I can know the Holy Spirit. I can know His ways and I can know Your will for my life and for the lives of others. Help me to grow, help me to know, help me to learn how to work as Your instrument by the power of the Spirit—in Jesus' name. Amen.

Chapter 3

God's Divine Ability Is Yours

---

*The ability available to you is equivalent
to the revelation you have of the Word of God.*

Now there was at Joppa a certain disciple named Tabitha, which by interpretation is called Dorcas; this woman was full of good works and almsdeeds which she did. And it came to pass in those days that she was sick and died; whom when they had washed, they laid her in an upper chamber. And forasmuch as Lydda was nigh to Joppa, and the disciples had heard that Peter was there, they sent unto him two men desiring him that he would not delay to come to them. And Peter arose and went with them. When he was come, they brought him into the upper chamber; and all the widows stood by him weeping, and shewing the coats and garments which Dorcas made while she was with them. But Peter put them all forth, and kneeled down, and prayed; and turning him to the body said, Tabitha, arise. And she opened her eyes; and when she saw Peter, she sat up. And he gave her his hand, and lifted her up, and when he had called the saints and widows, presented her alive. And it was known throughout all Joppa; and many believed in the Lord.

Acts 9:36-42 KJV

Good news always travels fast! Already the headlines about Peter ministering healing to Aeneas had spread to Joppa. In Joppa, the people were busy preparing to bury a wonderful Saint named Tabitha. Tabitha was a Christian and she was well known for her alms and good deeds. According to custom, they had washed her, put her in an upper chamber and were getting ready to bury her body. Someone though, upon hearing the news of Aeneas, called for Peter! When Peter arrived, he found Tabitha's friends and family mourning and weeping—in anguish over their loss.

*Hadn't Jesus sent His disciples to heal the sick,
cleanse the lepers, and raise the dead?*

Revelation – The Access Point to Power

God has given each of us a mandate to do the works of Jesus on Earth. The works, however, will not be done by might or by power. They can *only* be done by His Spirit. *"If anyone ministers, let him do it as with the ability which God supplies"* (1 Peter 4:11a).

In the Kingdom of God there are different graces. The *ability* available to you is equivalent to the *revelation* you have of the Word of God. The Church has missed it in thinking that God gives to some bountifully and to others sparingly. Smith Wigglesworth raised somewhere between eighteen to twenty people from the dead. For years Saints have thought, *"Well that's just Smith Wigglesworth. He's just special."*

All of the power of God is available to help you be the Christ-kind of Christian. However, the only way for you to gain access into God's unlimited ability is through revelation. The Bible says that you should pray for the Spirit of Wisdom and Revelation.

What does revelation do?
It causes you to know in part.

What do you do with the part you know?
You prophesy and preach it!

You cannot preach what you do not *know*. If you only preach *what you've learned* in Bible school, it will not profit anyone. However, when what you've learned becomes your personal persuasion—then you will have a revelation! Someone with a revelation *knows* that God has taught them! When you are standing on a revelation, you will preach it with conviction—with absolute assurance that God will back it up. God always backs up His Word! The Spirit of God will enforce and validate the revelation He has deposited into you.

Peter didn't show up in Joppa to raise Tabitha from the dead *"if it be God's will."* He didn't come to pray a nice prayer and comfort the family with, *"If God raises her, that's fine. If He doesn't, He doesn't."* No, Peter had a revelation! There was power that was backing up the revelation that was stirring within him. He was going to minister with the ability that the Holy Ghost provides!

"And they went forth, and preached every where, the Lord working with them, and confirming the Word with signs following" (Mark 16:20). *"I will never leave thee, nor forsake thee. So that we may boldly say, the Lord is my helper..."* (Hebrews 13:5-6). *"For I am not ashamed of the gospel of Christ..."* (Romans 1:16). *"Let us therefore come boldly to the throne of grace"* (Hebrews 4:16) (KJV).

When can you come boldly?

You can walk in boldness when you have a revelation! If your life isn't threatened, it's very easy to walk in boldness! During times of adversity, however, your revelation will sustain your boldness.

The Lord said, *"I will never leave thee nor forsake thee."* The Word of God is your point of contact—it gives you access to His Spirit at all times. Through the Holy Spirit, revelation becomes alive *in you*. Where you go, He goes. If you do what He tells you to do, He will not be absent. He will be there to provide the power! Once this becomes a revelation *in* you, then you too will be able to boldly say, *"The Lord is my helper; I will not fear what man can do to me!"*

You must have a revelation of His promise to *"never leave thee nor forsake thee."* Without that revelation, the Holy Spirit will be limited in His ability to work in you and through you. You may just end up operating by the grace and sovereignty of God! If you do this, you'll limit God and you will see *very little* of the results that belong to you as a faith walker. *"Now the just shall live by faith"* (Hebrews 10:38).

Removing the Mourners

Carrying the ability of the Holy Spirit, Peter went to Joppa to raise Tabitha from the dead. As soon as he arrived, he kicked out all of the people that were weeping and mourning. *Circumstances can overcome you.* As a believer, make the decision to allow the Word of God to challenge your regular routine and schedule. Do not allow contrary things that have been cycling for years to continue unaddressed. If you have the ability to take care of it, do so.

In one of our crusades, there was a woman who had a large tumor in her breast and scar tissue on the back of her neck and on her shoulders. I called her forward by a word of knowledge and laid my hands on her back. God ministered to her and *instantly* healed her! The following day she went to her doctor to be tested. The doctor was shocked to see that the large tumor had dissolved and that the scar tissue had disappeared. He was so shocked, in fact, that he paid for the test himself! You see, this doctor had been the one to diagnose the tumor in the first place. He knew where the tumor was and he knew where the scar tissue had been.

The woman was instantly healed through a miracle of God. Actually, this was not a healing — this was an instantaneous miracle. The Bible says, *"They shall lay hands on the sick and they shall recover"* (Mark 16:18). Any believer can lay hands on the sick and expect them to recover. In this example, a *power gift* brought about an immediate miracle. The power gift was preceded by both revelation and a divine utterance. Once the divine utterance took place, God backed up His Word by a manifestation of the Spirit.

Peter got rid of the people who had already made the decision to bow the knee to the circumstance. They were sorrowing because Tabitha was dead. Jesus said, however, *"Let not your heart be troubled"* (John 14:27). You cannot be mindful of an impossibility and, at the same time, expect to overcome it. The only way to deal with impossibility supernaturally is to be mindful of the report of the Lord! You must remain *absolutely untouched* in your spirit about the lying circumstances that face you.

Jesus had to do the same thing in His earthly ministry. He had the Spirit without measure, but even God in the flesh *could do no mighty works in Nazareth.* Jesus had to make sure that He protected His anointing. *How did He do this?* He moved the contrary elements out of His realm of influence. He moved them right out of His circle of experience. If you have contrary forces around you, they can affect the gifts of the Spirit. The weeping and mourning of the world can hinder the gifts from operating in your life. You have to protect what God has given you. This means that you have to separate yourself from the influence of the flesh.

There are churches where the Holy Ghost is not welcome. He would like to operate in a certain way, but it doesn't mesh with their schedule or experience. I've preached in churches where I have had a hard time flowing in the gifts of the Spirit. The Holy Ghost wasn't welcome, so His expression was stifled in their midst. Although they didn't mean to stifle the Lord, they were doing it without even knowing it. The Holy Ghost requires an atmosphere of appreciation. He requires an invitation to manifest Himself.

You must put a *demand* on the anointing! You must prepare the atmosphere. You must place a demand on a minister in order to get something out of him. Peter knew this and put the mourners out for a reason. He put them out because he knew he needed to get with God. He needed to tap into the ability of the Holy Spirit.

Obtaining Grace Through Prayer

Peter knelt and prayed. The Word of God does not tell us exactly what he prayed, but I'll tell you what he *did not* pray. He did not pray, *"God, raise her from the dead!"*

Is that shocking to you? Jesus *commanded* Peter to go and raise the dead. In Jesus' earthly ministry, every time He dealt with the dead, He gave a command: *"Arise!"*

What was that command? It was the oracle of God.

What was that ministry? It was the ministry that operated by the ability of the Holy Ghost. The Bible calls it *authority* and Jesus has given us that authority. The Bible also says that we have the *ability*. The ability of God is the *dunamis*—or the miracle working power that comes to enforce the authority that we have.

When Peter spoke the words of God—through *the identity of Jesus* and *by the ability of the Holy Ghost*—resurrection life came. Peter did not pray that God would raise Tabitha from the dead. *He knew the will of God.* He would never have journeyed to Joppa if he had not been confident of the will of God.

The thief comes to steal, kill, and destroy. Tabitha died before her time. The will of God, however, was to raise her from the dead. Remember what Jesus asked the Pharisees, *"Is it lawful to do good on the Sabbath day, or to do evil…to save a life or to kill"* (Mark 3:4)? He was saying, *"Use common sense! When you face a situation, don't just blindly say, 'Maybe it's the Lord's will.' Think about it!"* Realize who the devil is and who God is. If you know what the will of God is, then you will be able to hook into the Spirit of God. Once you know *for a fact* that the devil desires to kill people prematurely, then you can know *for a fact* that the will of God is to raise them from the dead. The next step is to utilize the help of the Holy Ghost to raise the person up!

So why was Peter praying? He was praying that he might receive upon him and receive within him the strength of the Spirit of God. He needed the ability of God to deal with the situation supernaturally. The Bible says, *"The effectual fervent prayer of a righteous man availeth much"* (James 5:16 KJV). The Bible also says, *"He that speaketh in an unknown tongue edifieth himself"* (1 Corinthians 14:4 KJV). When you pray in an unknown tongue—you edify yourself—you build your spirit man up. I believe that Peter was praying to the Lord, boldly coming to the throne of grace. He was not at the throne begging for the resurrection for Tabitha! He was there to obtain grace to help in time of need.

The Grace We Need

Grace provides what God has already granted. The Bible says that we are saved by grace through faith. We are saved by the grace of God. Yet there are people going to Hell, in spite of this free gift of grace. They are perishing because they haven't put faith in the grace of God!

We are filled with the Holy Ghost by the grace of God. There is no one that has earned the Holy Ghost! It's impossible because He is an unmerited gift—*a gift of grace.* We receive the gift of the Holy Spirit by putting faith in the grace of God. There must be an application of faith to receive grace from God.

The Word of God says, *"Man shall not live by bread alone"* (Matthew 4:4). Do you eat food every day? Jesus said that man should not live by natural food alone, but by every *rhema* Word that proceeds out of the mouth of God! The *rhema* Word is not going to come to the unbelieving person. A person walking in unbelief is going to have a hard time hearing the *rhema* Word of God. You must put faith in the grace to receive the promise of fresh manna every day.

Peter was receiving grace to help in time of need. That grace would provide the anointing and the ability to do the job effectively. It was Peter who wrote, *"If any man minister, let him do it as of the ability which God giveth"* (1 Peter 4:11 KJV). If it is God who raises the dead, then why do we need divine ability? The believer has to receive the ability that the Holy Ghost gives.

Peter started praying in the Spirit. He was praying boldly before the throne of grace to obtain two things: his *identity in Christ* and the *ability of the Holy Ghost*. He did not just want to say, *"Get up."* He wanted to speak as the oracle of God! He wanted to minister as "Peter entwined with God"—his life completely *"hid with Christ in God"* (Colossians 3:3). He wanted his *new identity*, which is seated with Christ above principalities and powers, *to do the talking*. He wanted the person who knows that death has been plundered—*to speak*. He wanted the person who holds the keys of death, Hell, and the grave to say, *"Tabitha, arise!"* The only way to do that was to throw the doubters out! Once he had silenced the noise of the flesh, he then hooked into the Spirit realm to receive the ability that the Holy Ghost gives. Peter penetrated Heaven.

Walk in the Spirit

Just like Peter, Smith Wigglesworth used his own faith to reach into the grace of God to receive the anointing. Jesus said, *"'I will never leave thee, nor forsake thee'...So that we may boldly say, the Lord is my helper"* (Hebrews 13:5, 6).

What does the Lord help us do? He helps us heal the sick. He helps us raise the dead. He helps us save the lost. He helps us touch the world. It's not natural help, but it's the supernatural ability that the Holy Ghost gives. It only comes to the people who want it and to those who know how to walk in the Spirit. You have to want it!

Peter prayed and the anointing came upon him—then the revelation came. We have the ability to *put off* everything from the natural realm and *put on* the Lord Jesus Christ and the anointing of God. When you go to church, you don't have to leave the way you came! Unfortunately, many Christians today have been trying to do a miracle "off memory." They want to do a miracle. They try to do a miracle, but they don't have the inspired utterance. They've become dull to the Word of God. They say, *"Didn't we read that Scripture last week?"* It's not what you remember that resurrects the dead — it's the revelation that you walk in *now*! The Holy Ghost will take what you remember and revive it, but only the Holy Ghost can do that.

When revelation comes, inspired utterance follows. When inspired utterance comes, power follows. Raising Tabitha from the dead required inspired utterance.

Who was Peter talking to? He was talking to Tabitha! *"But Peter put them all forth, and kneeled down, and prayed; and turning him to the body said, Tabitha, arise."* That is inspired utterance! That is the oracle of God! Boldness like that can only take place when a person knows their identity in Christ! It can only come from a person who is walking with the Lord *right now*, who is in fellowship with the Word *right now*, and who is in the Spirit *right now*.

The inspired utterance came and then the power came. That gift of power touched Tabitha's physical body and cured her from what she originally died from. If it hadn't, she would have been resurrected for a moment—only to topple over and die again! First there had to be inspired utterance, or the *good news*. The good news was *"Arise!"* Peter had good news and he was not ashamed of it. He had a supernatural boldness through the Holy Ghost. In Tabitha's situation, we can see several manifestations or gifts of the Holy Ghost in operation. She had to be raised and she had to be cured!

You can't *manufacture* the gift. You can't *make* it happen. You can't *produce* it. That's where so many Christians fall short! The Church has tried to reduce a miracle to natural principles. They have tried to do it religiously, but it can't be done that way. Sooner or later you have to learn how to get into the Spirit! You have to learn to operate with God.

One day, we'll get lost in the Spirit. There will be services where we will forget about the time, forget about the order of the service, and be lost in the Holy Ghost. When this happens, it will be chaos in the city! It won't be limited to the church building! People will be lost in the Spirit at home. On the street, cars will pull over and people will fall down under the power. They will call the fire department and say, *"The building is on fire!"* But it will just be the Holy Ghost! It's going to happen, but we're going to have to get in the Spirit.

> **That the God of our Lord Jesus Christ, the Father of Glory, may give unto you the spirit of wisdom and revelation in the knowledge of Him. The eyes of your understanding being enlightened; that ye may know what is the hope of His calling, and what the riches of His glory of His inheritance in the saints. And what is the exceeding greatness of His power to usward who believe, according to the working of His mighty power.**
>
> **Ephesians 1:17-19 KJV**

Paul is writing this to believers who are already baptized into the Body of Christ and baptized with the Holy Ghost. Paul, by the Holy Spirit, is saying to them, *"I'm praying for you so that God will give you the Spirit of Wisdom and Revelation in the knowledge of Him."* He is not praying that they would know *about* Him. He's praying that they would know *Him*. When you know someone, *you know what they know*. This is an important principle. The Bible says that *now* we know in part. Regardless of how much we grow, we will still just know Him in part. This *in part* is nurtured through the Spirit of Wisdom and Revelation.

Some people have a hard time knowing Him. They know very little about Him or they only know Him in the experience of salvation. It's not enough to know the Lord only in light of your salvation experience. You have to grow in God. To do so, you need the Spirit of

Wisdom and Revelation to be active in you. God wants the Spirit of Wisdom and Revelation to reveal Himself to you. When this happens, you won't only know God, you will know what God knows. You will see what God sees, you will say what God says, and you will do what God does. You will have a revelation of Him that came by the Spirit of Revelation that was sent to your spirit.

Express Your Gift

You have to cultivate your spirit. You have to develop your spirit in God and become sensitive in the Spirit. Let your spirit do the talking by praying in the Holy Ghost. Develop your language! Some believers still talk like little babies in the Holy Ghost! I've even heard some preachers pray in tongues like babies. You must put faith to your prayer language!

If I preached to you in an unknown language and joined the end of every word with the beginning of the next, you wouldn't know what I was saying! I don't do that because *I have faith*. Words are only intelligible if they are articulated properly. In the same manner, you must apply faith to praying with other tongues. If you really believe that you are full of the Spirit, then act like it! Pray in tongues as if you believe it is a language! Don't say in your heart, *"I'm not going to think about what I'm saying because it might not be God."* When you pray in an inhibited manner, your spirit is not getting the opportunity to express itself.

Put some faith to your tongues—it will give your spirit confidence! *"But ye, beloved, building up yourselves on your most holy faith, praying in the Holy Ghost..."* (Jude 1:20 KJV). Not only will you yield yourself to the Holy Spirit, but the Spirit will be invited to speak into your life. As you practice this, you will edify yourself on your most holy faith. In so doing, you will grow in God!

How will you ever be able to prophesy in a known language or give a word of knowledge if you are afraid of being wrong? If you can't put faith to tongues, you'll have a hard time putting faith to a language that everyone understands! *Express your gift!*

Eyes of Understanding

...the *eyes of your understanding being enlightened*; that you may know what is the hope of His calling, what are the riches of the glory of His inheritance in the saints.

Ephesians 4:18

Through faith we understand that the worlds were framed by the word of God, so that things which are seen were not made of things which do appear.

Hebrews 11:3

"*The eyes of your understanding being enlightened*" is referring to your heart's understanding. "*Through faith we understand that the worlds were framed by the Word of God*" is referring to trusting in the Lord with all your heart—leaning not to your natural understanding. There is an understanding in God that bypasses natural knowledge. It's an understanding that is enlightened by the Holy Spirit or the Spirit of Revelation who lives in you.

What does He show you?
He shows you revelation knowledge
from the Word of God.

Someone might say, *"Oh, I had a revelation yesterday."* Yesterday's revelation won't help you today! Someone who walks into their house at night doesn't say, "*I don't need to turn the light on today because I had the light on last night."* No, the light you turned on last night won't help you today. *"I don't understand why I fell down and bumped my head today! I mean, the light was on last night!"*

People wonder, *"Why am I not getting the results today that I got yesterday?"* You had a revelation yesterday! Yesterday, the light was on! You may remember how it looked last night, but last nights recollection won't do you any good if the lights are off.

The eyes of your understanding are enlightened when you fellowship with the Holy Ghost. As you walk in the Spirit, you will know what the hope of His calling is. You will be intimately acquainted with the riches of the glory of His inheritance in you. Hope is something realized.

When you love someone, you find out all you can about them. It's the same with your relationship with the Lord. The Spirit of Wisdom and Revelation will show you things about the one you love. When you discover a part of Him, then you know Him. You know Him and you can put faith in what He has said. As you practice knowing Him, you will come into the full understanding of the hope of His calling—Christ in you the hope of glory.

You are on an earthly mission that never stops—an ever-increasing lifestyle in Jesus. You are pursuing Him, not because He's your example, but because He lives in you. As you take the limits off of Him, people will see Him in His fullness through you.

> **And what is the exceeding greatness of his power to usward who believe, according to the working of his mighty power.**
>
> **Ephesians 1:19 KJV**

There is a great and an exceeding power that is available to you. Tabitha wasn't *believing* to rise from the dead. She didn't have faith for it—she had already died! It was Peter who was doing the believing because it was Peter who had a revelation. He had a revelation of the exceeding greatness of God's power toward him (Peter) who believed, according to the working of His mighty power. Peter had a revelation and by that revelation, he apprehended the power. By the power he apprehended, he exercised authority. By the authority, the power of God came, the gifts of the Spirit operated and a resurrection from the dead took place.

The Oracle of God

And my speech and my preaching were not with persuasive words of human wisdom, but in demonstration of the Spirit and of power.

1 Corinthians 2:4

Earlier you learned that, *"The manifestation of the Spirit is given to every man to profit withal."* You also learned that, *"If any man speak, let him speak as the oracles of God; if any man minister, let him do it as of the ability which God giveth, that God in all things may be glorified through Jesus Christ."*

Jesus is glorified and people benefit from the Spirit when the Spirit is in *manifestation* (not just in residence) through a vessel. Paul told the church at Corinth, *"When I came to you, my speech and my preaching was not with man's wisdom and the enticing words of it, but it was in demonstration of the Spirit and power"* (1 Corinthians 2:4). That means that his words carried demonstration. They carried *manifestation*. He wasn't necessarily talking about a manifestation of the *gifts* of the Spirit, but he was referring to a manifestation of the *power* of the Spirit. This manifestation could have been laughter, weeping, being slain in the Spirit, or falling into a trance. Whatever it was, it was a visible witness of the power of God working with the servant of God.

Paul told them that the manifestation of the Spirit was given so that their faith would not rest in the wisdom of man. As a legitimate apostle, he was constrained to preach the same Gospel that the Holy Spirit had revealed to him. He was not going to preach another gospel. However, he had the option to preach the Gospel either in the power of God or with the enticing words of man's wisdom.

You *can* preach the good news in a powerless way. How is this possible? It's only possible if you preach it in the flesh, preach it off memory, or just toss out some good Biblical principles. Paul said, *"I didn't come with the enticing words of man's wisdom! I didn't come to break down the Gospel to you psychologically or theologically. I determined to come to you in such a way that my words and my preaching would be in demonstration of the Spirit and power!"* That means he came in the

Spirit. Paul came to speak as the oracle of God so that their faith would not rest in the wisdom of man, but in the power of God.

Faith that Rests in Glory

Do you know what the problem in America is? Our faith rests in the wisdom of men! It's not for lack of hearing the Gospel. It's that people haven't seen the Gospel preached in demonstration of the Spirit and power. There are not many people manifesting the Spirit and causing us to "profit withal." We may know the Gospel, but our faith is not in the power of God.

People panic when the Holy Ghost comes on the scene! He interrupts their schedule. He disrupts the order of their service. They fear that things could go wrong!

Why is this? It's because they don't know how to work with the Spirit. People think the Holy Ghost is dangerous. He isn't when you know Him! There's absolutely no danger in manifesting the Holy Ghost. You can count on His power.

Some may warily say, *"But we've heard that people can get off into the gifts of the Spirit and mess up!"* No, it's only the abuse and the misuse of the manifestation of the Spirit that creates a backlash. You can take any good thing and do too much of it. Yes, there are people who abuse and misuse what is meant to be a blessing. However, the Holy Spirit is not just prescribed by God, it's the only way a believer can live in the Spirit! Living in the Spirit is not a suggestion; it's a command.

Paul said, *"I came so that your faith would rest in the power of God rather than in the wisdom of men."* Daily, you can walk in the power of the Spirit. It's *easy* to get in the Holy Ghost! During praise and worship have you ever sensed the glory of God? You can do that every day! You don't have to wear a choir robe to touch God. You can do that any day and anywhere! You can get in the Spirit *all the time*!

Choose This Day

> Now we have received, not the spirit of the world, but the spirit which is of God; that we might know the things that are freely given to us of God. Which things also we speak, not in the words which man's wisdom teacheth, but which the Holy Ghost teacheth; comparing spiritual things with spiritual.
>
> **1 Corinthians 2:12-13 KJV**

We didn't receive the spirit of the world. We received the Spirit of God so that we might know the things that are freely given to us of God. The spirit of the world will not know the things that are freely given to us of God. A Christian that is not walking in the Spirit can succumb to the domination of this world. Paul said that he didn't come with the enticing words of man's wisdom, but he could have!

Why didn't he? Paul determined that he was going to go to them in the Spirit.

How should a Christian face life? You should face life the way you choose to face it—for *this day*. You can actually choose to face it under the influence of the spirit of the world.

Does that mean that the spirit of the world lives in that person? No, we have not received the spirit of fear. A fearful Christian is someone who has chosen the spirit of the world.

Does that mean that they are possessed by the spirit of fear? No. The way you *choose* to live this day is the way you *will live* this day!

You have received the Spirit of God so that you might know the things that are freely given to you of God. There are certain things that are freely yours, but you won't know what those things are without the Spirit of God revealing them to you. God wants to reveal the things to you, but you won't apprehend them unless you get a revelation of them. These revealed things won't be tangibly expressed in your life unless you believe for them. We have to see them through the Spirit before we see them manifested in the natural.

What does this have to do with the gifts of the Spirit? The gifts of the Spirit are freely given by God. Yet some Christians still walk around saying, *"I wonder what my gift is?"* Who gave them the spirit of the world? Didn't they receive the Spirit of God that they might know the things that are freely given to them of God?

You ought to know what's available *to you* through the Holy Spirit! Cultivate what the Lord has given you and allow Him to manifest in you and through you. The gifts of the Spirit, spiritual maturity, the wisdom of God—*all* these things—have been freely given to you by God! The only way to know them and to identify them is by the Holy Spirit.

The Natural Can't Receive the Supernatural

> **Which things also we speak, not in the words which man's wisdom teacheth, but which the Holy Ghost teacheth; comparing spiritual things with spiritual (or fitly joining together Spirit-revealed truth with Spirit-taught words).**
>
> **1 Corinthians 2:13 KJV**
> (parentheses added by author)

After you receive a revelation, you talk the revelation and then you experience the revelation. The utterance and the power will come after the revelation. Without a revelation, you won't have anything to say. The power comes *after* the utterance.

You can have a revelation and never act on it or see the power of it. Some will say, *"I don't understand why I have to do it like that? I don't understand why I have to do it that way."* When the Holy Spirit is influencing your spirit, you will understand and know the things that are freely given to you. You'll know that God's way is the right way. Spirit-revealed truths with Spirit-taught words are fitly joined together.

"The natural man receives not the things of the Spirit of God" (1Corinthians 12:14). Do you know that you walk in the natural? You live in the real world. I know the text is talking about a person who is unsaved, but none of us are saved spirit, soul and body...yet. The Bible says, *"Be not conformed to this world; but be ye transformed by the renewing of your mind, that ye may prove what is that good, and acceptable, and perfect, will of God"* (Romans 12:2). If you don't renew your mind, you can't *prove* the good, acceptable or perfect will of God. If your mind isn't renewed you can't *see* the good, acceptable or the perfect!

Why doesn't the natural man receive the things of the Spirit of God? *"For they are foolishness unto him; neither can he know them, because they are spiritually discerned"* (1 Corinthians 2:14). A carnal Christian is not ready to receive the manifestation of the Holy Ghost in their life. The manifestation of the Spirit is a "thing of the Spirit." The natural man can't receive it because he hasn't been tuned into the things of the Spirit. You cannot walk in the natural and count on supernatural help. The Holy Spirit is only sent to help you live the Christ-kind of life. He can anoint you to be like Jesus, but He can't force you to walk in the Spirit!

People have been taught that someone can be out of line with God in their character but still operate out of the gift that is on their life. It is true that the Bible says that the gifts and callings of God are without repentance. However, there are people that believe that they can learn from a person who is practicing adultery, as long as they have the gifts in operation. In other words, as long as their working miracles, they must be okay by God! They won't operate in the gifts for long, however. The grace of God might give someone a little space, but the fountain *will* dry up! It won't take long. If someone is doing miracles and they are not walking like Jesus, they may simply be operating off of the faith of another person. They may be operating off of a gift on someone else's life.

If you walk in unbelief, the power of God will dry up in your life. I'm not referring to gross sin, but on slacking off on worship and praise; walking away from the congregation of the Saints; harboring resentment, etc. If you step away from the *Spirit-walk*, the light and the anointing of God won't be there anymore. The gifts of the Spirit will no longer operate through you like they did in the past. If you are still hearing the Spirit of God, He will deal with you on what needs to be corrected. He may still try to use you, but you will be confined to a certain level that you chose to make your boundary. You will not be able to grow beyond this barrier unless you walk in the light of the Spirit.

An Earth-Shaking Revival

> And great fear came upon all the Church, and upon as many as heard these things. And by the hands of the apostles were many signs and wonders wrought among the people; (and they were all with one accord in Solomon's porch. And of the rest durst no man join himself to them; but the people magnified them. And believers were the more added to the Lord, multitudes both of men and women.) Insomuch that they brought forth the sick into the streets, and laid them on beds and couches, that at the least the shadow of Peter passing by might overshadow some of them. There came also a multitude out of the cities round about unto Jerusalem, bringing sick folks, and them which were vexed with unclean spirits; and they were healed every one. Then the high priest rose up, and all they that were with him, (which is the sect of the Sadducees,) and were filled with indignation. And laid their hands on the apostles, and put them in the common prison. But the angel of the Lord by night opened the prison doors, and brought them forth, and said, Go stand and speak in the temple to the people all the words of this life.
>
> **Acts 5:11-20 KJV**

> *The greatest revival the world has ever seen is getting ready to come into its fullness.*

Remember when the disciples dealt with Ananias and Sapphira? Peter had a word of knowledge. That word of knowledge was crucial. It was devastating. The word of knowledge literally removed people who had allowed Satan to fill their hearts. They instantly died! When that happened, great fear—or godly reverence—fell on the Church and on all those who heard about it.

People magnified the Word of God that was spoken through the lips of the apostles. They magnified the Word of God and were not even daring to join the Church! The people in the world were afraid because of what might happen! Nevertheless, people *were added* to the Church *daily*. They got saved and then they joined the Church. The people brought the sick and laid them in the street so that the shadow of Peter might touch them and bring healing to their bodies.

What was it that gave the Holy Ghost such an awesome avenue of expression in the midst of those people? The people were prioritizing the will of God. They sought the Kingdom of God first. One of the greatest things that the Lord will ever do in the Body of Christ is to get us to be of one mind. The Lord wants us to stand together as *one*—to guard one another, defend one another, love one another, respect one another, to stop being critical of one another, and to stop being divided from one another. God's will is for us to come to the realization that the individual blessing is *dependent* on the corporate blessing.

Do you want the power of God in your life? If you do, you must seek what God is doing through the revelation of the vision that is being preached from the pulpit. God has a plan for each of our cities, our nations, and the world. We are excited about it, but we have to remember that it will not happen *just because God said it*. There has to be a *response* at our end to guard the vision. There have been enough church splits, enough failures, enough sin and enough embarrassment for the cause of Christ. We can't just settle for church attendance anymore. We must contend for something beyond that. We must contend for a citywide, a nationwide, a worldwide—an *Earth-shaking* revival that comes *through* men and women who have risen up to embrace destiny.

Beyond the Realm of Limitation

"And great fear came upon all the Church and upon as many as heard these things." Reverence and unity came upon the Church when God uncovered the devil. All of a sudden, they revered the Lord. All of a sudden, they united.

Do you know what that unity did? Not only did it add believers to the Church, but it opened the windows of Heaven to the Holy Ghost's miracle working power. Can you imagine a revival where everyone was healed? The people came and brought the sick to be healed. The disciples operated by faith, by anointing with oil, by the laying on of hands, and by the shadow (which is a sign and a wonder). They also operated in the manifestation of the Spirit—in the gifts. Jesus operated in the gifts when he put mud on the blind man's eyes. Healing doesn't necessarily just have to come by the laying on of hands. God is creative! He is not limited to a method. As a miracle working child of God, you must remain sensitive to divine direction. The Holy Ghost desires to address and meet each specific situation through the avenue that He chooses.

What was it that caused Peter's ministry to go outside of the realm of limitation? It was *those around him* who had vowed in their hearts not to give *any* place to the devil. If God will move like that in the area of divine healing, He will move like that in the area of finances. As a matter of fact, the Bible shows us that in this account, God moved in the financial arena first! God was moving in the arena of finances before Ananias and Sapphira ever got greedy. Immediately, the devil tried to use Ananias and Sapphira to kill or pollute the move of God, but the Lord *literally* took them out of the church. When He did, a great move of God erupted within the city. There is a great move of God coming *today!*

People wonder why Dr. Robin and I do things the way we do. Sometimes I tell people, *"If you don't like it, there's the door!"* You see, there are really two choices. We can have a mediocre ministry and join the "club," or we can strive for the work of God on the planet.

We have chosen the high call rather than the low call. All who would like to join us are welcome to come. We will take all who want to go with us to the high places in Jesus. We will see the will of God done in our lives and in the lives of those who join us.

CHAPTER 4

KNOWING GOD

―――◆―――

*You must let the Holy Ghost lead
you beyond what you know!*

Aperson who flows in the Spirit is a man of the Spirit. He or she is someone with sensitivity to God's realm—someone who has stepped outside the limitations of the natural world.

The Bible says, *"Trust in the Lord with all thine heart; and lean not unto thine own understanding"* (Proverbs 3:5 KJV). Your heart is the lamp of the Lord. It's where the Holy Ghost has chosen to make His permanent home. A Holy Ghost person chooses to lean upon revelation knowledge rather than natural understanding.

Revelation knowledge comes by the Spirit of God to show you the probability or availability of a divine promise. You may not know how the promise will come to pass, but you do know what must take place in the Spirit to cause it to happen. We know, for instance, that the anointing created the world. The world was created through speech or as stated another way, by *"calling those things which be not as though they were"* (Romans 4:17). The invisible substance becomes visible and natural. Through revelation we know the process that God uses to perform a miracle, however, we don't always know how it will transpire in the natural. We know that we are going to prosper, but we may not know who is going to open that door. We may not know who is going to be used by God to carry out that miracle. We know we are going to be more than conquerors, but we don't know how God is going to bring this about naturally.

God is saying, *"Don't limit yourself to how it's going to happen! Don't limit yourself to what you know with your natural mind or perceive with your natural understanding."* If you are going to be a Spirit-led person, you have to learn how to trust in the Lord with all of your heart.

A Radical Conversion

> And my speech and my preaching was not with enticing words of man's wisdom, but in demonstration of the Spirit and of power; that your faith should not stand in the wisdom of men, but in the power of God.
>
> 1 Corinthians 2:4

Paul was a man who was radically converted. You may have had a radical conversion yourself, but if you didn't—you still have a radical God who is able to give you a radical encounter with Him.

As faith people, we are not called to pursue experiences, but we do pursue a daily experiential relationship with the Lord. In other words, we're not looking to see angels or to see things that are far out or fantastic. We're not seeking an experience. However, because we're born of God and the Lord is our friend, we press into and believe for a daily experiential fellowship with Him.

The Apostle Paul was radically transformed. *How did he do it?* He really didn't try! He was on an assignment to destroy the Church and to bring the people of God into bondage. As he was minding his own business, a light from Heaven—brighter than the noonday sun—shined upon him. The force of that light knocked him to the ground (that's a demonstration of the Spirit). A voice then said to him, *"Saul, Saul, why are you persecuting Me?"* Severely startled, Saul asked, *"Who are you, Lord?"* If a light shined from Heaven and knocked you down, *you* would call the source of it "Lord" too!

What about the devil's supernatural ability? Not one of us needed the devil's supernatural power to be in bondage. Before you were saved, the devil bound you and kept you under his heel through natural means. When you received the Lord Jesus Christ, you received the God-given ability to detect who the Holy Ghost is. You were given the ability to know the voice of the Lord, to not follow a stranger and to be able to comprehend who God is. When Saul, a religious man seeking after truth, encountered the Spirit of God—he immediately knew *who* he had run into. There was no question.

An Enemy Called Unbelief

If Paul wanted the Corinthians' faith to rest in the power of God—then today—God wants your faith to rest in *His power*. God hasn't changed his mind. He's not saying, *"Now today, I would like you to rest your faith on an intellectual gospel."* No, the Lord hasn't changed his Gospel. He is the same yesterday, today and forever.

Paul said, *"I am not ashamed of the gospel of Christ, for it is the power of God unto salvation to everyone that believeth"* (Romans 1:16 KJV). The good news is that the power of God is available to everyone who *believes*. The power demonstration is directly related to faith in the promise.

All over the world, I've met people who have a form of godliness and deny the power of it. Those of you who are studying this book have fallen in love with God. You have stored up a zeal for Him—and *God is fanning that flame inside you*. You want more of the reality of the anointing. You desire more of God now, than every before.

Understand this: If you do not maintain a tenacity for the things of God, the spirit of the world will get on you. The Bible says the spirit of the world is a spirit of fear. *"For God hath not given us the spirit of fear; but of power, and of love, and of a sound mind"* (2 Timothy 1:7 KJV). The spirit of fear can get on the believer. At one point, it had already influenced Timothy. Paul had to write to him and tell him to stir the gift of God, which was in him. God didn't give Timothy the spirit of fear, but it was affecting him.

What is fear? Fear is the opposite of faith. Some would define fear as being afraid—afraid of dying, afraid of a dog, afraid of the storm. Fear, however, can be disguised in the simplest statement of unbelief. Fear can be hidden in an immovable believer who refuses to allow the Word to change them. If you're growth feels sluggish, it's because you've allowed a certain amount of *unbelief* or *fear* to taint you. You've become a hearer of the Word and not a doer.

Say this out loud:

I'm chosen by God to be used mightily! I'm chosen to be used supernaturally with power demonstrations of the

Holy Ghost! Therefore, I choose to contend for the faith that was delivered to the Saints!

Discerning of Spirits

Years ago, I was ministering at a church in New York. God had begun to break in among the people and the Holy Spirit was breathing upon the ministry. The people were laughing in the Spirit and falling down under the power. When a breakthrough like this happens – in a life, in a ministry, in a city, or in a nation—the devil will always attempt to quench the power demonstrations of the Spirit. He *hates* the Gospel backed up with power!

As the people were worshipping the Lord, I closed my eyes and in my spirit, I saw thirty people hugging each other in front of the church. I saw the power of God come upon them and all of them being slain in the Spirit. As I opened my eyes I saw the choir singing and worshipping the Lord. The witness of the Spirit said, *"That's them."*

They turned the service over to me and I asked the choir to come forward. The whole choir—about thirty people—came to the front. When they did, I said, *"Hug each other!"* Immediately, they were slain under the power of God and praying with other tongues!

What is it when thirty people are slain in the Spirit under the power of God? It is the demonstration of the Spirit and of power! People were healed and delivered. The anointing of God bore witness to that church.

The Bible teaches that through the discerning of spirits you can see into the Spirit realm. Many people misunderstand discerning of spirits to mean *discerning of devils*. The discerning of spirits, however, is simply the ability to look into the realm of the spirit. In the realm of the spirit, you could see Jesus, you could see the Holy Ghost—or as the Spirit wills—you could see the glory cloud, angels, demons, or just have a vision. The Bible says, *"I will pour out my spirit upon all flesh; and your sons and your daughters shall prophesy, and your young men shall see visions...."* (Acts 2:17). When you are full of the Holy Ghost, He will begin to birth in you an ability to perceive certain things by the Spirit. If we would give ourselves wholly to the realm of the Spirit of

God, we would see some mighty things! We would see miracles in our daily life!

What stops us from experiencing this? Quite simply, it's unbelief. When you know who your enemy is, then you know how to deal with him. When you know the source of your battles, you know how to kill its influence. The problem is unbelief. It's not God! God hasn't become weak—He's the same yesterday, today, and forever! God hasn't gone deaf—He still hears the prayers of His Saints!

Why didn't God show me that whole church in New York hugging one another? Why didn't He slay the whole church in the Spirit? The Lord was ready, but the church wasn't. He could only move among those who had committed themselves to a purpose. The people in the choir were unified—they were all responsible for the same thing. Their responsibility linked them together to a purpose. This common purpose and unified agreement gave God the right to move in and bring about an activation in their lives.

I guarantee you that there were people in the congregation that were living for themselves, prioritizing their own lives and living without a vision. Instead of being touched, they were just stirred to excitement. They could have, however, also been stirred by the Spirit to desire more.

Intellect or Inspiration?

On another occasion, we were ministering at a church in Atlanta. The pastor had been teaching the people for three weeks on being slain in the Holy Ghost. He knew what was going to happen when we ministered and he wanted the people to be ready. He explained to them through the Word of God what it was and what the Holy Spirit had in store for them. He even told the women that they could wear trousers on the day of the meeting if they wanted to, and they did!

As we ministered Sunday morning, the altar was filled with people. There were about twenty people standing at the altar and I exclaimed, *"There's the anointing!"* At that very moment, the power of God swept in and knocked all of them to the floor! When God does something to your physical body, it's only because the Spirit of God has already begun to do something in your spirit man. God began to fill them, energize them, activate them and impact them with the supernatural anointing of the Holy Ghost.

The only way to be led by the Holy Ghost and to operate in power demonstrations is to be *full* of the Spirit. You can't be full of the Spirit unless you maintain a Spirit-filled life. It's impossible to maintain a Spirit-filled life if you are dominated by unbelief. If only the Holy Spirit could just get a hold of your mouth, grab your tongue and speak through you! However, that's not the way God works. Where's the faith in that?

The Holy Spirit will inspire and influence. He allows your mind to operate. Human beings—*intelligent* creatures—have the ability to allow a shallow brain to short circuit the power of the living God. Subconsciously, people stop the Spirit from flowing through them because the things of the Spirit are foreign to them. They can't dissect it with their intellect. They can't comprehend it naturally. The Bible says that it's not by might or by power, but it's by the Spirit—that means *the anointing*.

Trusting in the Holy Ghost

And my speech and my preaching were not with persuasive words of human wisdom, but in demonstration of the Spirit and of power.

1 Corinthians 2:4

The apostle Paul is saying, *"Listen! My message is dependent upon the Holy Ghost to demonstrate the power of God. Only the power of God can inform and validate the message that I'm preaching."*

The Bible recorded that the disciples went preaching everywhere, *"the Lord working with them and confirming the Word with signs following"* (Mark 16:20). That means the Holy Ghost was working with them to confirm the Word. Their message was dependent upon the Spirit for demonstration.

The disciples only preached the things that kept them in a position of dependency upon the Holy Ghost. It takes some Holy Ghost boldness to preach something that only God can bring to pass. When people say, *"God can heal you, but we don't know if He will. He can save you, but we don't know if that's His intention today,"* then they have just detached themselves from their dependency on God. They've unhooked from His power. They're really saying that they don't trust that the Holy Ghost is going to show up after they preach.

Why would someone not trust the Holy Ghost?
They don't know the Holy Ghost!

Why would someone not trust the Spirit that Jesus sent to equip them to do the work? It's because they haven't seen a pattern or an example of someone who is dependent on the Spirit for demonstration. All they've seen are preachers who have a form of godliness but deny the power of it.

Jesus sent the Holy Ghost to enable us. Unbelief, however, will stop a person from being filled to overflowing on a continual basis. That person is hindered because they have not heard the promises regarding the Spirit's effectual activity in their life. There's no place in the Kingdom of God for people who will not trust the Holy Ghost. There is no such thing as a Gospel without the Spirit.

"I thank my God, I speak with tongues more than ye all" (1 Corinthians 14:18 KJV). Paul said that he prayed in tongues more than the *whole Corinthian church!* It is no wonder that he could say,

> **My message was not made up of words that were cloaked in philosophy, but they were effectual words that were reliant upon the power and the demonstration of the Spirit! Listen! I am so full of God's Word in my life that when I preach a message, I say, 'God has promised this, therefore, God will do this for anyone who will believe. God has said this, therefore, God will perform this on behalf of anyone who will believe.' And then I put myself in a place of dependency where I have to work with the Person that God has sent to enable me to do**

supernatural works on behalf of the Lord Jesus Christ!

1 Corinthians 2: 1-4 Wuest

The child of God must develop a relationship with the Holy Spirit! When they do, there will be no limits to what they will see in their life! You may be thinking, *"Oh, but I have problems—my bills are not paid!"* Your problem is that unbelief is causing you to walk in the flesh! If you will walk in the Spirit, *your bills will be paid.* It is *abnormal* for a Christian to have needs in their life that are not met. It is *abnormal* for a Christian to have unfulfilled godly desires. You are only limited by unbelief.

Troubleshooting Your Faith

The word *demonstration* is the Greek word *apodeixis*. It means *manifestation, demonstration,* or *exhibition.* Paul's message was dependent on the Holy Ghost exhibition or manifestation of power. The Spirit is in you all the time, but He's an invisible Spirit.

Have you ever put a key in the ignition of your car and turned it, but the vehicle wouldn't start? Wondering what was wrong, you may have opened the hood to find out if the battery was working properly. Seeing that the battery cables are connected, you know that it's possible that the juice is there—but you can't see the juice. So you troubleshoot the situation. Putting the two battery cables together, you put it to the test. If the battery is dead, there will not be any sparks. If the battery is alive, the sparks will shoot out.

By the same token, if the battery of your spirit man has gone dry, it may not be detectable on the outside. There may be juice, or it may be bone dry. You are put to the test when you are in a place where you *know* what God has promised, but the situation is not cooperating with it. It's an embarrassing thing to take out your cables, put the two together and not find any sparks!

Wouldn't you rather just see enough sparks to prove to the enemy and everybody else that God has some juice running through your vessel? As Paul said, *"I'm dependent upon exhibitions and manifestations of the Spirit that will prove that the Gospel in me is the dunamis of God unto salvation to anyone who believes!"*

You might be saying, *"Maybe if I keep quoting the Word, I would believe it."* Maybe if you would believe it, you would quote it! Some people try to do it in reverse. They try to say it over and over—thinking that if they just keep on saying it, they'll somehow end up believing it.

The Spirit of God is called the same Spirit of Faith. The Bible says that we have received the Spirit of Faith. I have believed and that is why I have spoken. *Why do we speak?* We speak because we believe. We speak because we are dedicated to encouraging someone else to believe! *Why invest the time in doing this?* Once another person believes, then we have the opportunity to release the power of God in us and allow the Holy Ghost to bring deliverance into that life. Paul said, *"I put myself in that position all of the time. I came preaching that kind of Gospel because that's what God has called me to do."*

...In order that your faith should not be *resting* in human philosophy but in God's power.

1 Corinthians 2:5 Wuest

Your faith should rest in the power of God. Notice the word *rest*. Paul is saying, *"Listen! Make sure your faith is not based upon what you have intellectualized. Don't base your confidence on what you have assumed that you know. Make sure it is based upon the power—the anointing and the Spirit of Almighty God."*

What does this mean to you? It means that *you* are going to have to have encounters with God in fellowship! You are going to have to have encounters with God in prayer. You're going to need to have encounters with God in worship because that is the realm through which the anointing will increase in your life. The Bible said, *"He anoints my head with oil."*

What does your cup do? It runs over. That's manifestation! That's exhibition! That's demonstration of the Spirit!

When does your cup run over? Your cup runs over after God anoints your head with oil! The Psalmist said, *"I will be anointed with fresh oil."*

How often will this happen? Daily!

How does your cup run over? Your cup will run over as you utilize your faith to appreciate and to *prioritize* the Holy Ghost, God's report, and the Spirit realm. The day that you make the choice to live in the natural, whether willingly or unwillingly, you're going to suffer. You will experience a shortage of the anointing in your life.

I have to sing! I have to worship! I have to praise God! I'm not satisfied to just *listen* to anointed music when I drive. I will open the sunroof, roll down the windows and blast the stereo. I will sing along with it! I'm not satisfied with limits! I want all that I can get and I want the anointing of God to reach out and get a hold of somebody else for the glory of Jesus!

The anointing of the Lord is available to you today!

Answers to the Questions

As His divine power has given to us all things that pertain to life and godliness, through the knowledge of Him who called us by glory and virtue.

2 Peter 1:3

With all of my heart, I believe that life's questions can be answered through the Word of God. *He has given us all things that pertain unto life and godliness.* It is not God's will or God's best for you to have unanswered theological or doctrinal questions. He wants you to have answers.

I'm not insinuating that we are going to know *everything* in every situation. We are, however, going to have *sound doctrine* and *sound theology* if we desire it from the Lord. If that wasn't available, Paul would not have told Timothy that there will come a day when people would not tolerate sound doctrine (2 Timothy 4:3).

If sound doctrine were something that we would understand better in the "by and by," then it wouldn't be available in the *here and now*. Paul said it was available. Paul said that he was preaching it. He said, *"If any other person preach to you another gospel, let him be cursed"* (Galatians 1:8).

Paul said that a day will come when people will not tolerate sound doctrine. They'll heap to themselves teachers having itching ears. There will be so many different views and opinions preached by false teachers that the people will be deceived.

I want you to say this:

Sound doctrine, right division of the Word of God and being led by the Holy Spirit belong to me in Jesus' name. Amen!

Pumping Spiritual Iron

That he would grant you, according to the riches of his glory, to be strengthened with might by his Spirit in the inner man.

Ephesians 3:16

How are you strengthened? By His Spirit!
Where are you strengthened? In your inner man!

He didn't say that you're strengthened by a book or that you're strengthened by a Scripture, although God will use those things to strengthen you. Did you know that you can read the Scriptures intellectually and not get anything out of it? You can read a book theoretically and not spiritually benefit from it! As a matter of fact, you can attend church in the realm of the flesh and never change!

So what is Paul saying? He is talking to the Ephesians. They are born again, Spirit-filled believers and he's telling them, *"God will grant you, according to the riches of His glory, to be strengthened with might!"* Would you like to be strengthened with might?

Do you know what might is? Might comes from the Spirit of Might and Power—*that's the Holy Ghost.* That is the creative, the miraculous, the divine living Spirit whom God sent to equip you and to enable you to perform what He has called you to do!

He will grant you to be strengthened with might by the Holy Ghost—by the anointing—by the power of God that is within your inner man. Why didn't He say, *"in your head?"* Your head cannot be strengthened with might! Your head can only be renewed to the Word of God. The might that flows through you is channeled from the Spirit of God into your spirit. The Bible says, *"The spirit of man is the lamp of the Lord"* (Proverbs 20:27). God has put His spiritual deposit within you.

What would hold you back from this experience? Once again, the answer is unbelief! Lack of knowledge will also hinder you every time. Also, if you insist on the flesh and refuse the Spirit, you will not cash in on the benefits of being strengthened with might in your inner man.

Why would someone not allow the Holy Ghost to strengthen him? There are several reasons, one being unbelief. The other is that the child of God hasn't been taught that they are a spirit. If they haven't been taught it, how can they expect to walk in it?

Emaciated Believers

As a human being, you've been educated to use your mind. You've been trained to use your body and your senses. You have been thoroughly versed in the use of all that is natural.

Most churches simply tell the new believer, *"Congratulations, now you are going to Heaven."* While that's true, they don't tell them anything more! There is so much that God has made available, but lack of knowledge prevents the baby Christian from moving beyond the elementary principles of faith. Their spirit man doesn't grow and they aren't strengthened in the Lord or in the power of His might. Strength in the spirit will only come by desiring the pure milk of the Word and then by feeding upon strong meat. Growth comes by developing a relationship and a communion with the Holy Ghost.

How does faith come? Faith comes by every *rhema* that you hear. It comes by hearing and hearing comes from every *rhema* that proceeds out of the mouth of God.

How does life come? Man does not live by bread alone. If a person doesn't eat, they will look emaciated. If your child didn't eat for a month, you wouldn't say, *"Oh sweetheart, you look great!"* No, you would look at that child and say, *"You look terrible! You are going to eat now!"*

If you eat—you develop an appetite to eat more. If you don't eat, you lose the appetite that you have. In the Church world today, Saints have lost their appetite for the Word of God. There was once a day when they were so hungry that they couldn't eat enough! If you had anything in your spiritual refrigerator, they would raid it! If you knew one revelation, they would pry it out of you! There was an insatiable hunger for the Word of God.

What would make a person hungry for God like that? The Holy Spirit is the Agent who develops your appetite for the Word. It is He who wants you to have Jesus in your life. Jesus is the Word, but if the child of God doesn't have an appetite for the Word, they will not have an appetite for Jesus! A child of God without a spiritual appetite will not experience the tangible manifestation of His presence.

What did the Holy Ghost come to do? The Holy Ghost came to develop a hunger for the things of God. Jesus said, *"They that hunger and thirst after righteousness will be filled"* (Matthew 5:6).

Why would a person not hunger and thirst after righteousness? They prioritized other things and their spiritual stomach shrank. They started pushing that spiritual plate away. If you are accustomed to eating, your stomach will grow—and instead of pushing the plate away—you will ask for seconds!

Some Christians have allowed the spirit of the world to rob them of their appetite for the Word of God. It no longer smells as good to them. They no longer crave it. They're not hungry for the things of God and they don't know why. If you stop eating, you lose strength.

How is God going to strengthen His people with power? Paul said it in this way, *"I'm praying that the eyes of your understanding would be enlightened."* In other words, *"I'm going to pray that the Holy Ghost will give you a revelation of the importance of getting together with Him. He wants to lead you into a place of communion with the Word! In that place, God will strengthen you with might by His Spirit in your inner man!"*

This is the avenue through which God is going to open the Spirit realm to us. This is how we are going to become supernatural! We will not become supernatural because God *sovereignly decided* that it was time. We will only become supernatural when we begin to hunger and press into the realm of the Spirit.

I want you to say this:

> *Holy Spirit, You're welcome today and every day of my life to continue tugging on me and inspiring me. It is my desire to follow You and be strengthened in my spirit with the might of the Lord.*

Does Christ Feel at Home in Your Heart?

That Christ may dwell in your hearts by faith.

Ephesians 3:17

That the Christ might finally settle down and feel completely at home in your hearts through your faith.

Ephesians 3:17 Wuest

Why would Christ not feel at home? Christ will not feel at home in your heart if there is an unbelieving influence. If you are born again, you can be sure that you have godly desires. There's a difference, however, between desires stirred up and desires oppressed. Faith will stir up desire. Unbelief will compress or oppress desire. When your desires are suppressed, they are no longer alive. If your desires are dead to you, then others will not be able to see what the Holy Ghost has put on the inside of you.

Christ really feels at home in the lives of those who are *doers* of the Word. Jesus said, *"If you do My commandment, then I will love you. My Father will love you, and We will come and make Our abode with you"* (John 14:23).

We know that Jesus lives in every Christian, *so what was He really saying?* Jesus was saying, *"I'm going to live with you in a manifested form. I'm going to demonstrate power on your behalf because you have become a doer of My Word."*

Doing the Word is building up your spirit man. It's building yourself up on your most holy faith. It's developing a sensitivity to the Spirit of God.

Several years ago we developed a friendship with a couple that had been associate pastors in a very powerful Baptist church. They had gotten Spirit-filled and God had opened the Scriptures to them about deliverance. They began to learn about casting out devils. When their denomination learned about it, they were ejected out of their church! They had the call of God on their lives but never mentioned the call to us. At the time, they were running a television station and they were content in that.

Once while we were ministering in their city, we met up and fellowshiped together. We were talking about a lot of different things, and all of a sudden I said, *"Shhhh!"* Everyone stopped talking. *"I just feel that we need to pray"* and I began to pray in tongues. As I said the first couple of words in tongues, a wind flooded that room! When the wind hit that room—it hit that couple and they began to sob. We laid hands on them and the prophetic began to flow. We prophesied, we read their mail and God ministered to them. It was an awesome visitation of God.

It's imperative that we develop a sensitivity to the Holy Ghost. How do you know when a truck is coming? How do you know when someone's in the room? How do you know when a natural event is transpiring? God has granted you an ability—through your humanity—to evaluate, to access and to analyze what you sense in the natural world. Yet, people often think it's weird when you're sensitive in the Spirit. In reality, your spirit was around before your body ever developed!

Before your body developed, your spirit was alive! We were born and then we developed in the natural. We grew. Some people are "smart" in the natural. They specialize in rumors, in lies, and in sensual earthly wisdom.

When you're full of the Holy Spirit, you'll begin to develop a sensitivity to the Spirit. As you develop that sensitivity, you'll know what the Spirit is doing. You'll know when something is wrong and you'll know when something is right! You'll know when God is doing something.

If you are full of the Spirit, you will be strong in your spirit. Not one leader in the ministry world has ever fallen into sin while they were strong in the Lord and in the power of His might! No one has fallen into sin while they were strengthened with might by His Spirit in their inner man.

What happened then? Somewhere along the way they lost their appetite for the Word. They lost their desire for the Spirit, but kept on going. The battery cables were connected, but no one could see whether there was juice.

How do you know when someone is not walking in the Spirit? It's easy to detect. Usually, they know a great deal about the natural, but they know *very little* about the Spirit. Some, who have fallen into sin, are people who used to know a lot about the Spirit. You see, it's not a "once and for all" thing. If you don't use it, *you lose it!* It doesn't go away—it's in you—but God wants *you* to stir it up into expression! He wants His power to be expressed through you.

Say this out loud:

I'm going to be strong and mighty in the Lord!

Experiencing God

[*That you*] may be able to comprehend with all the saints what is the breadth, and length, and depth, and height; and to know the love of Christ, which passeth knowledge, that ye might be filled with all the fullness of God.

Ephesians 3:18-19 KJV
(brackets added by author)

Paul prayed that you might be strengthened with might by His Spirit in your inner man. He prayed that you would comprehend with all the Saints the limitlessness of God and that you would be filled with all the fullness of God. He prayed that you would know the love of Christ, which passes knowledge.

That word *know* refers to an experiential knowledge. It is *to experience* the love of Christ. Paul also said that nothing shall separate us from the love of God, which is in Christ Jesus (Romans 8:38, 39). He must have had an experience with that love!

How do you have an experience with the love of God? You do not experience it through intellect. I know intellectually religious people who would kill someone in the name of God! The Bible says that you understand the love of Christ—which passes natural knowledge—in your spirit man. This is possible because you have the *Knower* in you! The Holy Ghost lives in you and He will make spiritual truths known to you.

The Spirit realm is the realm through which God functions. It's the realm where miracles transpire, breakthroughs happen and visitations come. Remember the prophet and his servant! The prophet went to God and said, *"God, open his eyes so that he would be able to see that there are more on our side then there are on their side"* (2 Kings 6:17)!

Paul prayed that the eyes of your understanding would be enlightened. He was really saying, *"God, open the Ephesians eyes! Open the understanding of their spirit man so that they can see what is available to them by the Holy Ghost! Open their eyes so that they can flow in the Holy Spirit."*

> **...that ye might be filled with all the fullness of God.**
>
> **Ephesians 3:19b KJV**

How much of the fullness of God is available? It's *all* available—God is not holding anything back. If you are full of *all the fullness* of God, then you will be strong with might in the inner man! Paul didn't say that the Ephesian church was already full of all the fullness of God. The Ephesians were full of the Holy Ghost, but he prayed that they might be filled with *all of the fullness* of God!

We are Christ's Body. We are filled with the fullness of him that filleth all and all (Ephesians 1:23 KJV). If we're in Christ, we're positionally already filled with all of the fullness. We can be continually filled and experience this fullness in our daily walk. It's something that is available to the child that is filled with the fullness of God.

Confess this out loud:

> *I'm not interested in a theory. I want an experience! I want a manifestation! I want a demonstration, an exhibition of the fact that the Greater One lives on the inside of me! The only way for me to see this is to develop a relationship with the Spirit of God in me. I must begin to pray and meditate in my heart on the things of the Spirit—so that I can expand the boundaries of my spiritual life in Christ Jesus.*

Supernatural Results

Now unto Him that is able to do exceeding abundantly above all that we ask or think, according to the power that worketh in us.

Ephesians 3:20 KJV

Do you know that the power working in one person may not be equivalent to the power working in another person? Paul prayed that you might be filled with all of the fullness of God. Only the person who has an experiential knowledge—*a revelation knowledge*—of the love of Christ is going to step into that fullness! This is a person who has been rooted and grounded in love. It's not something that automatically drops on you because someone prayed for you. The revelation comes because you made a decision to pursue it. Paul said that a person like that would be filled with all of the fullness of God!

The Word is saying, *"Allow the Holy Ghost to develop in you the kind of power that exceeds all that you can think and ask. Then God, who is able to do exceeding abundantly above all that you ask or think, will be able to perform it according to the power at work in you!"*

The only reason we don't have more power is because we limit our experience with God to our rational mind. People can't even pray three sentences in tongues before they begin to think, *"I wonder if I'm saying the right words?"* Perhaps they drift back into the natural realm, carried away mentally by some pressing concern or desire. People can't even sing in the Spirit without opening one eye to see if anyone is watching them.

People like this are limiting their experience in God to their thought life. Do you want Him to do above all that you can ask or think? If you desire this, then you will need to develop the kind of power that exceeds your thought limitations. You will need to exercise your spirit man so that His power will usher you into the miraculous.

You *must* let the Holy Ghost lead you beyond what you know! To participate in this, you have to yield to God and go off into the Spirit! There isn't a danger in this. As you go there in God, the Spirit of God will cause the Word to become alive in you. When the Word is alive in you, the nature of God is alive in you.

As you yield to the influence of the Spirit, the Holy Ghost will remind you of the things Jesus said. He won't speak of Himself, but He will show you things to come according to Scripture. When He stirs these things in you, it will *impart* and *impact* you with the spiritual force you need to see the miracle working power of God!

God said that He could do *exceedingly* more than we could ever think! Most Christians are just trying to get God to answer their petition. Yet, God said that He could do more than a person could ever ask for.

Why isn't everyone experiencing the full manifestation of this promise? To walk in this revelation, we must allow the Holy Ghost to develop us with the kind of power that is *bigger* than our intellect, *bigger* than our ability to ask, *bigger* than our ability to envision, and *bigger* than our ability to limit! If you desire supernatural results, you must get in the realm of the Holy Ghost!

> **He who did not spare His own Son, but delivered Him up for us all, how shall He not with Him also freely give us all things?**
>
> **Romans 8:32**

In other words, how can He *not* do it? When you are in the Spirit realm—the very things people stagger at are the things that you know God will do! *You know* God will do even more because you have already thought of it! He can do more than what we think or even ask! The power in us is greater than what we're thinking and more than what we're asking. If God is going to do it, He will do it according to the power at work in us.

If a Christian has a hard time believing God to be healed of a headache, then He isn't going to be able to enable them to walk in divine health. If a Christian doesn't believe that God can pay their bills, then He isn't going to be able to make them millionaires or cause them to increase financially. *It is according to the power at work in them!*

Lay hands on yourself right now and say this:

> *The Spirit of God will lead me. The Word of God will live in me. I'll see things by revelation. I'll perceive things by revelation. I'll know things by revelation. It won't be my thoughts. The Word of God and the mind of Christ will give strength to my heart. Through that strength, I will be able to experience the power of God in my life. In Jesus name! Amen!*

Chapter 5

The Price of Power

Your invested interest in your gift will determine the level of heat, fire, and anointing activated in your life!

Wherefore I put thee in remembrance that thou stir up the gift of God, which is in thee by the putting on of my hands, for God bath not given us the spirit of fear, but of power, and of love and of a sound mind.

2 Timothy 1:6-7 KJV

Paul told Timothy, *"I'm reminding you to fan that inner flame—the gift of God that is in you."* The word *gift* in the Greek is *charisma*, meaning *gratuity, endowment, miraculous faculty*. Notice that Paul didn't say, *"You don't have it."* Paul said, *"You have the gift! Now give it some attention! I'm reminding you to fan it!"*

When you fan something, it gets hotter and brighter. That means that your gift can become weak from lack of attention. There's an anointing in you that if neglected, may only smolder weakly in your life. The power that is in you can become weak if you ignore it.

Ever Present Power

You have already learned that the Lord will do exceeding abundantly above all that you can ask or think according to the power at work in you.

What kind of power is at work in you?
Are you fanning it?

Are you remembering it?
Are you pumping it?
Are you priming it?
Are you stirring it up?
Are you continually meditating upon it?
Are you rehearsing it?
Are you allowing the gift to hear what excites it?
Are you bringing the gift—the endowment—around the kind of atmosphere that sets it loose?

or

Are you abandoning the priorities of the Spirit for the natural realm?

Your vested interest in your gift will determine the level of heat, fire, and anointing activated in your life! It will be determined by the priorities you have. Even, the thoughts you think will determine the kind of power that will emanate from your spiritual life! *Your thoughts will affect your results!* People just think, *"Well, I believe in the Holy Ghost,"* and then they aren't even getting their bills paid! They don't know that it is according to the power *at work in them*! Your prayers are answered according to the power at work in you.

Only *Word-power* has an ability to claim something God has promised. It can't be a *religious-word-power* or a *memory-word-power* - it has to be a *living-Word-power*. The Holy Ghost will take the promise and cause it to live in you *today*. *A today Word* will enable you to walk in ever-present power. It will be alive like fire. When you are walking in a today word, you can claim what belongs to you and see it come to pass!

Why is it that people can come to church, read the Bible and still live defeated?

Nothing can substitute your relationship with the Lord! Your relationship with your God is the avenue through which the Holy Ghost causes Jesus to live in your life! The Holy Ghost *breathes* upon your spirit man. As He breathes on your inner man, the Lord Jesus Christ or the Word that was sown in your heart rises up and becomes a rhema Word. It becomes a Word for the *now*! He becomes a miracle worker for the now! He becomes a provider for the now!

Paul said, *"I'm reminding you to stir up the charisma! Stir up the spiritual endowment! Stir up the miraculous faculty! Stir up the deposit, which is in you!"*

The deposit is in your spirit. You can't stir up this Holy Ghost deposit if you're operating in the flesh. You can't do it if you're operating under the dictates of a natural mind. You can't do it if you're overridden with cares and burdens. You can't do it by spending your time trying to solve problems in the natural realm.

The only way to stir this gift is to prioritize the deposit that is in your spirit. Paul said, *"God did not give us the spirit of fear!"* Fear is unbelief. Unbelief will stop the answers from coming your way. The spirit of fear will suppress the expression of your gift. Before long, you'll become a weak Christian who says, *"Do you really think God will do that for me?"* The spirit of fear will cover and weaken, but God said, *"Fan the gift!"*

Develop an unshakable assurance in the power in you. Develop your gift to the point that its strength *exceeds* what you can think—until it takes you *beyond* what you can petition God for. Grow to the place where you can boldly say, *"He can do not only what I ask, but exceeding abundantly above all that I can ask!"* Develop an assurance that will take you beyond your ability to petition God! As you develop this force, this fire, this deposit in your inner man—you will bypass the borders of human limitation. You will walk in the assurance and the unshakable conviction that God will do exceedingly abundantly above all that you could ever ask or think!

Do Not Neglect the Gift

Paul had a radical transformation. He had a radical experience with the Spirit. He prayed in tongues. He stirred up the gift. He came with demonstration. His messages relied on the Holy Spirit.

Paul tells Timothy how to do it:

Let no man despise thy youth; but be thou

> an example of the believers, in word, in conversation, in charity, in spirit, in faith, in purity. Till I come, give attendance to reading, to exhortation, to doctrine. Neglect not the gift that is in thee, which was given thee by prophecy, with the laying on of the hands of the presbytery. Meditate upon these things; give thyself wholly to them; that thy profiting may appear to all.
>
> **1 Timothy 4:12-15 KJV**

Paul tells Timothy to remember to read the Scripture, to keep sound doctrine, to be an example to believers and to be fervent in the Spirit, in faith, and in purity. Then he adds, *"Don't neglect the gift. Don't neglect the spiritual deposit that is in you, which was given you by prophecy through the laying on of the hands of the presbytery."* Through the laying on of hands, the presbytery imparted a spiritual deposit to Timothy. Paul is telling him, *"Don't neglect that deposit!"*

If you neglect the gift, you will become weak, through unbelief, in your inner man. This doesn't mean that unbelief is *in* your inner man. It means that unbelief is pushing and suppressing the gift of God that is in you. It is keeping your gift from becoming influential in your life!

Paul then tells Timothy, *"Meditate on the things that I'm saying to you."* Paul is exhorting his son in the faith to remember the gift, to think on it and to stir it up. He goes on to say, *"Give thyself holy to them that your profiting may appear to all."* In other words, *"Keep on giving yourself! Stay committed! Keep prioritizing the spiritual gift that God has put in your life!"* The gift in you is the Holy Ghost. The Bible says, "Believe on the Lord Jesus, be baptized, and you shall receive the gift of the Holy Spirit." The gift is profitable to you and me. *"That thy profiting may appear to all."* The word *profiting* is the word *advancement* or *furtherance*. Do you want to be advanced? The word *appear* is the word *shining*, or to *manifest*.

Paul is saying:

"Listen! If you would be an example... if you would give yourself to reading the Scripture...if you would give yourself to the gift that's in

you—remember it, stir it up, cultivate it—if you would meditate upon spiritual things and give yourself over to them… then your furtherance and your profiting would appear! If you do these things, everyone will see the manifestation of profit in your life. They will see this manifestation because the power at work in you will have enabled God to do the things that He has promised to do for you!"

Do you want people to see you succeed and prosper?

People say, *"If the Lord said that He's going to do it, then why doesn't He just do it?"* The Lord never said that He's going to just do it! *He told you* what *you must do* in order to enable Him to do it! He's not going to do it in spite of you! He's going to do it *through* you!

As a man thinks in his heart, so is he. You cannot fool God. The only way that you can receive from Him is to allow His Spirit to remove any inferiority, fear or lack of knowledge from your mind. Allow the Holy Ghost to impact you with a conviction and a supernatural strength in your inner man so that… *you'll know—that you know—that you know*! Then the power working in you will cause your profiting to appear to all!

Putting the Anointing to Work

In this account, Jesus and the disciples are ready to go to Gethsemane. The Lord is ready to be betrayed and turned over into the hands of sinners.

Jesus said to His disciples,

> **"When I sent you without money bag, knapsack, and sandals, did you lack anything?" So they said, "Nothing." Then He said to them, "But now, he who has a money bag, let him take it, and likewise a knapsack; and he who has no sword, let him sell his garment and buy one. So they said, "Lord, look, here are two swords." And He said to them, "It is enough."**

> But Jesus said to him, "Judas, are you betraying the Son of Man with a kiss?" When those around Him saw what was going to happen, they said to Him, "Lord, shall we strike with the sword?" And one of them struck the servant of the high priest and cut off his right ear. But Jesus answered and said, "Permit even this." And He touched his ear and healed him. Then Jesus said to the chief priests, captains of the temple, and the elders who had come to Him, "Have you come out, as against a robber, with swords and clubs? When I was with you daily in the temple, you did not try to seize Me. But this is your hour, and the power of darkness."
>
> Luke 22: 35-36, 38, 48-53

Jesus was a man anointed by the Holy Ghost. As a man, He walked in a hundredfold manifestation of the anointing. Jesus said to those that would believe on Him, *"He that believes on me, the same works that I do shall he do, and greater works than me shall he do."* How did Jesus intend to accomplish this? *"I am going to My Father, and I will send them the anointing!"* In other words, *"the way I did it—by the anointing—they are going to do it!"*

However, just because you have the anointing doesn't mean that you will walk in it! Your spirit man must receive it! Your priorities must shift! When your heart lines up and you choose to walk as a spirit-being, your life will be filled with the power of God. You can choose to walk as a natural being or you can choose to walk as a spirit-being. If you let the Spirit have His way, the anointing will go to work in your life!

Supernatural Help

Jesus asked the disciples an astonishing question. He said, *"When I sent you without money bag, knapsack, and sandals, did you lack anything?"* They answered, *"Nothing."* Then Jesus said, *"Now, he who has a money* bag, let him take it, and likewise a knapsack; and he who has no sword, let him sell his garment and buy one." Earlier He told them not to take anything and now He's telling them to take some things.

Were you ever confused about that?

This is what the Holy Ghost is teaching us: When Jesus was here as a man, He was the instrument through which the Holy Ghost moved in the life of the disciples. They didn't lack anything because Jesus' faith and His anointing sent them out. His authority and the anointing upon Him, *personally*, was what provided for them. He told them, *"Go! And whatever they put before you, eat! Heal the sick, and tell them the Kingdom of God has come!"*

Ministers of the Gospel have an anointing that will cover people. Thank God for that covering! Some people would not be able to stand on their own without it! We were all there at one point and some are at that place right now. God will use the anointing on the life of a ministry gift to sustain another believer, to hold them up. There will come a time, however, when the Christian will have to stand on their own two feet.

His anointing went with them, and they never went without a meal! They never went without a place to sleep. They never needed money. They never lacked anything! The personal presence of Christ covered them and supplied all their needs. He told them, *"Don't even take a money bag!"* So they went out and didn't take money, didn't take food and they didn't lack!

Now Jesus says to His disciples, *"…he who has a money bag, let him take it, and likewise a knapsack; and he who has no sword, let him sell his garment and buy one."* Jesus said this because He knew that the hour of darkness had come. The one who was using His anointing to provide for them was going to use His anointing in another direction: to become the sacrifice—*to pay their price*! Without Jesus in their midst, the Holy Ghost would not be able to supply their needs. He couldn't because the Holy Ghost was not *yet* given! The Shepherd was getting ready to be smitten and the sheep were going to be without supernatural help for a season.

Natural Help

Jesus said to His disciples, *"It is better for you that I go. I will send you the Spirit. When the Spirit comes, He will show you things to come. I will go and prepare a place for you. Where I go you know, and the Way you know"* (John 14:3).

The disciples protested, *"We don't know the way! Show us the Father!"*

Jesus replied, *"He who has seen Me has seen the Father."*

He was telling them about a coming time when the Spirit of God would come to them and help them to have the Christ-kind of results. For a time however, there would be a lapse in which the hour of darkness would come. Jesus was willingly going to use His faith to place Himself in the very heart of darkness. He was on a mission. If Jesus had neglected to pay the price for us, we would not have access to the Holy Ghost today!

The Bible calls Jesus the gift of God, yet people become accustomed to Him. He's God's gift! The greatest gift God could ever give you is Jesus. He gave you the Spirit of Christ to anoint you—*to live in you*—so that you could see Christ's results manifested in your life!

Jesus was telling His disciples, *"Listen! Now there's going to be trouble. I'm going to be taken. Do you understand?"* Of course, Peter didn't. He rebuked the Lord. Jesus then said, *"Get thee behind me, Satan! Peter, Satan has desired to sift you as wheat, but I have prayed for you, that your faith would not fail. And when you are restored, strengthen your brethren!"* Then He added, *"You will deny me three times before the cock crows."*

Then He said to the disciples, *"Take a money bag with you. Take a knapsack and sword too."* Why Jesus? *"You're going to need natural help. My anointing won't work for you! When I become sin, My anointing will be inactive until justice is satisfied. It will be inactive until I come out of the grave with all the power in Heaven and in Earth! My anointing will not work for three days. My anointing won't work while I'm in captivity."*

While Jesus was in the grave there was no anointing available for the disciples. They couldn't have their needs met supernaturally. They couldn't minister in Jesus' name until He rose from the dead. They couldn't have any miracles by His anointing because His anointing had stopped.

The Bible said that He became sin. The anointing can't operate in sin. Jesus became sin! Jesus never sinned, but when He became sin—He became sin to the fullest. He took it upon Himself. When He did, His anointing ceased to operate.

In the Garden of Gethsemane Jesus prayed, *"My soul is sorrowful even unto death. Father, if it is possible, let this cup pass from me. Nevertheless, not My will but Yours be done."* He drank the cup in the garden. When He made the decision to go to the cross, it was sealed.

When Judas showed up with his entourage, Jesus said, *"Will you betray the son of man with a kiss?"* That was a Word of knowledge.

> **And while He was still speaking, behold, a multitude; and he who was called Judas, one of the twelve, went before them and drew near to Jesus to kiss Him. But Jesus said to him, "Judas, are you betraying the Son of Man with a kiss?" When those around Him saw what was going to happen, they said to Him, "Lord, shall we strike with the sword?" And one of them struck the servant of the high priest and cut off his right ear.**
>
> **Luke 22:47-49**

Peter thought, *"Forget it! I'm not waiting for an answer!"* I'm going to fight! He took out his sword and chopped off the soldier's ear!

Permit Even This

Jesus had been in meditation and communion with God. The book of John tells us what He was praying, *"God, I'm praying that they would be one as We are one."* The entire fourteenth, fifteenth, sixteenth, and seventeenth chapters of John are an account of His communion with God! Jesus was talking. He was stirring up the gift of God that was in Him! He was speaking the Truth into the Earth!

"Father, glorify Me with the same glory I had with You before the world was!" He was taking hold of His identity! He was taking hold of an awareness of who He was in God and what He had come to do. This was His mission!

He was praying for the Church. He was telling the disciples His identity and what the Holy Ghost would help them to do. He was telling them where He was going and what He was going to prepare for them. Jesus *kept on talking* until His faith was so built up, until the gift was so strong in Him, until He was so deep in the Spirit realm—that He was ready to go to the cross in the supernatural power of the Spirit!

When they came to take Jesus and Peter chopped off the ear of the soldier, He said, *"Permit even this."* In other words, *"Let Me do this—let Me put his ear back on."* He was in the Spirit! He was in the anointing! He was out there in the Holy Ghost because He had been speaking. He had been praying. He had been communing with His Father.

He had been declaring, *"I'm the Vine! I'm the Door! I'm the Good Shepherd!"* He had been saying, *"I had glory with You, Father, before the world was! You always hear Me, Father!"* He prayed for believers. He prayed for those who would believe as a result of His disciples' words. He prayed for the Church. He was anointed!

While Judas was still approaching, Jesus said, *"Are you going to betray the Son of man with a kiss?"* He had a Word of knowledge! At that point, you would think Judas would have had the sense to say, "Sorry!" Looking at him Jesus asked, *"You come against me as a thief?"* Jesus knew the whole thing! He said, *"Allow it to be so,"* and He put the man's ear back on.

It's Better for You That I Go

And for their sakes I sanctify Myself, that they also may be sanctified by the truth.

John 17:19

Jesus prayed this right before Judas showed up to betray Him. Several chapters of prayer, talk and preaching from this night preceded His arrest. In the thirteenth chapter of John, Jesus talks about the Holy Ghost and how He will come after Jesus leaves.

Jesus says,

> **And I will pray the Father, and He will give you another Helper, that He may abide with you *forever*—the Spirit of truth, whom the world cannot receive, because it neither sees Him nor knows Him; but you know Him, for He dwells with you and will be in you.**
>
> John 14:16-17

Jesus was telling His disciples, *"Previously, I told you not to take a money bag or a knapsack and you didn't lack a thing. Everything was provided for you. Now I'm telling you to take what you can for right now. I'm going to go and ask the Father and He will send you another Comforter. I will not leave you as orphans; I'm sending you another Comforter!"*

They cried, *"But why do you have to leave, Jesus?"*

"As long as I'm here alone, you are going to need Me to get your needs met. You're going to need My supernatural presence to substitute the purse and substitute the sword and substitute all those natural things. But I'm going to pray the Father, and He will send you another Comforter. I won't leave you orphans! When the Spirit of God comes, the world won't be able to receive Him, but He will abide with you forever! The world cannot receive Him because it doesn't see Him. It operates by what it sees. But you know Him!"

The disciples wondered, *"Lord, how will we know Him?"*

"You've met Him through Me! He dwells with you! He's been walking with you, teaching you in Bible school and taking you around the nation! But He shall be in you! After the cross, I won't have to be with you—I'll be in you through the Person of the Holy Ghost!"

If the twelve disciples could have every need met and never lack; if twelve people could walk in divine health and never have sickness; if twelve could be taken care of—around the clock—just because He was with them, then *how much more* is that available to us because He is in us through the person of the Holy Ghost?!

The disciples had faith because they saw the Lord. When He said, *"Go there and make preparations for the Passover. You will meet a man. Tell him I need the guest chamber to have supper, and he will take you to an upper room,"* they believed Him. Everything He said happened exactly as He said.

Now Jesus tells them, *"You know the Spirit of truth. He's been with you. But when I leave, I'll pray and send Him, and He will be in you."*

> **Most assuredly, I say to you, whatever you ask the Father in My name He will give you.**
>
> **John 16:23**

Jesus was saying, *"Don't panic because I'm leaving! Was it good for you while I was with you these three and a half years? Did you throw your net into the sea and catch so many fish that your net broke? Don't panic! When I send you the Holy Ghost He won't just be with you, He'll be in you! And because He's in you, whatever you ask the Father He will give it to you!"*

Time to Grow Up

Why do we pray and not get what we prayed for?
Why do we see people pray and not get anything?
Why do we see people ask and not receive?

It is according to the power at work in you! While Jesus was with the disciples, they really didn't need to pray like they should because the Master was doing all the praying! The Pastor was doing the praying! They didn't need to do anything. They just needed to ask Him and His faith provided what they needed.

It's like that with parents and children. Parents take care of their children. They provide for them and the children have no concept of what is required to provide for a household. When they grow up, they learn that you have to work for the money! Like children, the disciples didn't have to use their faith when Jesus was with them.

"I'll send you My Spirit, and whatever you pray the Father in My name He will give you." The same Spirit that operated in Jesus would be operating in them. Jesus was showing them how to flow in the Holy Ghost! The way He fellowshiped, they were called to fellowship. The way He prayed, they were called to pray. A disciple is like their teacher.

"Until now you have asked nothing in My name." They couldn't ask in His name. You can only ask in His name if you are full of His Spirit! *"Until now you have asked nothing in My name. Ask, and you will receive, that your joy may be full"* (John 16:24).

The power of the Spirit in you will lead you to pray with great plainness of speech. When you pray in the name of Jesus, anything you pray will be done because of the power flow coming through the indwelling Spirit.

Jesus speaks to the Father in front of His disciples and says, *"For their sakes I sanctify myself, that they also might be sanctified through the truth"* (John 17:19). In other words, *"Father, I'm setting Myself apart so that they would be set apart through the truth."* He's the Word. He was the Word before He was conceived. The world was created by Him. Why would the Word need to sanctify Himself?

Jesus is saying, *"Father, I'm setting Myself apart for the purpose of the cross. I'm setting Myself apart, sanctifying Myself—for the cross—for death—and for burial. Through this act, my disciples will be sanctified and set apart as well. Then they'll no longer need Me to walk with them; they'll have Me living in them!"*

The Church spends a lot of time acting like—*Christ in us, the Hope of Glory*—is weaker than Christ with us, two thousand years ago! The *only* difference between then and now is that you couldn't ignore Him two thousand years ago! The only way someone could shrug Him off then was to blatantly reject Him or betray Him. Today, you may not see Jesus walking down the street, but there is a Spirit in you who bears witness of His presence in your life. You must cultivate your spirituality!

The Power to Pay the Price

> **Judas, having received a detachment of troops, and officers from the chief priests and Pharisees, came there with lanterns, torches, and weapons. Jesus therefore, knowing all things that would come upon Him, went forward and said to them, "Whom are you seeking?"**
>
> **John 18:3-4**

How did Jesus know all the things that were going to happen to Him? He knew through the gifts of the Spirit. He knew by the manifestations of the Holy Ghost! He was walking in the Spirit, and in doing so, received the supernatural help of the Holy Ghost.

People wonder, *"Why didn't God show me that thing ahead of time?"* Were you walking in the Spirit? If you would walk in the Spirit, you would start knowing things by the Spirit of God. You would have divine clarity and direction. Jesus knew all things by the Spirit.

He said to the band of men, *"Whom are you seeking?"* but He already knew the answer.

The band of men replied:

> **"Jesus of Nazareth." Jesus saith unto them, "I am *He*." And Judas also, which betrayed him, stood with them. As soon then as he had said unto them, I am *he*, they went backward, and fell to the ground.**
>
> **John 18:5-6**

That was a power demonstration! Jesus answered, *"I am He."* If you look at the word "He" in the King James Version of this verse, you will see that "He" has been added by the translators to better clarify the text. The literal rendering of this text is, *"I am."* *"As soon then as He had said unto them, 'I am,' they went backward, and fell to the ground."*

What was it that knocked them down? The power in the *"I AM!"*

Paul told Timothy, *"Meditate upon these things; give thyself wholly to them."* Give yourself wholly to these things! Jesus prayed until He sweat great drops of blood! He made a decision: *"I am the Lamb of God, slain from the foundation of the world. I know Who I am. I already know where I'm going. I know what I came here for and I know what lies ahead for Me."* He meditated upon these things until the life of the Holy Ghost rose up within Him. That gift rose up so strong that there was no room for the world to hinder His purpose. There was no threat that was going to stop Him from going to the cross supernaturally.

His battle was not in deciding whether or not He was going to the cross. His battle was that—in such dire circumstances—He needed *supernatural power!* He needed supernatural power to enable Him to complete His mission. Without that power, the whole sacrifice would have been worthless.

The Bible says, *"(He) through the eternal Spirit offered himself without spot to God"* (Hebrews 9:14). When Jesus said, *"Father, I sanctify Myself,"* He was saying, *"Father, I know I am He. I know I'm the Lamb of God. I know I'm the Good Shepherd. I know I'm the Son of God. I know that I'm the Messenger of the Covenant. I know that I'm the Head of the Church. I know that I'm the one whom You sent, and I know where I'm going. I'm setting myself apart for that task so that You will be able—through the Spirit—to set them apart, anoint them, and use them."*

Jesus looked at Judas and said, *"Did you come to betray the Son of man with a kiss?"* Then Judas kissed Him! If a person has not been meditating on the Word, they won't be able to stand in the face of adversity and say, *"You found me, devil! You found me and I'm going to fulfill my purpose. This is why I am here."*

Jesus looked at them and said, *"Whom do you seek?"*

They said, *"Jesus of Nazareth."*

He said, *"I am."*

In other words, *"You have found Him! It's Me! I'm ready! Let's go! That's what I came for! I am anointed right now, by the Spirit of God, to supernaturally give My life for others!"*

When He said, *"I am,"* the power of the anointing that had filled Him knocked them down! They fell down under the power of God!

That's how it is with a preacher who has prayed and meditated! That's what will happen when someone has spent time with the Holy Ghost! The cables are hooked up to the charge of Heaven—and that charge, that electricity—is in their voice! They can say, *"Hey!"* And the power of God will go through you from the top of your head to the soles of your feet!

When Jesus said, *"I am,"* they fell to the ground. Can you imagine being there? This man says, *"I am,"* and you and your whole company fall to the ground! When they got up, they had wild looks on their faces. They were probably thinking, *"Okay, what in the world just happened to me?"*

The Garden of Gethsemane

Then He asked them again, "Whom are you seeking?" And they said, "Jesus of Nazareth." Jesus answered, "I have told you that I am He. Therefore, if you seek Me, let these go their way," that the saying might be fulfilled which He spoke, "Of those whom You gave Me I have lost none."

John 18:7-9

The disciples were going to need natural help after Jesus was taken into captivity, but as long as He was with them, His anointing delivered them from anything that could come against them. He was prayed up! He was ready! He said, *"I am He,"* and the men who came to arrest Him fell down!

Do you know why the Holy Ghost did that? The power of God was demonstrating that the devil was not the one in charge in the garden! Jesus was in charge through the anointing of the Spirit! The devil wanted to kill the rest of the disciples, but Jesus wouldn't allow it. The devil wanted to sift Peter, but Jesus had prayed for him!

When the men got up off the ground Jesus said, *"I told you I am He! Now, leave these alone! You came for Me, now leave these be!"* Through

His anointing He kept the lives of His disciples!

Jesus knew that the devil was a thief. He knew that the thief wouldn't just settle for the Son of God alone. He would try to come after the others. He would go after Peter, kill him and then go after John. If the devil could kill all of the disciples he could destroy the foundation stones upon which the Church was being built!

Jesus said, *"I have the power to give My life and I have the power to keep the ones the Father has given Me! I know the devil is a thief and I know the only way to keep the ones God has given Me is to be so anointed—so full of the supernatural power of God—that when the showdown at Gethsemane comes, every one in the spirit realm will know that I'm in charge! The devil is not taking Me! I'm giving My life! You came for Me. Leave these others alone!"*

> *What if Jesus had not been in the anointing?*
> *Some of His disciples would have died!*

What Jesus said determined whether or not Scripture would be fulfilled in His own personal life. People think, *"The Lord is going to do this thing because the Lord is sovereign."* The Lord says that we are more than conquerors, but if you live like a failure, that Scripture is not going to be fulfilled in your life. Jesus said, *"I know the devil is a thief, but I'm not going to let him take My disciples! I'm going to keep My disciples!"*

Peter, of course, took the sword and chopped off the soldier's ear. Jesus immediately said, *"Allow this! Let me operate in the anointing and help you as far as I can! The anointing is going to lift and leave you. However, when I rise from the dead, I'll pray the Father, and the anointing will come back upon you. When the anointing comes, He won't be with you—He will be in you! If He paid your bills when He was with you, He'll pay your bills when He is in you! If He healed you when He was with you, He'll heal you when He is in you! He'll be in you and whatever you ask my Father, He will do it—but allow Me this! Let Me put the anointing to work on your behalf while I can, Peter. Put your sword away!"*

In the Garden of Gethsemane Jesus had prayed earnestly, *"My soul is sorrowful even unto death! Father, if it is possible, let this cup pass from me! Nevertheless, not My will but Yours be done."* Jesus was full of the Holy Ghost! He had prayed through! He was so full of the Spirit that

He would not allow His mind to dictate His course of action. *"The cup, which My Father has given Me, shall I not drink it?"*

Jesus took the soldier's ear and put it back on. He was in charge!

Beyond the Grave

The devil had entered into Judas. He had driven the mob to cry, *"Crucify Him! Crucify Him!"* He knew the Scriptures: *"Cursed is everyone that hangs on a tree."* The devil thought, *"If He only gets on the tree, He'll be cursed. If He's cursed, He can't bless anyone else…and if He's cursed and dies, that's the end of it!"*

When they nailed Jesus to the cross, Satan said, *"Now, the only Anointed One—the one who went about doing good and healing all—the one to whom I said, 'What have I to do with you, Jesus, Son of the Most High God? Don't torment me!' Is cursed! He is cursed! He is sin!"*

Jesus died and went to Hell. Satan scoffed, *"Ha—Now, that's the end of Him!"*

The only problem with his evil plot was that Jesus didn't have any sin! He took our sin upon Himself so that He could take it from the Earth and cast it into Hell. When it was time, Jesus said, *"Satan! I just came down here to drop something off!"* He shook that sin off and left it in Hell! *"Now, give Me the keys of death, hell, and the grave!"* He commanded Satan and then took the keys and rose from the dead!

> **And after eight days His disciples were again inside, and Thomas with them. Jesus came, the doors being shut, and stood in the midst, and said, "Peace to you!"**
>
> **John 20:26**

The doors were shut. The same disciples had spent the last three and a half years running around the country, casting out devils and

healing the sick. Now they were huddled inside a room with the doors shut!

Do you know what they were doing? They were holding on to their swords! There was no anointing! There was no covering! There was no protection! There was no Covenant Keeper! They had locked themselves away in the safety of that room.

Suddenly Jesus walks in! He says, *"Peace be unto you!"* He evidently didn't use the door – He just walked in. Thomas was there too. Now Thomas was the one who had declared, *"I will not believe that Jesus is alive and well unless I put my finger in His nail prints and thrust my hand into His side. I'll just never believe it!"*

Why did Thomas doubt? Thomas doubted because his intellect told him that there was no reversal for such a curse. He saw what happened to Jesus! Jesus had been mutilated. His head was swollen. His beard was ripped off. His body was ripped open. His back was whipped. His flesh was shattered and smashed. His body was totally overcome by the ravages of sickness and disease from the curse that He took upon Himself. Thomas had a hard time believing that there was a power available that could reverse such a hopeless condition.

Power Paid for in Full

> **The eyes of your understanding being enlightened; that ye may know what the hope of His calling, and what the riches of the glory of his inheritance in the saints, what is the exceeding greatness of his power to usward who believe, according to the working of his mighty power, which he wrought in Christ, when he raised him from the dead, and set him at his own right hand in heavenly places.**
>
> **Ephesians 1:18-20 KJV**

The situation looked utterly hopeless, but the energy of the Holy Ghost reached into that grave and raised Jesus unto life again! The Bible tells us that the power that raised Jesus Christ is available to us today! In the Scripture above, Paul is praying that our eyes would be enlightened so that we would be able to comprehend this glorious power and understand that it belongs to us!

The doors were shut, yet this flesh and bone Person walked right in through the walls! Jesus showed up and walked into their midst without a scar—just the holes in His hands, the holes in His feet and the opening in His side. He was healed! The marks that were left in His body were not left as a bruise or a wound. His body was healed and glorified by the power of God!

He now lives in a glorified body that derives its strength from a different Source. The first body had its life in the blood. The glorified body is living by the anointing! The anointing is what gives Him life!

To Thomas He said, *"Handle Me and see; a ghost doesn't have bones as you see Me have."*

Thomas said, *"My Lord and my God!"*

Jesus said, *"Because you see, you believe. You are still intellectual; you're still natural. Blessed are they, which have not seen, and yet believe!"*

For forty days He was with them, showing them the anointing. One time He appeared to them while they were out fishing and asked, *"Children, do you have any fish?"* They said, *"We didn't catch anything."*

He said, *"Throw your net on the other side."*

Why hadn't they caught anything? They didn't have the anointing! They threw the net on the other side and caught so many fish that they almost drowned! This time their net did not break. One of them had a thought and said, *"It's the Lord!"* Immediately, Peter threw himself into the water and swam ashore. When they arrived on the shore, Jesus had already cooked some fish!

After Jesus rose from the dead He had all power in Heaven and in Earth! Before His resurrection, Jesus was a man anointed by the Holy Ghost. He didn't turn stones into bread. He didn't operate in creative power. He emptied himself of that creative force and walked as a man anointed by the Holy Ghost. He said, *"Give Me the loaves and the fish, and the anointing will multiply it."* He said, *"Go out and throw a hook into the water and get a coin out of the mouth of the first fish you catch."*

Jesus is standing on the shore. He's the resurrected Christ. By the time the disciples got to shore, he had the fish cooked and ready to eat! Fish just swam out of the lake and jumped on the grill! He said, *"All power in Heaven and in Earth is given unto Me!"* The authority on planet Earth has been regained. It was given to the Lord Jesus Christ and to His Church!

After appearing to His disciples, the Holy Ghost caused Him to elevate and then to ascend into Heaven! It happened right in front of His disciples. They stood there and watched! He then sat down at the Father's right hand—far above principalities and powers!

Today, that same Spirit is living in you! The Holy Ghost is living in you to give you the Christ-kind of results from within!

> If you want God to do something,
> *He's going to do it from within you!*

CHAPTER 6

THE MYSTERY OF GODLINESS

―――◆―――

*The power is in you
to fulfill His promises toward you!*

In order to see demonstrated power, you must have indwelling power. Nothing will manifest that does not reside. If you see light manifesting when you turn on the switch, it's because there is power connected to the switch. That connection is empowering the manifestation of the light. When you put your foot on the gas pedal, your car will only manifest what's under the hood.

To benefit from the anointing that resides in you, you must understand what has been deposited in you by the Holy Ghost.

> **These things write I unto thee, hoping to come unto thee shortly; but if I tarry long, that thou mayest know how thou oughtest to behave thyself in the house of God, which is the Church of the living God, the pillar and ground of the truth. And without controversy great is the mystery of godliness: God was manifest in the flesh, justified in the Spirit, seen of angels, preached unto the Gentiles, believed on in the world, received up into glory. Now the Spirit speaketh expressly, that in the latter times some shall depart from the faith, giving heed to seducing spirits, and doctrines of devils.**
>
> **1 Timothy 3:14-4:1 KJV**

In other words, Paul was telling Timothy, *"I'm hoping to come to you soon, but if I'm delayed, these things should help you to learn how to behave*

The Mystery of Godliness

yourself in the Church, the house of God, the place that is called the pillar and ground of Truth."

Church is a place where living members join together. It's where the anointing is. It's not in the brick and it's not in the carpet—the anointing is in the believer! A church is not a church unless there is a fellowship between believers—unless they have *koinonia* or things in common. It's only a church if God has set someone whom He anointed, and appointed to minister to that body.

Paul tells Timothy, *"I want you to know, as a minister, as a pastor—how you should behave yourself in the house of God."* We are the house of God! We are the Church of the Living God—the pillar and the ground of Truth. Paul then gives Timothy the key to the Church, *"Without controversy, great is the mystery of godliness: God was manifested in the flesh."*

The Bible says that in the beginning was the Word; the Word was with God; the Word was God; and the Word became flesh (John 1:1, 14). This is called the incarnation or the mystery of godliness. The world cannot receive the mystery of godliness because the world cannot understand how God can become a human. The world cannot imagine how a virgin could conceive a child that is God manifested in the flesh.

What kind of power did it take for the *Living Spirit Word* to become flesh, bone and blood? What did it take to be conceived as a child; to be born into the Earth realm; to live; to grow; to minister; to die; and to rise again on behalf of humanity? It took some demonstrations of power! *That is the mystery!*

The mystery of godliness is beyond controversy, beyond debate, beyond argument. It is this: Almighty God, with all of the power within His Word, laid aside His creative force, laid aside His deity and became a human. He was born among us and grew up to become our Redeemer!

The Bible says that He was justified by the Spirit. That occurred when the Spirit of the Lord came upon Him at thirty years of age. John the Baptist baptized Him at the river Jordan. As Jesus rose up out of the water, He was baptized with the Holy Ghost! It is important to remember that although God became flesh, He did not perform one miracle until the anointing of the Holy Spirit came upon Him! When He began to minister, humanity witnessed *God manifested* in the flesh.

The Bible says, *"You shall call his name, Emmanuel."* Emmanuel literally means God with us—as if He were *in* a tent or *in* a tabernacle. In other words, on the outside of the tent you couldn't really tell, but nonetheless, He was God with us. This is the mystery of godliness: that Almighty God would incarcerate Himself in the limitations of a human body. That He would live and minister, displaying through the words he preached and the things He did, the will of Heaven for mankind!

Another Mystery

The Bible cautions us that in the last days men are going to depart from the faith. In other words, if we want to stay on track with God, we shouldn't necessarily look to the theologian or the denominational leader. We should look back and find out how the Church started. What did the apostles preach? What did Jesus prophecy? If what we see today lines up with those things, then we need to follow it. If it doesn't, then we need to forget about it!

The Bible warns us that in the latter days people will give heed to seducing spirits and doctrines of devils and that ultimately, they would depart from the faith. There is only one faith. It is called *the faith*. Any faith that is not *the faith* comes from seducing spirits and doctrines of devils.

> **For the mystery of lawlessness is already at work; only He who now restrains will do so until He is taken out of the way. And then the lawless one will be revealed, whom the Lord will consume with the breath of His mouth and destroy with the brightness of His coming. The coming of the lawless one is according to the working of Satan, with all power, signs, and lying wonders...**
>
> **2 Thessalonians 2:7-9**

According to the Word of God, there are two extremes. One is the mystery of godliness manifested in the Head of the Church—in the Rock of Ages—in the King of Kings—in the Lord of Lords—in Jesus Christ: godliness manifested in the flesh. The other extreme is the mystery of iniquity. Whether it is the mystery of godliness or the mystery of iniquity, both will be manifested through people. Godliness will be manifested through a human, and iniquity will also be manifested through a human.

The mystery of iniquity was already at work while Paul was preaching. The Bible tells us, however, that something or Someone will withhold the full manifestation of satanic power. This full manifestation is the Antichrist, or the anti-type of Christ. Christ is the only begotten Son of God. The Antichrist will be the only begotten son of Satan. Jesus Christ is God manifested in the flesh. The Antichrist will be Satan manifested in the flesh.

The mystery of iniquity was already at work two thousand years ago. The full manifestation of the king of iniquity, or the child of doom, cannot be manifested yet because there is Someone holding him back. There is Someone withholding him—Someone causing him to tarry. That *Someone* is the Holy Spirit within the believer! While the Body of Christ is here—and the mystery of godliness is still manifested in the flesh—the powers of darkness will be held back. As long as Christ is living within you, the powers of darkness will be restrained from their full manifestation. The Bible says that now we're holding him back, but when we are taken out of the way, a full manifestation of the Antichrist will come with all kinds of lying signs and wonders.

The Results Are Abnormal

Powerless Christians are paranoid about signs and wonders. They are so out of touch with the Holy Ghost that they are ready to accuse the devil of what God is doing! They are quick to say, *"The devil does miracles!"*

The mystery of iniquity is at work and Satan is preparing the way for the Antichrist. We see the mystery of iniquity manifesting today in psychics. You could turn on the television and hear a psychic tell you your name or tell you your initials. You could hear a psychic tell you what you've been through.

That's not abnormal. Ever since the fall of man, a choice has been made available to the human race. The choice is to be led by a familiar spirit or to be led by God's Spirit. Both realms are available. You can choose godliness or iniquity, Heaven or Hell, the power of God or the power of the devil. Today we are seeing an intensified onslaught of satanic power because the heathen are pressing into the supernatural realm and allowing spirit beings to direct them.

In the last days men will depart from the faith. *What is the faith? The faith* is the mystery of godliness manifested in the born again child of God. Human beings are departing from that mystery and giving heed to seducing spirits. They are saying, *"We don't have to name Jesus Christ as the Lord of our life. We can have supernatural gifts operating in our lives through Buddha, through Mohammed, through Krishna and through the new age! We can have supernatural access through whatever means we choose!"*

In the Church today, religious people are lifting their hands and praying little powerless prayers. God wants His Church to be full of believers living by the power of the Holy Ghost!

Lay your hands on yourself and say this:

> *I'm not afraid of the Holy Spirit. I'm not called to control the Holy Spirit. I will learn about the Holy Spirit, so that He can manifest the power of God through me and draw people to my Lord and Master, Jesus Christ!*

The Bible says, *"He revealeth the deep and secret things. He knoweth what is in the darkness, and the light dwelleth with Him"* (Daniel 2:22 KJV). There is nothing hidden that will not be made manifest. Jesus said that whoever will seek will find, yet the Church doesn't believe that! They say, *"We'll understand it better in the by and by."* Why don't we just seek it and find it while we are here now? Why don't we find the Truth while we still can live the Truth?

Whosoever asks will receive! *"If any man lack wisdom let him ask of God and He will give it to him if he asks in faith, nothing wavering"* (James 1:5). This is referring to the wisdom of the Holy Ghost! The child of God should be proficient in flowing in the Spirit. They should be so learned in the Spirit, that when someone accuses them of being abnormal, they can take them straight to the Scripture and show them the truth.

People have come up with the excuse, *"The Bible says that in the last days the devil is going to do miracles."* That's not what the Bible said! It said, *"Before that happens, you who are not doing miracles, will depart from the faith! You, who are not doing miracles, will give heed to seducing spirits and doctrines of devils!"* The Church started with miracles, so if there aren't any miracles taking place, someone must have departed from the faith!

We're not abnormal—they are! If they are not tongue-talking, they're abnormal! If they're not living by the power of the anointing of the Spirit, they're abnormal. That's how the Church was born! We don't want to depart from that faith! We want to come closer to it!

This Is Your Time!

Whereof I am made a minister, according to the dispensation of God which is given to me for you, to fulfill the Word of God.

Colossians 1:25 KJV

Paul is telling the Church that He is a minister. As a minister of the Gospel, he's been given a time period to fulfill the Word of God. *What is that time period?* It's for as long as he is alive! When He says, *"I'm now ready to be offered. The time of my departure is at hand. I have fought a good fight. I have finished my course. I have kept the faith,"* He will leave and will never again minister to the Body of Christ. His mission will be over; His dispensation of labor will have been done away with. Paul is saying, *"I realize I've been called to minister and that I have been given a time period—a span—to fulfill the Word of God."*

Christians say, *"I just hope that some way, some how, the Lord will get some glory out of my life."* Read this very carefully: You have a dispensation for a reason. Do you know what that reason is? It's to fulfill the Word of God! That's why you are on the planet!

> *How do you fulfill the Word of God?*
>
> *The Word says that you're a winner.*
> *You have a dispensation to demonstrate*
> *that you're a winner!*
>
> *The Word says that you're more than a conqueror.*
> *You have a dispensation to demonstrate*
> *that you're more than a conqueror!*
>
> *The Word says that you can do all things.*
> *You have a dispensation to demonstrate*
> *that you can do all things!*
>
> *The Word says that whatsoever you do will prosper.*
> *You have a dispensation to fulfill that*
> *and to prove that it's talking about you!*

"But I don't understand! This puts pressure on me! What if I don't succeed? What if I can't be more than a conqueror?"

If you try to do it on your own without the assistance of the Holy Ghost, it won't work. He is the Helper and He will enable you to cash in on the supernatural benefits that are available in Jesus. If the Church is falling short, it's because believers are trying to do it through legalism and law! We have bound ourselves with this thing called *order*. People say, *"Let all things be done decently and in order."* What they're really saying is, *"We need a law to bind the Spirit of God so that we can take control of our church services and take control of our lives."* So a denomination comes up with a law and discovers that it's dry and dead. People are trying to live Christianity through will power and mind power. You can't do it! You need the Holy Ghost!

Say this out loud:

> *I can only fulfill the Word I believe. I can only believe*
> *the Word I receive. I can only receive the Word that's*
> *talking to me, and the Word will only talk to me when I*
> *see it through revelation.*

When the word becomes *rhema* to you, you can put your name on it! When your name is on that Word, then you *know* why you're here! We have a *dispensation* given to us to fulfill the Word of the Lord—to fulfill the mystery! We've been given a time span to fulfill, to execute, to verify, and to demonstrate the Word of the Lord.

> **Even the mystery which hath been hid from ages and from generations, but now is made manifest to his saints, to whom God would make known what is the riches of the glory of this mystery among the Gentiles; which is Christ in you and the hope of glory.**
>
> **Colossians 1:26-27**

To the Jews, Christ is a stumbling block. To the Greeks, He's foolishness—but to those who believe, Christ is the wisdom of God and the power of God (1 Corinthians 1:24). Before you can have a demonstration of power, you have to know what kind of power lives on the inside of you!

Religion said, *"Let's not get prideful; we want to be humble!"* And it wrote stupid songs, published stupid hymnals, and built stupid churches! Meanwhile, in the heathen world that has no legalism in their spirituality, the witch doctor is doing alright! The warlock is doing just fine! The psychic is doing well! *Why?* They're not bound to legalism! They're open to whatever spirit will come their way! They have an understanding of the spiritual realm, while most Christians have only a mental concept of the letter of the Word. Christians are afraid of the Holy Ghost because they haven't received biblical teaching about the Spirit of God.

You cannot be open to the Spirit of God and receive a scorpion! You cannot be open to the Spirit of God and receive a stone! You cannot be led astray, deceived, bound up or involved in demonic activities when you're a child of God that is full of the Holy Ghost! It can't happen! However, Christians that are afraid of the Holy Ghost are bound up! They are bound by the spirit of fear!

Christ is the wisdom of God and Christ is the power of God! There's power living in you!

I Am the Way

The mystery of God is God manifested in the flesh. We saw Him manifested in the flesh in the life of Jesus. He said, *"It's expedient for you that I go away. If I don't go away, the Comforter will not come. I'm going to send you the Spirit of Truth, whom the world cannot receive because it seeth Him not, neither knoweth Him, but you know Him, because He's with you"* (John 16:17).

How was He with them?
Godliness was manifested in the flesh!
Where is godliness now?

He's with you and shall be in you! I will go away, but I will come again and I will send you another Comforter.

John 14:16

Jesus was saying: *"The same godliness, the same mystery, the same awesome demonstration of power that was manifested in Me, is going to be shed upon you through the Spirit of God! It will fill you with the same identity, the same potential, and the same supernatural privileges that are operating in Me! You will receive it on the day of Pentecost, and from then on it will be available to anyone who will believe. For the promise is unto you and your children, as many as the Lord, our God, shall call!"*

Jesus told His disciples, *"Where I go, you know, and the way, you know."*
They protested, *"We don't know where You are going! How do we know the way?"*
Jesus responded, *"I am the Way."*

He was saying, *"I am going to the presence of God, and you know the way there."* We've interpreted this one dimensionally saying, *"That means no man cometh to the Father in eternity except by Jesus."* Yes, that's true, but nobody comes to the Father today in prayer—*into the Holy of Holies*—unless he comes through the nature of Jesus Christ and through the Word of God!

Jesus was saying, *"Listen! When I send My nature to live in you, when I send My power to live in you by the Holy Ghost, you're going to be able to come boldly to the throne of grace and into the presence of God. Through Me you will have access to God's glory by the Spirit!"*

And the disciples said, *"Show us the Father!"*

Jesus replied, *"This is the Spirit of the Father talking to you! This is the Holy Spirit talking! Have I been so long with you, yet you do not know Me? He that has seen Me has seen the Father!"*

Some people have interpreted this to mean that Jesus and the Father are the same person. Jesus and the Father are one in *essence*, one in *unity*, one in *substance*, but They are two different Persons.

Jesus was saying, *"Why are you asking to see the Father? I am the express image of Him! If you've seen Me in action, you've really seen the Father in action because I'm the express image of His Person! As a matter of fact, the Words that I speak to you are not My Words! It's the Father in Me doing the talking! He is doing the works! If you don't believe Me by My Words, believe Me because of the works!"*

If the Spirit of God lives in you and inspires what you minister, what you believe, what you preach, what you herald—then there will be a manifestation of power that will verify the supernatural power of the one living on the inside of you!

Divine Energy

Godliness was manifested in the flesh two thousand years ago and it hasn't stopped manifesting. God continues to manifest that godliness in you and I. This is the mystery hidden from generation to generation but now is manifested to the Saints.

Manifested means revealed. It's a coming to the forefront. It's a revealing. For generations the mystery of God living in man had been hidden. No one had been able to apprehend it or comprehend it, but now that mystery has been revealed to the Saints. The mystery is Christ in you, the hope of glory (Colossians 1:27)!

The word Christ means the *Anointed One*. The mystery that has been hidden from generations was this: One day the Anointed One, the anointing, the divine nature, the supernatural Spirit of Faith—will live in the lives, in the bodies and in the spirits of men and women. The Anointed One will walk around on planet Earth—empowering and activating lives with His divine will! His will shall be done on Earth, as it is in Heaven!

Paul said, *"I have a dispensation to fulfill the Word of God—to fulfill the mystery that God lives in people! I have a life span to keep on demonstrating that God lives in me!"* Paul chose to live anointed!

Paul said, *"For me to live is Christ! I am crucified with Christ; nevertheless I live, yet not I, but it's Christ who lives in me! I've been given a dispensation to fulfill the mystery, to demonstrate the fact that Christ lives in you and in me, and by doing so, I hope to activate your faith! I didn't come with the words of philosophy. I didn't come with the enticing words of man's wisdom. I came in demonstration of the Spirit and of power—in demonstration of the Spirit that lives in me, so that your faith would not stand in the wisdom of men but in the power of God!"*

Unless someone comes to you demonstrating the power, you won't be able to put your faith in the power! That's the problem with most of the Church! People have been coming to us demonstrating the wisdom of man and we have put our faith in the wisdom of man. This has caused a lot of problems. You must see this! The more your mind opens up to it, the more you'll begin to allow God to do what He wants to do in your life. You'll begin to experience God and you'll no longer be afraid of Him.

> **…Christ in you, the hope of glory; whom we preach, warning every man, and teaching every man in all wisdom; that we may present every man perfect in Christ Jesus; where unto I also labor, striving according to his working, which worketh in me mightily.**
>
> **Colossians 1:27-29 KJV**

The Kenneth Wuest translation says it like this: *"…To which end also I am constantly laboring to the point of exhaustion, engaging in a contest in which I am controlled by His energy which operates in me in power"* (Colossians 1:29 Wuest).

Paul is saying: *"That's why I work and why I push it—and sometimes I'm at the point of exhaustion. However, I engage in a realm where, all of a sudden, His divine energy begins to operate in me! His resurrection life begins to operate in me and my physical body starts benefiting from Christ in me, the hope of glory. This has given me the potential of being inhabited by the resurrection life of his divine nature!"*

That means there is a fight of faith, which the believer is involved in. There is a fight to get out of the realm of natural laboring and into the realm of God's rest! The Bible says, *"Labor to enter into His rest."* The Bible also says that, *"God inhabits the praises of His people."* This is always true, isn't it? Yet, some people won't offer up the sacrifice of praise because it's *work!* It is work to really praise God. It's work because you have to watch your mind.

When you praise God, are you thinking about the bills? Are you thinking about the car breaking down or are you just numb? If you don't approach God with your heart, then you aren't praising Him! It is hard work to praise God because you have to push out of the realm of the natural. You're leaving the outer courts and walking into God's presence! The way to His presence isn't through the corridors of feelings!

Paul said, *"At times, I'm at the point of exhaustion. But what I do is engage in an activity that causes His force, His power, and His energy to work in me powerfully!"* He's talking about resurrection life! If you would learn to fight like that, to praise like that, and to pray in tongues like that—a force will come upon your physical body and energize it. That force is the anointing that is already resident on the inside of you. The anointing, which is greater than you, will cause resurrection life to operate in your body. It's a demonstration of the Spirit!

> **But if the Spirit of him that raised up Jesus from the dead dwell in you, he that raised up Christ from the dead shall also quicken your mortal bodies by his Spirit that dwelleth in you.**
>
> **Romans 8:11 KJV**

He will make alive your mortal body!

Endless Knowledge

> **How that by revelation He made known to me the mystery (as I have briefly written already, by which, when you read, you may understand my knowledge in the mystery of Christ).**
>
> **Ephesians 3:3-4**

God is trying to get us to understand the revelation Paul had. The Holy Ghost wants us to walk in the realm Paul walked in!

Wouldn't you like the devils to say, *"Jesus we know, and (your name here!) we know"*? Paul walked in a supernatural realm because of his revelation of the mystery of Christ. Anyone who will allow the Holy Ghost to bring the revelation of the mystery closer will grow in that revelation and begin to see more power manifested in their lives! The potential is endless! *"He that believeth on Me, the works that I do shall he do also, and greater works than these shall he do!"*

> **By which, when you read, you may understand my knowledge in the mystery of Christ, which in other ages was not made known to the sons of men, as it has now been revealed by the Spirit to His holy apostles and prophets.**
>
> **Ephesians 3:4-5**

At some point, somehow, we placed our trust in the wrong thing. If we can't trust the Apostle Paul and his writings or the Holy Spirit to cause the Word to live to us, then our trust is in the preacher's theology degree. Our trust is in the seminary that he went to.

Paul gives his qualifications: *"By revelation the Holy Spirit made known to me the mystery that I'm telling you. When you read you will understand my revelation and my knowledge of the mystery of Christ. This was the mystery that was hidden for ages but now is made manifest unto the apostles and the prophets by the Spirit."*

Paul's not saying that the apostles and the prophets of today will add to the Bible. What the Spirit revealed to the apostles and prophets in that day is already recorded. However, we could live a lifetime trying to exhaust the revelation in the Word that's already written – *and never do it!* People are casting away Scripture rather then attempting to live their life to reach the extent of the revelation that is invested in just one Scripture.

This mystery is revealed to the apostles and the prophets by the Spirit. That means the Holy Ghost inspired the Scriptures. The Bible says that no prophecy or Scripture is of any private interpretation (2 Peter 1:20). If man, then, does not hold the key to interpreting the Scriptures, who is qualified? It is the Holy Ghost who is able to interpret Scripture in light of Scripture! He will bring the pieces together and will bear witness with your spirit. You'll *know* it is divine Truth!

The Gift of Grace

Whereof I was made a minister, according to the gift of the grace of God given unto me by the effectual working of His power unto me, who am less than the least of all saints, is this grace given, that I should preach among the Gentiles the unsearchable riches of Christ.

Ephesians 3:7-8 KJV

In other words, *"I have a grace gift that was given to me through the effectual working of God's power."* It is through God's power that gifts are imparted! Paul said, *"Because of the abundance of the revelations there was given me a thorn in the flesh, a messenger of Satan, to buffet me"* (2 Corinthians 12:7 KJV). Religion read that and wrongly reasoned, *"God didn't want Paul to become prideful because of all the revelation he was given, so He hired a devil to beat up on Paul in order to keep him humble."* That's what religion said!

This is what Paul said: *"I approached God three times saying, 'God, help me! You know Satan keeps sending people to stone me and throw me in jail!' And the Lord answered me saying, 'My grace is sufficient for you.*

You have the effectual working of My power already on the inside of you, Paul! I've given you the gift of grace, and, through that gift, you can rise up to claim the deliverance I have promised you! You can put the devil behind you!"

Three times he asked God and three times he got the same exact answer: *"You don't need help from Heaven. My grace, the gift of grace that you have in you, the mystery of Christ in you, the effectual working of the power in you, is enough! Godliness is already in you Paul!"*

People in the church pray the same way: *"God, why don't you do something?"* If the child of God would listen, they would hear God say, *"The Holy Ghost is enough. I've already done it."*

An Invitation to Partake

Paul wrote to the Church, *"God shall bruise Satan under your feet shortly!"* He had put to work what God said! Putting the devil under his feet, he rose up to fulfill the law and the plan of God. *"That I should preach to the Gentiles the unsearchable riches of Christ; to make all men see what is the fellowship of the mystery (Christ in you, the hope of glory!), which from the beginning of the world has been hid in God, who created all things by Jesus Christ!"*

Paul gives the mystery a lot of attention. He wants you to know by revelation that Christ is literally living in you! Paul wants you to know how you can allow the Holy Ghost to live His supernatural life in your life! *"I've been anointed. I've been called. I've been given the gift of grace. I've been chosen by God and given a dispensation to fulfill the Word of God so that I can cause all men to see what the fellowship of the mystery is!"*

There is a great invitation from God to us: *"Come on and partake in the fellowship! Partake in the koinonia! Partake in having things in common with Me! Live in the realm where Christ is in you and My power is at work in you!"* Christ is in us; therefore we can have boldness. We can access the presence of God. We can have confidence and faith in Him. That's a great invitation, but you can only have it if you see it.

Speaking of his call, Paul said, *"I'm called to get men to see that there is a fellowship in the mystery available to them. It had been hid in God, who created all things by Jesus Christ, from the beginning of the world."*

To the intent that now unto the principalities and powers in heavenly places might be known by the church the manifold wisdom of God, according to the eternal purpose which he purposed in Christ Jesus our Lord, in whom we have boldness and access with confidence by the faith of Him.

Ephesians 3:10-12 KJV

Paul is writing to the Church, *"I'm trying to get every man to see the fellowship of the mystery that was not available to any other generation! I'm trying to show you where the power is. I'm trying to show you Christ in you, the hope of glory! He's in you and I'm trying to get you to see that I have an understanding of godliness manifested in human flesh. I want you to partake of the nature and the power of Christ. I want you to let Him live in you so that all the principalities and powers would see godliness manifested in the Church!*

God was writing about you! You should put your name there! You too should say, *"To the intent that now unto the principalities and powers in heavenly places might be known by* (your name here) *the manifold wisdom of God."* God wants you to have a revelation of the mystery so that the devil will see that mystery operating in you! He wants His Church to show the devil the manifold wisdom of God!

How are the principalities and powers going to see the manifold wisdom of God in demonstration? The only way they will see it is when Christ in you, the hope of glory, begins to demonstrate Himself victorious! The devils said, *"Jesus we know, and Paul we know,"* because it was being made known through Paul to the principalities and powers that God had a secret! They thought they killed Jesus, but instead God multiplied Him! There used to be one Jesus casting them out; now God had multiplied the Lord in millions of believers.

This is why the devil fights the Holy Ghost! He really doesn't mind if you read the Bible. He doesn't mind if you go to a dead church. He doesn't even mind if you live your life by Christian principles. You see, you won't do any damage to his kingdom unless the hope of glory—*Christ in you*—is manifested in mighty demonstrations of the Spirit!

You Are What You Eat

Paul prays for the Ephesians church:

> **(I do not cease) to give thanks for you, making mention of you in my prayers, that the God of our Lord Jesus Christ, the Father of glory, may give unto you the spirit of wisdom and revelation in the knowledge of Him; the eyes of your understanding being enlightened; that you may know what is the hope of His calling, and what the riches of the glory of His inheritance in the saints.**
>
> **Ephesians 1:16-18**
> (parentheses added by author)

These are Spirit-filled Christians, but Paul is telling them that they are still not proficient. He is saying, *"You still don't have a grasp of it yet. You're not growing in the mystery of Christ. The indwelling Spirit or the power of God in you is important to your daily life and victory!"*

God will use wisdom and revelation as the avenue or doorway through which the Spirit can be strong in your life. *"That the eyes of your understanding would be enlightened so that you would be able to see."* God has to get you to *see it* before He can get you to *receive it!* You can't receive what you do not see by revelation. It's impossible for you to claim it or benefit from it. It's like having a million dollars in your house, but not knowing where it is! That million dollars won't do you any good if you can't see it! It is the same with a revelation. You have to see it. You have to know that it's there to partake of it. *"I'm making mention of you in my prayers continually so that the Spirit of God, the Father of glory (that means power, anointing, and splendor) would give you the Spirit of wisdom and revelation in the knowledge of Him."*

In the Garden, the devil told Eve that if she ate of the fruit—she would be like God, knowing good and evil. The devil, however, was lying because God does not *know* evil—*not the way she knew evil after eating the fruit.* Eve *experienced* evil by doing it and God never did that. The devil lied! Once you partake of evil, you become a servant to evil.

The Spirit of wisdom and revelation in the knowledge of Him is an experiential understanding of God. It's an *experience* in God. It doesn't mean to know *about* Him. There are people who have gone to church for thirty years and still don't really know God. On a lesser scale, someone could live a week without an encounter with God, but they will only live off of the strength of that last encounter. Paul wanted you to have a revelation so that you could have an ongoing experience. He wanted you to have wisdom, to have an *experiential knowledge* of God so that you would have an ongoing fellowship—an ongoing relationship and an ongoing encounter with godliness. He wanted you to be a partaker of godliness!

The Bible says that Jesus learned obedience by the things He suffered. Once again, preachers have misinterpreted this and taught, *"When you suffer, you learn how to be obedient. Even Jesus learned how to be obedient by suffering!"* If that were the case, and disobedience is sin, then it's only logical to conclude that Jesus was in sin before He learned to be obedient. Yet, that same preacher will tell you that Jesus was without sin.

Can we think and still be a Christian?

Suffering didn't teach Jesus how to be obedient! Jesus said, *"I always do the things that please My Father."* He said that before He was whipped, before they pulled His beard, before they spit on Him, before He suffered anything at the hands of men! *"I always do the things that please my Father."* Then what does it mean? It means that God had never *experienced* the sufferings of man. Oh yes, He had empathized with them, He had understood the sufferings of man, but He had never suffered in the way that man suffered.

Jesus could not give you what is His *until* He took what was yours! He put on *your* humanity and He went through *your* suffering. He experienced obedience from a human viewpoint for the first time. He learned. He had an *experiential knowledge* of obedience in the midst of suffering. Experiencing it firsthand, He was obedient through suffering so that He could qualify to be our High Priest. He experienced obedience in the midst of suffering so that He could tell every believer, *"I've been through that; I know that by experience; Yes, I learned that by experience; I've been through what you're going through! That's why I can help you! That's why I can uphold you!"*

Experiencing God

Jesus learned by experience. We need the Spirit of wisdom and revelation so that we can experience God. You can't experience God without the anointing, but there are people who are never moved by the Spirit of God. They are never moved—they just go through the religious motions. *Where is the Lord in all of it?*

Paul said that you need the Spirit of wisdom and revelation so that you can come into an experiential life in God—so that you can experience the anointing and experience the glory. The fellowship of that mystery is in these things! Where God is, *there is power*. Where the presence of God is, the will of God can be enforced and claimed *by believers*. He said, "Where two or three are gathered in My name, there am I in your midst" (Matthew 18:20 KJV)!

"The eyes of your understanding being enlightened; that you may know what is the hope of His calling." The hope of your calling is Christ! *"For me to live is Christ!"* The hope of my call is to be like Jesus, to be transformed from glory to glory!

You have been predestined to be conformed into the image of His dear Son! What do you need to do to fulfill that calling? *You need a revelation.* You need to see *who* Christ is in you. When you see this, *you will know the hope of your calling.* As you walk in this calling, people will begin to see Christ alive on the inside of you. They'll encounter the victory, the joy, the anointing, the liberty, and the wisdom of the Lord Jesus Christ Himself because He lives on the inside of you by the Spirit of God!

"And what is the exceeding greatness of His power toward usward who believe, according to the working of His mighty working power" (Ephesians 3:19 KJV). He said you need the Spirit of wisdom and revelation so that you would know how overabundant His power is towards you!

It's not mental belief; it's experiential faith! When you have the wisdom and the revelation of the knowledge of Him, you will have the fellowship with the anointing that lives in you. You have a knowledge of the hope of your calling!

What is fellowship? The Bible says that it's like looking at the Word, or looking at the Lord with an open face. It's like looking into a mirror. When you look into a mirror, that mirror tells you what you look like. In the same way, the anointing is telling you what you look like. It's a reflection of the glory within! That's an experience!

The Bible says that faith cometh by hearing and hearing by the *rhema* Word of God (Romans 10:17). Faith explodes beyond the limits of your life when you have an experience with God. If God is there, He'll talk to you! When the anointing is upon you—as you're having fellowship and communion with the Holy Ghost—the *Spirit of revelation will flow* and *the rhema will come*. Once you believe according to the working of His mighty power, you will see the *exceeding greatness* of His power toward you (who are believing)!

The Rhema Life

Jesus walked in on the mourners and said, *"Why are you crying? She's asleep!"* They laughed Him to scorn, but He kicked them out. Jesus was walking a rhema life!

Paul did as well: *"I have been given a dispensation to fulfill the Word of God, even the mystery, which is Christ in me! If I know that I'm living the life of opportunity right now, then the words of Christ are living in me and I'm living in those words! When those words say, "Go! Do what I told you to do!" Then I receive the faith that comes by that rhema! That faith is according to the working of the power of that mystery that is at work in me. Once I have the faith according to the working of the power that is in me, then I see the exceeding greatness of the potential available to help me to do what I'm called to do! I'm walking a rhema life!"*

Jesus said the same thing:

> **I did not come to destroy the Law, I came to fulfill it, to verify what is written about Me, "Lo, I come in the volume of the Book that is written of Me to do Thy will, O My God."**
>
> **Hebrews 10:7 KJV**

He set His heart and His faith in agreement with the Holy Ghost in order to fulfill what was written about Him.

You and I have discovered that God wrote something about us:

> **That they would make known the manifold wisdom of God by the Church to the principalities and powers.**
>
> **Ephesians 3:10**

In other words, *"I am here right now—in this dispensation—to embarrass the devil and show him that Jesus is more than enough in my life! Once I know that—then the mystery in me, Christ in me, the anointing in me, the power in me, the Word in me—is alive! I'm living in that Word—and that Word will talk to me! I'm a person with purpose! My priorities are to do the will of Him who sent me! 'As my Father has sent Me, so send I you!' When my priorities are in order, the Word talks to me."*

Faith cometh by hearing, and hearing by the rhema Word. *What kind of faith is it?* It is faith according to the power that is at work in you. It's the faith that the *rhema* brings! It's the knowing that *"I know that I know that I know!"* When you have the faith that is according to the power at work within you, then you will *see* the exceeding greatness of that power in your life! When you see it, you are able to do what God has called you to do! The power is in you to fulfill His promises toward you!

All the Power There Is

> **Giving thanks unto the Father, which has made us meet to be partakers of the inheritance of the saints in light; who hath delivered us from the power of darkness, and hath translated us to the kingdom of His dear Son, in whom we have redemption through His blood,**

> even the forgiveness of sins who is the image of the invisible God, the firstborn of every creature; for by Him were all things created, that are in heaven, and that are in earth, visible and invisible, whether they be thrones, or dominions, or principalities, or powers; all things were created by Him, and for Him, and He is before all things, and by Him all things consist and He is the head of the body, the church; who is the beginning, the first born from the dead; that in all things He might have preeminence. For it pleased the Father that in Him should all fullness dwell.
>
> **Colossians 1:12-19 KJV**

God delivered us from the power of darkness. We were delivered legally by Jesus, but we are delivered literally—*by experience*—through the Holy Ghost! Christians can walk in bondage even though the Deliverer lives in them. The anointing is what destroys the yoke, but it is the *manifested power in you* that will *enforce* the victory of Calvary in your life!

He has translated us into the Kingdom of His dear Son. Positionally, we live with God, in Christ. *"If you are risen with Christ, seek those things which are above, where Christ sits, for you are dead and your life is hid with Christ in God"* (Colossians 3:1)! That's where we are!

In Heaven we will feel the presence of the Lord. The glory is going to be awesome! The Bible says that there's no need for the light of the sun because the glory illuminates the entire city (Revelation 21:23). Think about it! When that final blast of glory comes, our physical bodies are going to change to be just like His. We will be immortal!

The power you have available to you now, is exactly what will be available to you in eternity. There won't be any more power available to us! There is just one promise that is not yet available to us—the glorification of the physical body. That, however, is the *only* promise in regards to life and godliness that you cannot secure now through the power in you! Divine health is for you *now!* Physical healing is for you *now!* Abundance and prosperity are for you *now!*

What kind of power did God make available to you? Jesus said, *"All power in Heaven and in Earth is given unto Me."* The mystery of godliness is God in us. *"For in him (Christ) dwelleth all the fullness of the Godhead bodily"* (Colossians 2:9 KJV). Bodily! It's not *some of the fullness* of the Godhead, but it's *all of the fullness* of the Godhead. In His Body resides the fullness of Him that filleth all in all! *Who is His Body?* It's the Church! We are His Body! There will not be one ounce of power available in Heaven that is not available to us *now!*

In Christ, dwells all of the fullness of the Godhead bodily. This is the mystery. It's a mystery to us because, no matter what measure of anointing we currently operate in, we're going to spend the rest of our lives growing in it. We'll never exhaust it! God is not holding the supply back. He has given it to the Church through Jesus Christ! You don't have a part of Jesus—you have *all of Jesus* living on the inside of you!

The Hiding Place of His Power

In whom we have redemption through His blood, the forgiveness of sins. He is the image of the invisible God, the firstborn over all creation.

Colossians 1:14, 15

Christ is the image of the invisible God. He is godliness manifested in the flesh. He is the express image of His Person. He is the firstborn of all creation. He is the first one of the new breed, the born again being, the new species, the new creation. *"He that is in Christ is a new creation; old things are past away, and all things have become new"* (2 Corinthians 5:17). Christ is the image of the invisible God and He is the firstborn. The firstborn is the image of the invisible God, and the second born, the third born, the fourth born, etc. should resemble the firstborn!

The Bible says that we have been predestined by God. It was God who took the mystery and hid it, *in Himself,* for generations. The prophets tried to uncover it. They searched diligently for it, yet they could not apprehend it. *Why?* The mystery was hidden! It was not revealed! It wasn't revealed when Jesus was walking the shores of Galilee. It wasn't even revealed while Jesus was preaching. This mystery wasn't revealed until the Holy Ghost came down from Heaven and indwelt believers, enabling them to be partakers of the same nature. All of a sudden, they started acting just like Jesus!

The apostles looked into the Old Covenant, *and the Holy Ghost who knows how to interpret Scripture*, brought Truth to them and led them to write the New Testament. He revealed the mystery to the apostles and prophets so that they would, in turn, make it known to us!

God reserved the preeminent position for Jesus. He called Jesus the Forerunner *(that means others are running right behind Him)*. He called Him the Firstborn *(that means other brethren were born after Him)*. Then He hid that mystery in Him, knowing all along that He had predestined us to be conformed to the image of His dear Son. *Who is His dear Son?* His dear Son is His image! *Who are we?* We are the image of His dear Son, if we get a hold of that revelation and let the exceeding greatness of His power work in us! *What will happen then?* The things Heaven has provided for you will begin to operate in your life!

The throne of your life is not big enough to house you *and* Christ. You have to make up your mind: either *you* live or you let *Him* live!

You are not a Christian unless you died by faith with Christ; were quickened in Christ out of the grave; and now live in Christ and Christ in you. You have traded your nature for His nature; your limitation for His power; your weakness for His strength; your sin for His salvation! You've traded it, and the Spirit of God will help you to make that trade forevermore!

He's the firstborn of every creature, and all things exist by Him. He's the Head of the Body, and in the Body dwells all the fullness of the Godhead. *"To know the love of Christ, which passeth knowledge, that ye might be filled with all of the fullness of God"* (Ephesians 3:19).

It Has Begun!

Without controversy, great is the mystery of godliness: God was manifest in the flesh, justified in the Spirit, seen of angels, preached unto the Gentiles, believed on in the world, received up into glory.

1 Timothy 3:16

He was received up into glory, *but it doesn't stop there.* The Bible doesn't say that Christ is the end—it says that Christ is the beginning! *"I am the beginning and the end!"* He's the one who lived here physically for thirty-three and a half years and then left and came again through the Holy Ghost! The same one, who did miracles two thousand years ago, will do miracles today *in* you and *through* you! When He was received up into glory, it wasn't the end! It was the beginning. Christ *is* the beginning!

Christ is the firstborn from the dead. When Christ died, He died spiritually. In Isaiah the Scripture refers to *deaths* (plural). Jesus did not only die, He made His soul a sacrifice for sin. That means that after He died and was in the grave, He was born out of the grave from death unto life. The only way that you can be born again is to be buried *with Him* for your transgressions, and then born again out of the grave *in Him* for justification and newness of life.

He was the firstborn from the dead. That means there would be others born from the dead after Him. When Jesus rose from the dead, Old Testament saints rose from the dead as well!

And what is the exceeding greatness of His power toward us who believe, according to the working of His mighty power which He worked in Christ when He raised Him from the dead and seated Him at His right hand in the heavenly places.

Ephesians 1:19-20

The kind of power available to us is the kind of power that raised Jesus out of the grave. It's the same power that healed His mutilated, deformed, beaten up physical body! It's the same power that took Old Testament Saints, who had died and become dust and raised them to life again! They walked around the streets of Jerusalem ministering and sharing the Good News (Matthew 27:52, 53)!

He is the firstborn from the dead that in all things He might have preeminence—*the position of priority*. Preachers, however, have made Him the *only* one. They have told believers, *"He used to do it,"* or *"He can do it when He wants to do it."* That's a lie! The reason you can do what He has called you to do is because He did it *personally* first—and He'll do it again through you now! He is the first and we come after!

Lay hands on yourself and say:

> *Thank you Lord, for the power resident in me. Thank you for the anointing of God that will never fail—that will always see me through! Thank you for the exceeding greatness of Your anointing on my behalf!*

Chapter 7

The Tabernacle of Power

―――――◆―――――

*Tabernacles made with hands
are not what God desires!*

Much of what the disciples saw the Lord do, they didn't understand. They didn't even understand when He took the time to explain things to them. They walked with Him for three and a half years. They saw Him do what He did and they heard Him say what He said. They asked Him questions and listened to His answers, but they could not comprehend.

What's Next?

The disciples really didn't know *how* Jesus did what He did. They didn't know a lot about doctrine. Even when He rose from the dead, they asked Him:

> **Therefore, when they had come together, they asked Him, saying, "Lord, will You at this time restore the kingdom to Israel?" And He said to them, "It is not for you to know times or seasons which the Father has put in His own authority."**
>
> **Acts 1:6-7**

During the countdown to Gethsemane, Jesus was talking to His disciples and preparing them. He was saying, *"Now I'm going to leave and give you over to the tutelage of and teaching of the Spirit of God. When the Spirit of God comes, He will remind you of what I said. You're going to need to be reminded through revelation, and you'll say, 'Oh! That's what He meant when He said that!' He will show you things to come."*

You've heard it said many times before: *"...And He will show you things to come"* (John 16:13). Preachers have taught that this meant that the Holy Ghost would reveal things pertaining to eschatology to the disciples. Of course, He did that, and they wrote about it. However, do you know what He will show you? When you get alone with God, He will show you what is *coming*. He will show you what kind of things that you need to prepare for and how you need to walk that day. The Holy Ghost will enable you and empower you for what is coming!

Miracles On Credit

When the disciples were walking with Jesus, they were doing miracles by His authority. They weren't doing miracles through their own anointing—they didn't have an anointing! The Bible said that He took them aside and gave them authority to cast out unclean spirits.

The disciples took this authority and went in His name. From the standpoint of Calvary, however, His name wasn't *yet* given. The disciples were using His name *on credit!* While they were under the covering of this Anointed Teacher (who was literally the House of God) they went out and, through delegated authority, did exactly what He told them to do. The Spirit of God backed up their words on His behalf.

The disciples didn't have an anointing of their own. They couldn't have an anointing of their own! You cannot receive the anointing unless you are born again, and you can't be born again without the shedding of blood. The blood had not yet been shed.

One day they tried to cast out a devil and failed. Jesus had to step in and help them. Afterwards they asked the Lord, *"Why couldn't we cast it out?"* Jesus answered, *"Because of your unbelief."*

Unbelief is the by-product of not hearing a rhema Word. When you have a rhema experience, you will have faith. When you're walking with God in the *now*, you'll have an inner assurance for the *now*. When you're walking in prayer with God, you'll know that He is with you to perform. Faith comes by hearing and hearing by the rhema Word! The disciples were operating without a rhema Word. Jesus said, *"Howbeit this kind cometh not out but by prayer and fasting."*

The disciples saw Jesus pray, but they could not enter into His dimension of prayer. They said, *"Teach us to pray!"* Jesus taught them the *Lord's Prayer*. Since they didn't have the Holy Ghost to inspire them through prayer, they needed help to pray as they should. As Paul wrote, *"We know not how to pray as we ought."*

Jesus taught them to pray, *"Thy Kingdom come. Thy will be done on Earth as it is in Heaven."* By and large, Christians pray that as a passive prayer! In other words, they look forward to a day when God will sovereignly perform His will on the Earth. However, Jesus said, *"Go in My name, and these signs will follow you!"* After the provision of the Holy Ghost was made, the Lord's Prayer ceased to hold the same degree of relevance for the believer. It was a form or pattern that Jesus gave to His disciples before they had been endowed with the Holy Ghost. After the Spirit of God filled them, they were able to enter into the same prayer dimension that Jesus participated in.

As believers, we will see a measure of His Kingdom come in our lives. Some will see thirty, some will see sixty, and some will see a hundred fold. When we say, *"Thy Kingdom come,"* we are saying, *"Thy Kingdom come in me by the power of the Holy Ghost—who has come to give me a revelation of Your will—so that I can claim it in the earth realm and see it manifested in my life!"* That's the good fight of faith! We're not fighting to *win* the victory. We're fighting to *claim* a promise that Christ has provided through His death, burial, and resurrection!

Godliness Manifested in the Flesh

And He said to them, "Assuredly, I say to you that there are some standing here who will not taste death till they see the kingdom of God present with power." Now after six days Jesus took Peter, James, and John, and led them up on a high mountain apart by themselves; and He was transfigured before them. His clothes became shining, exceedingly white, like snow, such as no launderer on earth can whiten them.

And Elijah appeared to them with Moses, and they were talking with Jesus.

Mark 9:1-4

As Jesus prayed, He was transfigured before the eyes of His disciples! Jesus had the Holy Ghost, but His disciples had not yet received the Spirit. Up until that point, no one other than Jesus had the ability to pray the kind of prayer that brings power. He was praying and the power was in Him. The Bible doesn't tell us what He prayed, but I guarantee you, He was praying by the inspiration of the Spirit within Him! The Bible says that the Words He spoke were the Words of the Spirit of God.

Suddenly, His face began to change. From head to toe, he began to glow with a brightness greater than the sun! The glory inside of Him came forth and radiated from His physical body! Now that's a demonstration of power! *What were the disciples seeing?* They were witnessing *Godliness* manifested in the flesh! The Jesus that they saw is the *same Jesus* who is living in you! He is now glorified and He's alive in you!

He changed before their eyes and they saw the House of God manifested. As they witnessed the glory coming out of Him, they saw Elijah and Moses talk with Him. One account said that they talked to Him about His coming death and the sufferings.

What does Moses represent? He's the mediator of the Old Covenant. God covered his eyes and passed in front of Him. Moses saw God from the back! So profound was this experience—this tiny glimpse—that his face shone with a reflective glory so bright that the people told him to veil his face. They couldn't handle the residue of the glory on His face! In the New Testament, it is recorded that the veil is taken away.

Moses was the Law. The Law was the schoolmaster that was supposed to lead us to Christ. The schoolmaster used symbolism. It relied on shadows of things to come—types and lessons that were given to lead us to a life of experience with Christ.

The prophet represented the promise. Jesus said, *"Go, search the Scriptures because the prophets talked about Me."* Elijah was a type of the Head of Prophets. He is someone who was glorified. He's old, but he's not dead! He was translated to Heaven and never died.

What an awesome experience! Three disciples—Peter, James and John—who just *happened* to become pillars of the early Church, had this glimpse before the crucifixion. They saw the glorified Christ! They saw the fullness of the Godhead bodily manifested! Do you know what Jesus called it? *"The Kingdom of God come with power!"* He had told them, *"You will not die until you see the Kingdom of God come with power!"*

The *Kingdom of God come with power* was God manifested through a human vessel. There was no doubt that the glory was in that vessel! *When did this transformation come?* Jesus was transfigured *as He prayed!* Oh yes, God was in Him all along, but the manifestation of the glory didn't come while they were *on their way up* the mountain. It came while Jesus was caught up in the Spirit praying. All of a sudden, a supernatural law superseded the laws of the natural!

BANG!
GLORY MANIFESTED!
A body that was flesh was suddenly lit!
His face changed! His outfit changed!
It was full of light!
Everything radiated!

The disciples fell down on their faces under the power of the Spirit. They were afraid! They had never seen anything like this. They had never seen the anointing in Him physically manifested! The anointing was in Him all along, but if the anointing had been in manifestation twenty-four hours a day, the disciples would have spent three and a half years on their faces! They would have never gone anywhere! They would have been slain in the Spirit for three and a half years! The power was present all along, but the power was not in manifestation all the time.

The Spirit of God chose to manifest the power in different ways. Sometimes He would teach, and while He was teaching, people would believe on Him. That's the power of God in demonstration! The disciples saw Him do miracles. They saw Him raise the dead. They had never however, up until this point, watched Him pray until the glory manifested in His body. That's the Kingdom of God come with power!

Let Us Make Three Tabernacles

And Peter answered and said to Jesus, "Master, it is good for us to be here; and let us make three tabernacles; one for thee, and one for Moses, and one for Elias," for he wist not what to say; for they were sore afraid. And there was a cloud that overshadowed them; and a voice came out of the cloud, saying, "This is my beloved son, hear him." And suddenly, when they had looked round about, they saw no man any more, save Jesus only with themselves. And as they came down from the mountain, he charged them that they should tell no man what things they had seen, till the Son of man were risen or were risen from the dead.

Mark 9:5-9 KJV

Peter had been taught by the Law that a tabernacle was needed to house the glory. He had been taught that a tent, a building, a booth, the tabernacle of witness, the tabernacle of the congregation—*something* was needed to house the glory. When he saw the glory, he immediately reverted back to the Law. He reverted *back* to the thing that was supposed to bring Him *to* Christ. The anointing was present. When the anointing is present, it will always bring hidden things to the surface. The way Peter responded revealed that he was in error. Peter believed error because he was caught up in the type and shadow of the Christ to come. However, the *present* Christ was already manifested with him!

He saw the glory. He saw Moses. He saw Elijah. They appeared in glory with Jesus. Peter's first thought was, *"Let's build three tabernacles! That's what we need to do. We need to house God! We need to house the anointing! We need to house the glory! We need to build around it!"* All of a sudden, the cloud of glory came and God said, *"This is My beloved Son!"*

Do you know what God was saying? *"This is the end of man made* tabernacles! You won't be building another one! You are not going to put Me in a box any more! You will no longer put Me in a booth any more! I will not be on the outside. I am going to manifest Myself through tabernacles made with flesh! That's what I'm going to do and this is My beloved Son, in whom I am well pleased!"

Immediately the visitors disappeared and they only saw Jesus. Jesus said to them, *"Don't tell anyone what you have seen until I rise from the dead!"* They saw the things that would come to pass after His resurrection. They saw the Kingdom of God come with power! What is the Kingdom of God come with power? It's the mystery of godliness—*God manifest in the flesh*!

A Glorified Body

And Stephen, full of faith and power, did great wonders and miracles among the people.

Acts 6:8 KJV

Religion says, *"Now, we don't do miracles; God does miracles."* Stephen however—full of faith and power—did great wonders and miracles. We need to view the book of Acts as a success manual for Calvary!

Prior to Pentecost, only *one* Person was full of faith and power. After He rose and the promise of the Spirit was sent, one hundred and twenty were suddenly filled! Peter got up, preached, and three thousand were added to the Lord! Others preached and five thousand came into the Church. With so many people to tend to and more being added daily, seven deacons were chosen who were full of God's power. Stephen and Philip were among those who were chosen for this work.

The Kingdom of God had come with power into them. It had come through the power of the Holy Ghost. The demonstration that the Kingdom was at work is evidenced by the many signs and wonders that were accomplished through them! The book of Acts is the success of Calvary! It is not a dispensational book – it's a book that never ends.

They may have stopped writing it, but the book of Acts continues today in the lives of believers that are filled with power.

> **And all that sat in the council, looking steadfastly on him, saw His face as it had been the face of an angel.**
>
> **Acts 6:15 KJV**

There were seventy or eighty people in the council—religious people who sat and accused Stephen. As they looked steadfastly on him, his face began to shine as that of an angel. Perplexed, they wondered, *"What in the world is happening?"* His face was like the face of an angel! That was a manifestation and demonstration of the glory! They were seeing Christ in Him!

The Bible said that Stephen spoke with wisdom. The council could not refute his wisdom. Whose wisdom was it? It was wisdom of Christ operating in Stephen!

When God said, *"This is My beloved Son, hear Him,"* He was saying, *"This is My beloved Son! You won't have to build Him a tabernacle. From now on, My beloved Son is going to make you a tabernacle! In fact, He's going to make YOU His tabernacle. When He does, He's going to come back enforcing the power of His Kingdom through signs and wonders. He's going to break the bondage of the enemy through the anointing of God in you!"*

Stephen's face changed right in front of them! He looked like an angel and he preached to them saying:

> **Yea, ye took up the tabernacle of Moloch and the star of your god Remphan, figures which ye made to worship them, and I will carry you away beyond Babylon. Our fathers had the tabernacle of witness in the wilderness, as he had appointed, speaking unto Moses, that he should make it according to the fashion that he had seen.**
>
> **Acts 7:43-44 KJV**

Stephen was talking about the Ark of the Covenant. He was saying, *"When the children of Israel turned from worshipping God, God gave them over to the host of Heaven. They took up tabernacles for Remphan and for Moloch."* They had built man made tabernacles for the demon spirit of Moloch and the demon spirit of Remphan to live in. Stephen continued, *"God spoke to Moses and gave you the tabernacle of witness."* That was the Ark of the Covenant. The glory of God was supposed to dwell in the midst of the cherubim. The Law, the Word of God, the tablets of stone, was to be housed in that place. This was a type and a shadow of the house of God. The shadow was designed to ultimately lead us to Christ.

Stephen said, *"God told you to build it the way He commanded."* God didn't say, *"Go out and get some rotten wood and cover it with lead."* No, God said, *"Get some good wood and cover it with gold!"* That's just the tabernacle!

Do you know what the tabernacle is? It's the body! It's a box that holds the glory inside. God said, *"Put gold on the outside of it! Decorate it well!"* Why? The tabernacle—*the Body*—is a precious thing to God!

Don't Put God in a Box

> ...Speaking unto Moses, that he should make it according to the fashion that he had seen. Which also our fathers that came after brought in with Jesus (or Joshua) into the possession of the Gentiles, whom God drove out before the face of our fathers, unto the day of David; who found favor before God, and desired to find a tabernacle for the God of Jacob.
>
> **Acts 7:44-46 KJV**

David said to the Lord, *"Let us build You a tabernacle."* (Peter wasn't that far off the mark, was he?) David said, *"Let me build You a house!"* He wanted to build God a house. He could not envision God, in a box, being carried around itinerant! He wanted to build God a house!

Solomon built Him a house.

> **But Solomon built Him a house. However, the Most High does not dwell in temples made with hands, as the prophet says: 'Heaven is My throne, And earth is My footstool. What house will you build for Me? Says the Lord, Or what is the place of My rest? Has My hand not made all these things?'**
>
> **Acts 7:47-50**

Who is God's hand? Jesus! All things were made by Him, whether they're thrones, dominions, principalities, powers—all things were made by Him!

God said, *"You won't build me a house with your hands! My Hand has created everything! My Hand will build Me a house! When the time comes, when I'm ready to live in a house, I won't settle in a house made by man! I'll send My Hand, who created everything, and My Hand will become the first house! My hand will become a representative of every other house that would believe upon Me and believe upon His name. From then on, I'll have houses made by Me and built by Me to be inhabited by Me! I'm going to have tabernacles, just like My Son, all over the Earth!"*

Why did the Israelites carry a box with them? They needed the anointing! They had a schoolmaster. When they dedicated the temple of Solomon, one hundred and twenty of them rose up and sang with one sound (That sounds like in the upper room!): *"For the Lord is good! His mercy endures forever!"* Suddenly, the cloud of glory came into the temple and the priests could not stand to minister (They were slain in the Spirit!) because of the glory!

God spoke through Haggai: *"The glory of the latter house will be greater than the former, saith the Lord, and I will fill this house with glory"* (Haggai 2:9 KJV)! All of these things were types and shadows to teach God's people so that they would recognize the real thing.

Stupidity of the Heart

Peter didn't have the Holy Ghost on that mountaintop. He was still religious. When the Holy Ghost started moving, he got stiff! There are people who will get up and leave a church service when the Spirit of God starts moving. Their religion surfaces in the anointing.

Religious people say, *"I just believe we ought to be reverent in church!"* They get mad because they have a religious concept of reverence. I've been to churches where the people were so stiff, so formal and so unhappy that you'd think they lost their best friend! After service, we would go out to eat and the same folks that looked like they needed a resurrection from the dead would sit around the table laughing, telling jokes, and acting as if they were normal!

Why do people put on that religious face when they step into the house of God? Why do they have to act ugly when the Spirit of God is moving? When the anointing moves, everything that is still a type and a shadow will manifest! People will use the very Scriptures that God has given to teach us to flow in the Spirit, as grounds for *not* flowing in the Spirit! God never intended for us to merely know about Him. If that were so, the Old Testament would have been enough. He wants us to know more!

Stephen continued,

> **You stiff-necked and uncircumcised in heart and ears! You always resist the Holy Spirit; as your fathers did, so do you.**
>
> **Acts 7:51**

They're resisting the Holy Ghost operating through Stephen. He didn't say, *"You're resisting me,"* but he said, *"You're resisting the Holy Ghost."*

There's an unbelief that's based upon a lack of knowledge, and there's an unbelief that's based upon a hardness of heart. God knows the difference. Jesus asked the religious crowd, *"Is it lawful to do good on the Sabbath? To save a life, or to destroy it?"* They didn't answer.

He looked on them with anger, being grieved at the *stupidity* of their hearts (interpreted *hardness* in the King James Version). They weren't unbelievers because of a lack of knowledge. They were *willfully* obstinate. It was the hardness of their heart that was resisting the anointing. There's a *big* difference between the two. You cannot help someone who is determined to be a barrier to the Holy Spirit. God sees the difference between lack of knowledge and hardness of heart. If a person has the right heart, they will want to learn.

In the original language, "stiff-necked" is like a bull that refuses to allow the right yoke to be put on him. That's a great illustration of a religious person! Some people want to go to church and stay mad all their lives. You can't change those kind of people.

The Face of an Angel

Stephen was preaching, *"You have had God in a box. You have even built boxes for demon spirits and carried them around! You built God a house through Solomon, although David wanted to build one, but God said through His prophet, 'What house will you build me? Didn't My hand build everything? I don't live in tabernacles made with hands!'"*

No wonder his face shown like an angel! He was speaking out of the Spirit of God in him. God was giving those religious people a visible manifestation of the Truth he was preaching! *Stephen was the tabernacle!* He was the house of God. He was housing the glory—godliness manifested in the flesh! It was Christ in him, the mystery that God had hid and was now revealing! He was telling them, *"You have God in a box, but I have God in me!"*

He was ministering to them by the power of the Spirit. He was showing them types and shadows in order to lead them to Christ. The New Testament is not religion—it's experience! The New Testament is not a promise—it's receiving the promise! The Bible said, *"That the blessings of Abraham might come on the Gentiles through Jesus Christ, that we might receive the promise of the Spirit through faith"* (Galatians 3:14).

"You always resist the Holy Spirit; as your fathers did, so do you." If we put our trust in anything other than the Word, we become guilty of resisting the Holy Spirit. The Holy Spirit will only flow in line with

the Word. Jesus said, *"He won't even speak of Himself. What He hears of Me, He will deliver to you."* Jesus is the Word, and the Holy Spirit makes the Word alive to you.

The Jews put their trust in the signs that Moses showed them. They put their trust in the things Elijah did. They said, *"We're children of Moses. We're children of Abraham."* They put their trust in their heritage. They saw themselves as righteous people and looked at the Gentiles as dogs. They put their trust in shadows and types rather than allowing the Spirit of the Law to bring a revelation of the Law.

Throughout Old Testament history, every prophet that God sent spoke by the anointing. They didn't have the anointing living in them, but they were moved by the Holy Ghost. They were men of faith and the words they spoke were God-breathed. They saw the promises afar off, were persuaded of them, and embraced them.

The Case of the Empty Tomb

Jesus died and after three days, they couldn't find His body. It wasn't in the grave. They had put a Roman garrison around it to ensure that no one would steal His body. Despite their best efforts, Jesus rose from the dead anyway!

When the chief priests heard about it, they spread the rumor that Jesus' disciples had stolen His body. There was one hole in this theory, however, Jesus was showing up around town! For forty days He showed Himself alive by many infallible proofs, opening up the Scriptures, and speaking of things pertaining to the Kingdom. When He left, it was even worse than before! Instead of the movement dying out, the Spirit of Christ came and filled others! The Spirit anointed them and they become radical!

Having had years of practice, these people were proficient at resisting the Holy Ghost. They were not resisting Him out of ignorance—they knew that Jesus did miracles. In desperation, they had come to the conclusion that if they didn't kill Him, everyone would believe on Him. Their problem, however, had escalated dramatically since Jesus' resurrection. The disciples of Christ were now just like Jesus!

"You stiff-necked and uncircumcised in heart and ears! You always resist the Holy Spirit; as your fathers did, so do you." Why did Stephen

talk about their fathers? He talked about them because they were known for putting their trust in heritage. People today put their trust in their denomination, in their upbringing, and in what other people have said. Confident in tradition and in the convictions of others, people like this inadvertently resist the Holy Ghost! They repeat the mistakes of their fathers. These Jewish leaders could not receive the Spirit because they were putting their trust in heritage and religion.

> **Which of the prophets did your fathers not persecute? And they killed those who foretold the coming of the Just One, of whom you now have become the betrayers and murderers, who have received the law by the direction of angels and have not kept it.**
>
> Acts 7:52-53

They caught a man gathering sticks one day and stoned Him because He broke the Law. People get so religious that they want to create a standard that is higher than the standard Jesus gave. It's impossible to follow their standard! Jesus said, *"Forget about it! You think you haven't sinned? Let Me break it down for you: If you looked at someone and lusted after them, you already did it! You have received the Law and have not kept it."*

You can't do what you're supposed to do without the Holy Ghost! Tabernacles made with hands are not what God desires! He wants to live in us!

The Light Shown the Glory Came

Stephen may have had no idea that he was beaming like an angel. He was just preaching about the house of God, about being a tabernacle, and became so excited that he preached himself right into a vision!

> **But he, being full of the Holy Ghost, looked up steadfastly into heaven, and saw the glory**

> of God, and Jesus standing on the right hand of God, and said, "Behold, I see the heavens opened, and the Son of man standing on the right hand of God."
>
> Acts 7:55-56

Stephen told them by the anointing, *"You stiff-necked and uncircumcised in heart and ear! You always resist the Holy Ghost! As your fathers did, so do you. Show me one prophet your fathers did not persecute—and you killed Jesus—you murderers! You got the Law by angels but couldn't even keep it."* When they heard these things, they were cut to the heart and they gnashed their teeth.

Stephen was out there in the Holy Ghost! *Keep it to yourself, Stephen! Just pray in tongues or something!* At least Jesus folded the Book, gave it back, and sat down! *Not Stephen!* He wasn't going to sit down. He was in a vision!

When Stephen saw Jesus with the Father in Heaven, he must have thought, *"I see the heavens opened, but I'm here preaching to these deadbeats!"* They were gnashing on him with their teeth! Then he said aloud, *"I see the heavens opened and the Son of man standing at the right hand of God!"* Stephen was so full of God that he looked into Heaven and decided, *"I'm going there!"*

They said, *"That's it! We're going to kill you—tabernacle or no tabernacle!"* They cried out with a loud voice, covered their ears, and ran upon him with one accord. When you are full of anything, *it will manifest!* Stephen became so full of the Holy Ghost that he couldn't hold it back! He was out there! He was flowing with God and they were full of anger. *What are the odds that a group of religious people would all do the same thing at the same time?* They didn't rehearse this! There was a demonstration of the power of God, and it caused a reaction.

> Then they cried out with a loud voice, stopped their ears, and ran at him with one accord; and they cast him out of the city and stoned him. And the witnesses laid down their clothes at the feet of a young man named Saul. And they stoned Stephen as he was calling on God and

> saying, "Lord Jesus, receive my spirit." Then he knelt down and cried out with a loud voice, "Lord, do not charge them with this sin." And when he had said this, he fell asleep.
>
> Acts 7:57-60

Habitation of God

Saul was standing there, but he was not satisfied. He was going all the way with this thing. He wanted letters! He wanted the legal right to persecute the Church. He had a purpose, and he was on his way to fulfill it!

Paul, however, had no clue that he was well on his way to becoming the next tabernacle! He didn't know that God was going to give him the revelation of the mystery. He didn't know that he would personally proclaim the fellowship of the mystery to the known world.

The light shone. The glory came. This time it wasn't coming from the face of Stephen, but it was coming directly from Heaven! Its brightness exceeded the noonday sun. Saul couldn't close his ears or shut his eyes to it. It was so strong that it knocked him and the people that were with him down. *"And he fell to the earth, and heard a voice saying unto him, Saul, Saul, why persecutest thou me"* (Acts 9:4 KJV)?

When you persecute a tabernacle, you're persecuting the Body! You're persecuting godliness manifested in the flesh! *"Why are you persecuting Me?"* Paul answered the Light, *"Who art thou, Lord?"* Jesus told Him, *"I'm Jesus, and you're persecuting Me! I'm the one walking around in these people, and you're trying to put Me in jail. You're going there to throw Me in prison! Don't you know that I can knock you down?"*

Convincing argument.

Saul got up, but he couldn't see a thing. The theologian was blind. Theologians can tell you anything and everything you need to know about the tabernacle, and about the Holy of Holies. Saul could tell you anything about the Law, but all he had was a shadow.

He got up, but he couldn't see a thing. Then God commanded him, *"Go to the city and wait! It will be told to you what to do."* Meanwhile, the Holy Ghost spoke to Ananias in a vision, *"Go over there where Saul is praying. He saw you in a vision coming to lay your hands on him, that he might receive his sight."* Ananias asked, *"Is this the same Saul that I've been hearing about? Is this the man who has been killing the Saints?"* Obedient to the vision, Ananias went, and while he was on his way, he received *something* by faith.

When he entered the house he said to Saul, *"Jesus sent me to you to lay my hands on you so that you would receive your sight and be filled with the Holy Ghost."* He laid his hands on Saul, and scales fell from his eyes. Instantly, Saul received the Holy Ghost and became a tabernacle!

> **I know a man in Christ who fourteen years ago—whether in the body I do not know, or whether out of the body I do not know, God knows—such a one was caught up to the third heaven. And I know such a man—whether in the body or out of the body I do not know, God knows—how he was caught up into Paradise and heard inexpressible words, which it is not lawful for a man to utter.**
>
> **2 Corinthians 12:2-4**

Lay hands on yourself and say this:

> *Spirit of God, thank you for the fellowship of the mystery! Thank you that we can fellowship around the nature of Christ. Thank you that the divine nature can live in us. Thank you that Jesus is not far, but He's near me—He's in my heart and in my mouth. Thank you that we are the house, the habitation, the Body of Christ, the fullness of Him that fills all in all! Thank you for the dwelling places that you have made of us through Jesus. Thank you that this Body is the temple of the Holy Ghost, the habitation of God through the Spirit.*

Chapter 8

The Supply of the Spirit

The anointing will pay your bills.
The anointing will answer your questions.
The anointing will solve your problems.

The primary doctrine of the New Testament and the greatest achievement of Calvary is *God making people like Jesus.* The most miraculous miracle God ever did was to transform the hard heart of man into a heart of flesh. It was mercy that took the Law—the living Word—out of the realm of principle and legalism and put it into man. We are the literal habitation of God through the Spirit! The sooner we learn how to pursue this Truth, the faster we will become like the Master.

The Bible says, *"Greater is He that is in you than he that is in the world"* (1 John 4:4). It's a privilege to have God living on the inside of you! The greatest thing that you could ever do is to *live* the reality of *God living in you!*

The Message of Faith

> **This only would I learn of you, Received ye the Spirit by the works of the law, or by the hearing of faith? He therefore that ministereth to you the Spirit, and worketh miracles among you, doeth he it by the works of the law, or by the hearing of faith?**
>
> **Galatians 3:2, 5 KJV**

The Kenneth Wuest translation states it this way, *"This only am*

I desiring to learn from you. By means of law works did you receive the Spirit or by means of the message which proclaims faith?" In other words, Paul said, *"I want to learn something from you. Did you receive the Spirit through the works of the law, or did you receive the Spirit through the message that proclaims faith?"* The Wuest translation continues, *"Therefore, the one who is constantly supplying the Spirit to you in bountiful measure, and constantly working miracles among you, by means of law works is He doing these things, or by means of the message which proclaims faith?"*

This was a Spirit-filled church. The Galatians had come into the grace that brought them to salvation, but the religious people came in and began to add to the message of salvation by grace. They were telling the Galatians, *"It's not enough to believe in Jesus Christ as your Savior in your heart. It's not enough to confess Him with your mouth. You must keep certain holy days. You must keep certain feasts. You must be circumcised."*

Teachers came in and began to add legal law obligations to that which God said. So Paul asked the Galatians, *"Did you receive the Spirit because you worked for Him? Did you receive salvation because you worked for it? How is the One who is constantly supplying the Spirit to you in bountiful measure doing it?"*

Although the church was Spirit-filled, there needed to be a constant supply of the Spirit in abundance. We know that God is the source of the Spirit, but God has given the Church *ministers* that have been anointed to bring His Spirit close to man. The *hearing of faith* is essential to maintain a consistent lifestyle of being filled with the Holy Ghost.

Paul said, *"My message was dependent upon a manifestation of the Holy Ghost so that your faith would not be in the wisdom of men but in the power of God."* God anoints certain people to bring the Spirit to you with a promise, so that your faith would rise to an expectation that would enable you to receive the supply of the Spirit again!

Paul was asking them, *"Is the one who is constantly supplying the Spirit in bountiful measure doing it through the works of the law? Is He telling you that if you get up early in the morning, you'll get the Spirit? Is He telling you that if you do natural things, you'll be able to earn the Spirit?"* No! Through the proclamation of the Gospel, He is promising the provision of the anointing and stirring up your faith so that you'll expect it. The result should be a constant, bountiful supply of the

Spirit!

This tells us two things:

1. Preachers must preach the message with a promise that develops expectation.
2. People must allow faith to be stirred up in them so that they can receive the promise.

It is God's perfect will for you to have a consistent supply of the Spirit in bountiful measures!

Recommended Daily Allowance

Do you want more of the anointing?
Do you want more of the power of God?

If you do, then you must continually meditate on the doctrine of *godliness manifested in the flesh!* Think about it: *the Body of Christ is filled with the fullness of Him that fills all in all!* We have to look into every New Testament Scripture and into every Old Testament shadow that talked about the Church. We have to learn what God's will is for the average believer. If we do, we'll grow in the Spirit of Revelation and we will have an experiential understanding of being filled to overflowing with the Holy Ghost! When you *know* it, you'll be able to lay claim to what God has promised.

I want you to say this:

I cannot earn a bountiful supply. I cannot work for a bountiful supply, but I can believe for a consistent, bountiful supply of the Holy Ghost!

Right now you can be filled to overflowing with the Holy Spirit! As a matter of fact, there can be several infillings of the Holy Ghost in your life that will overflow on a daily basis! There can be multiple supplies of the Spirit provided for the believer, as needed, in a day. The New Testament tells us about times when the apostles were filled with the Spirit to overflowing more than once in a day. God may have bailed them out of jail earlier, but when they were brought in front of the council later in the day, the Spirit of God supplied them once again with an overabundance of His Spirit to speak supernaturally. They may have already had a miracle earlier, but when a situation demanded a supernatural manifestation, the Spirit of God was right there to supply them with an overabundance of the Spirit to act miraculously. *"I will be anointed with fresh oil!"* If we love righteousness and hate iniquity, God will anoint us with the oil of gladness daily!

The one who is *"constantly working miracles among you,"* does it through the proclamation or the message that proclaims faith. The Galatians were constantly seeing miracles! Their faith was reaping a consistent, overabundant supply of the Spirit. As a result, they were seeing a consistent manifestation of miracles in their midst! What could the Judaizers possibly add to that kind of faith?

Nothing!

When religion comes in and attempts to add to the pure faith that God has given, it's not for the benefit of God! It's for the benefit of the enemy. The devil knows that if we take faith and mix it with works, *we'll end up with failure.* He wants us to get so involved in trying to *work* for something that God is supplying, that we exhaust ourselves in attempting to reap a free gift.

Take As Directed

He therefore that ministereth to you the Spirit, and worketh miracles among you, doeth he it by the works of the law, or by the hearing of faith?

Galatians 3: 5 KJV

The original Greek says, *"He who is constantly doing miracles among you...."* There was someone who was having a consistent manifestation of miracles in the Galatian church! That's a power demonstration!

Miracle working power comes from God. The Bible said that the excellency of the power may be of God and not of us. As long as we are not the source, there is no limit to that power. If we were the source, there would be a limit. There would be a cap. There would be an impossibility. If God were dependent on our ability, we would reach a ceiling. There is *no limit* when God is the source!

There was a working of miracles in the midst of the Galatian church. There was a consistent performance. If two thousand years ago God's best was a *consistent working of miracles,* do you think it might be the same today? Do you think that if two thousand years ago God's best was a consistent supply—a bountiful supply of the Holy Ghost—then it must be the *same* today? You should never have one weak, weary or feeble day. *God is your Source!*

If we do experience weariness or weakness, it's not because the Spirit is far away. Somehow, somewhere—at some point—we took our eyes off the message that inspires faith. If a person doesn't have inspired faith, they can't lay claim to the provision of the consistent, bountiful supply of the Spirit or the consistent working of miracles!

I want you to say this:

> *If I keep my eyes on the message, if I keep the promise alive, I'll keep my faith in motion and I'll continue to see consistent miracles at work. I'll continue to have a consistent, bountiful supply of the Holy Ghost! Glory to God!*

Lay Claim to It

"...*That we might receive the promise of the Spirit through faith*" (Galatians 3:14). If it's by faith, it means that there is something God has provided that we have to receive. The only way we can receive it is through faith. The way we get faith is by hearing the message that inspires faith.

The word *proclaim* in the Greek is to *make plain, to manifest, to announce, to make known publicly or officially.* Why is the Gospel preached? It is preached so that you can have the manifestation of the revelation!

The word *"proclaim"* is the word *pro-claim*. Have you ever heard the derogatory remark that calls us *"Name it and Claim it"* people? The word *"proclaim"* starts with *pro* (as in *pro* and *con*). If you go to the dictionary, you'll find out that *claim* means *to demand as one's right* or *to assert ownership or title to*. Claiming means to assert your legal right of ownership to something!

When the Bible said, *"He who is doing miracles among you, isn't he doing it because there is a message that is proclaiming faith?"* Absolutely! Someone heard a message that said, *"Claim what is legally your right!"* It said it publicly and it said it officially! It inspired faith in the hearer and the hearer said, *"Do you mean a bountiful supply of the Spirit is consistently available to me? Do you mean to tell me that a consistent working of miracles belongs to me in my life?"*

Yes! That person then raised their hands without wrath or doubting and got so filled with the Holy Ghost that they were overrun by the Spirit! They had visions. They had dreams. They had revelations. They prophesied. They sang in the Spirit. They talked with other tongues. They lived their life in an anointed way! Every time they heard that message, it officially publicized their legal rights. It inspired faith and they laid claim to that which was rightfully theirs. Through faith they received what God had provided!

A Full House

A few verses later Paul writes to us, *"That the blessing of Abraham might come on the Gentiles through Jesus Christ, that we might receive the promise of the Spirit through faith."* He was saying, *"The only reason there is a Christ—the only reason there is a Gospel—is so that God can get the blessings of Abraham over to us that we can receive the promise of the Spirit through faith!"*

I want you to say this:

> *Every day that I live, I have a legal right to receive a bountiful supply of the anointing through faith!*

Have you watched people get filled with the Holy Ghost?
Have you come to a service and watched people leave happy?
Have you attended church and watched people get set free?
Did you wonder why God allowed others to leave without an assurance that something happened on their behalf?

The answer is very easy: *"That you might receive the promise of the Spirit through faith."*

It is imperative that we tune our ear to hearing the claim! When the proclamation of the Gospel comes—and the promise is set before my eyes—then my ear develops faith. I lay claim to what's legally mine, so that I can receive the bountiful supply of the blessings of Abraham and the anointing of the Holy Spirit in my life. I need faith in order to receive!

I want you to say this:

> *Without faith I cannot receive what God is giving me. I can't receive the financial blessings He's already provided. I can't receive the promotion, the spiritual maturity, the divine health, the right relationships, the open doors, the blessings of Abraham, the joy of the Lord, or any other thing. For without faith, it is impossible to receive from the Lord!*

Although the Word says, *"Without faith, it is impossible to please Him,"* it also says about the man who is double minded, *"Let not that man think he shall receive anything of the Lord."* God has given us certain things through Jesus. God has provided certain things through the Good News. Whether we receive them or not will be dependent upon whether or not we allow the Good News to impart faith into our hearts.

You are going to discover more and more about who you are as a vessel of honor, as the house of God, as a temple for the Holy Ghost. As this happens, you will desire to live your life recharging your body and refueling your spirit with the anointing of the Lord.

Excellent Choice

> **On the last day, that great day of the feast, Jesus stood and cried out, saying, "If anyone thirsts, let him come to Me and drink. He who believes in Me, as the Scripture has said, out of his heart will flow rivers of living water." But this He spoke concerning the Spirit, whom those believing in Him would receive; for the Holy Spirit was not yet given, because Jesus was not yet glorified. Therefore many from the crowd, when they heard this saying, said, "Truly this is the Prophet."**
>
> John 7:37-40

This is Jesus in action. Everything Jesus said, He said because of the anointing. He never said anything out of line with the perfect will of God. *Do you know why He stayed in the perfect will of God?* He never spent a day without a bountiful supply of the Holy Ghost! He said, *"The things I am saying, I am not saying. The Father in Me—the Spirit of God—is doing the work. He is doing the talking."* His choices were what provided Him with His excellence.

In other words, although God gave Him the Spirit without measure, He dedicating Himself to prayer like no other person previously recorded. If the anointing was operating *automatically* in Him, He wouldn't need to get up, go apart by Himself, and pray and seek God. However, it wasn't operating *automatically* in Him. He wasn't on autopilot! This was a Man who *knew* the importance of being anointed by the Spirit! If everything the Father said through Him was the perfect articulation or speech of the Holy Spirit, then He must have been giving Himself over to the power and to the anointing of the Lord *daily.*

Why did Jesus speak the perfect will of God?
Why were His Words the Words of wisdom?

Why is there nothing *in the Word that records a single statement of His that was out of line with God's will?*

It is *not* because He didn't have access to temptation.

The Bible said that He was tempted in all points like we are, yet without sin (Hebrews 4:15). That means the devil tried to get Jesus to say *something* out of line with God! Jesus was the Word and the Word became flesh. He chose to be the Word through His will and He spoke only of the things that work. In doing so, He was able to say, *"Every idle word that man will speak, he will give account thereof in the day of judgment. A good man out of the good treasure of his heart brings forth good things"* (Matthew 12:36).

He was saying, *"Listen! As a believer you ought to see to it that nothing you speak is idle—that everything you speak is by the inspiration of the Holy Spirit and in line with the Word of God! The Words that I speak unto you, they are Spirit and they are life!"*

He utilized His faith to receive a constant, overabundant supply of the Holy Spirit daily!

Discerning the Time

No one could discern what time it was in God, but Jesus knew exactly what time it was! When you are in the anointing, you'll know exactly what God is doing in that day. You can't be confused and anointed at the same time! You will know what God is doing when you have utilized your faith to receive a bountiful supply!

Jesus jumped up! He stood up and cried with a loud voice. *Do you know why He lifted His voice like that?* When you're anointed by the Holy Ghost with an *abundant* measure, you have a message burning inside of you! The revelation is loud! The Holy Ghost is saying, *"Now is the time for this! Now is the time for that! This is what God is doing now!"*

Everyone was looking for Messiah. Everyone was wondering when God would send the Redeemer. Jesus got up in the midst of this crowd of people, who had *no concept* of what time it was in God, and said,

In the last day, that great day of the feast, Jesus

stood and cried, saying, If any man thirst, let him come unto me, and drink. He that believeth on me, as the scripture hath said, out of his belly shall flow rivers of living water. (But this spake he of the Spirit, which they that believe on him should receive: for the Holy Ghost was not yet given; because that Jesus was not yet glorified.) Many of the people therefore, when they heard this saying, said, of a truth this is the Prophet.

John 7:37-40 KJV

He spoke a message of promise in the anointing—*a message of promise!* Don't ever allow the devil to frustrate you about the promises of God! Don't ever allow the devil to make you feel like the promises of God are not accessible to you—or that they're not for today! Any gospel that does not carry a promise with it is not Gospel at all!

Jesus stood up and said, *"If any man thirst let him come to Me and drink, and out of his belly will flow rivers of living water."* That's a promise! The anointing was upon Him and He was able to preach with promise. A man who does not preach with promise has no anointing upon him! Any humanist can preach without a promise. *"Well, you know, I can't promise you anything."* They have not received an overabundance, a bountiful measure, of the Spirit to preach with promise!

As He was giving that promise, people heard it. *What did they do with that promise?* They believed it! When they heard Him preach, many believed and said, *"This must be the Prophet!"*

Faith came to their hearts!

Jesus said, *"You can come and drink, and God is going to establish in you a river that has streams. Rivers of living water will flow right out of your core—if you'll make Christ the Source for your life! If you drink from Me, then out of your belly will flow rivers of living water!"*

He was talking about the Holy Ghost!

Keep Your Priorities Straight

And I will pray the Father, and he shall give you another Comforter, that he may abide with you for ever; Even the Spirit of truth; whom the world cannot receive, because it seeth him not, neither knoweth him: but ye know him; for he dwelleth with you, and shall be in you. I will not leave you comfortless: I will come to you.

John 14:16-18 KJV

The Head of the Church is preparing the disciples for the one that will come after Him. He is the one who will help them follow in His manner of life. He will help them to produce His kind of results. He was saying, *"Listen! Come to Me and drink, and out of your belly will flow rivers of living waters—just like the Scripture said."* Then He told the disciples, *"I'm going to ask the Father and He's going to give you another Comforter."*

Jesus prepared mankind for the Holy Ghost! We should spend our lives learning more about Him. It is my firm belief that if a Christian would choose to live in an anointed manner *(that means to use their faith to claim daily—a consistent injection of the supernatural abundance of the Spirit),* they would live their entire life healthy! They would live in a strong body. They would live with a keen mind. They would not go senile. They would not have a nervous breakdown. They would not lose their peace. They would live strong and healthy all of their lives.

If they would let the Spirit of God live in them that way, then the Spirit of God would make the Word live to them! If they would pursue that priority in their life, they would live prosperous. They would be able to receive everything that God has promised in the Gospel.

What is our potential in Christ? I believe that it is far beyond where we've ever gone! We can't even get there without the Spirit of God and we can't receive the Spirit of God to that measure without faith. We can't have faith unless someone preaches about what belongs to us— so that we can develop the faith to claim what's rightfully ours!

Miracle Provision

Jesus was promising, *"I will pray the Father, and He will give you another Comforter."* Why did He say, *"Another Comforter?"* He said *"another"* because He was the *first* Comforter! *How did He comfort His disciples?* He comforted the twelve by providing for them. When He first met Peter and Andrew He said, *"Cast the net in on the other side,"* and they did. All of a sudden, they had more than what they needed!

He said, *"Oh! You're in business for yourselves, but you're not doing very well, are you? Did you catch anything?"* They said, *"No."* He said, *"You toiled all night and didn't catch a thing? And you are fishermen? Cast your net in on the other side!"* MIRACLE PROVISION.

Peter was married. On account of the call of God, He spent three and a half years in Bible School, being mentored by Jesus. *What happened?* His wife was supplied for and provided for! The Teacher that Peter was following had the anointing of God upon Him. He was comforting him by supplying all of his need. Not one of them had a need.

As a matter of fact, one day there were thousands of people listening to Him preach. He talked so long that several days passed, and the people got hungry. The Lord comforted the *whole* crowd. He didn't operate off of deity, but He operated off of the anointing of God that was upon Him. He took something that was available and multiplied it beyond rational, mental, or human conception! Not only did He meet the need and comfort those who were hungry with natural supply, but His disciples gathered baskets full of leftovers!

The disciples were well acquainted with the Provider. Jesus asked them, *"When I sent you out without a money bag, when I sent you out without a knapsack, did you lack anything?"* They said, *"No."* As their Comforter, His anointing was supplying their every need. At the same time, He was training his disciples to develop an expectation for what was coming. When the anointing would become available to them, they would know how to put it to work. They would expect it to produce the same thing in their lives.

Jesus prepared them by teaching them the Word. He prepared them by telling them the Promise. He couldn't give them the Spirit; the Spirit was not yet given because Jesus was not yet glorified. John the Baptist had an experience with the Holy Ghost, but I believe that it was under Old Testament provision. He was a prophet, and the Spirit of God came upon him to bear witness of Jesus and to point the finger to Him. Jesus had the anointing in a different way. He was the Christ, the *Anointed One*. He had the anointing without measure.

Active Ingredient

He was their first Comforter, but now He was telling them, *"Where I'm going you know, and the way you know. I'll pray the Father, and He will send you another Comforter."* They said to Him, *"We don't know the way! We don't know where you're going! Show us the Father, and it's enough for us."* He answered, *"If you've seen Me, you've seen the Father."* In other words, *"You have already seen Me in motion. The power flowing in Me and the will done through My ministry is the exact will of the Father."*

Then He told them, *"I will pray the Father, and He will send you another Comforter."* In other words, *"Listen! When I'm glorified, our relationship will be different."* Today in the church Christians say, *"I wish I could just see the Lord and touch the Lord and walk with the Lord!"* No, you don't! That's regressing! That's going backwards!

In the beginning, the disciples had a relationship with Jesus that consisted of them asking Jesus for something and Jesus doing it for them. Jesus was telling them, *"It's no longer going to be like that! I will pray the Father and He will send you another Comforter. He's the anointing! He is the Spirit of God! When He comes upon you, He will give you a supernatural awareness of being a member in the Body of Christ. By My Spirit you will cry out, 'Abba, Father!' You will no longer need to ask Me anything. I will be in you doing the asking in My name, to the Father, so that the Father would be able to grant you, by the anointing, everything that you ask for!"* It was a *completely different* relationship! It was no longer about them relying on the Master, but about the Master living His life in them and through them by the Spirit of God.

The way He supplied their need two thousand years ago was by His anointing. He told Peter, *"Go out and catch a fish. Out of its mouth you'll get the coin to pay the tax."* He did it supernaturally! That's the same way He will do it today.

Two thousand years ago He did it off *His* anointing.
Two thousand years ago He did it off *His* prayer life.
Two thousand years ago He did it off *His* faith.

Today He is going to be limited by *your* anointing.
Today He is going to be limited by *your* prayer life.
Today He is going to be limited by *your* faith.

The good news is that we can be just like Paul. Paul said, *"I'm crucified with Christ, nevertheless, I live. Yet not I, but it's Christ who lives in me. The life I now live in the flesh I live by the faith of the Son of God, who loved me and gave Himself for me"* (Galatians 2:20)! Paul decided that he would not have any limits, that he would not fall short, that he would not wallow around in shallow waters. Paul decided that he would give the Holy Spirit full rulership and reign in his life. He decided to contend for everything that was provided for him in Christ! He got into a realm where—*daily*—he was living his life by the faith of the Son of God who loved him and gave Himself for him!

God is asking you, *"Do you want this? Do you want it with all of your heart?"*

Once you learn what it's all about, then you must do what is necessary to provide it. In other words, if you believe it is so, then *believe to the point of action.* Believe it to the point of releasing your faith, so that you would have the promises fulfilled in your life! If you don't believe it, then you will just hear it and never act upon it. You'll be like a lot of other Christians wondering, *"Why doesn't God do what He said He would do?"*

If we believe what He promised, then we will receive what He promised. The only way to receive what He promised is to receive a bountiful supply of the Spirit. This bountiful supply will enable you to walk daily in the divine promises of God – to see their manifestations in the here and now!

The Visible Became Invisible

Jesus was saying, *"I'm going to turn you over to the guidance of Someone else. He won't speak of Himself. Everything that's of Me, He will give to you. You won't see me walking around, but I will be in you through Him. I will never leave you. Just as you learned who I was during these last three and a half years, you're going to have to become acquainted with the Comforter."*

How did they find out about Jesus? They asked a lot of dumb questions! They asked some good ones, but they asked a lot of dumb ones too! They walked around with Him. They watched Him. They grew accustomed to Him. They spent time with Him.

"Now I'm going to go. I'm going to send you another Comforter." The Holy Ghost and Jesus were in agreement, so the disciples actually *saw* the ways of the Spirit walking around! For three and a half years, they *saw* the will of Heaven walking! Once that which was visible became invisible, they didn't have a problem recognizing the Spirit of God—they knew His ways!

If we know the Word, then we should have no problem knowing the ways of the Spirit. The Spirit never contradicts the Word.

The Church has been told lies about the Holy Ghost. Those lies have turned into strongholds that have short-circuited the operation of the Spirit. As God delivers us from those lies, we will see Him for who He really is. We will then allow the Spirit to empower the Word in us! The disciples saw the Master, knew what He did, and knew what the will of the Father was through Him. When the Spirit came, they were able to yield to the other Comforter.

Seeing the Invisible

Jesus said, *"He is the Spirit of Truth. He will abide with you forever."*

Say this out loud:

The Spirit of Truth has to be the Spirit of the Word because there's no truth outside of the Truth. Jesus is the Way, the Truth and the Life.

What is the Word? The Word is the mind of God. It is the Truth of God. When Jesus said, *"I'm going to send you the Spirit of Truth,"* He was saying, *"I'm going to send you the Spirit that is going to reflect into your life the Words of the Son of God, the mind of the Father, the perfect Truth that is heavenly in its source. I'm going to send you the Spirit of Truth whom the world cannot receive because it seeth Him not, neither knoweth Him."*

In the original language it says, "It does not see Him by discernment." The world does not see him by discernment. Even a Christian doesn't see the Holy Ghost in the natural! You didn't see the Spirit come upon you as a dove when you got baptized with the Spirit! He didn't come in a bodily form—He's invisible, even to the Christian. Jesus is talking about seeing with perception, or discernment. He said, *"The world cannot receive Him."* Why can't the world receive him, Lord? *"Because the world cannot discern Him, and the world does not know Him"* (John 14:17).

What would prevent someone from knowing the Spirit of Truth? If they're dominated by lies, they won't be able to see the Truth. Sometimes lies *sound* like truth. Sometimes a *little* perversion of the Word of God is enough to create a massive stronghold in the life of a believer. When that happens, they will not be able to receive the influence of the Comforter because the Spirit of Truth contradicts lies. You will contradict a lot of religion and a lot of theology when you preach the pure Truth of the Word of God!

Why would a person not be able to receive the Holy Ghost? Jesus said the world can't receive Him because it does not discern Him. It doesn't know Him. The Bible said that you will know the Truth and the Truth will make you free (John 8:32). A person who is *not* free does not know the Truth. They do not have an *experiential knowledge* of the Truth. Once you know the Truth, then you'll search for further Truth. You'll become receptive to more Truth.

Have you ever noticed that when a person is stagnant, they remain that way? However, when a person begins to flow, they continue to grow in the Truth. When the Spirit of God moved in your heart and you received His refreshing, you became turned on to the Word of God. You couldn't get enough of the Word! You tasted the Truth and that Truth sparked your spirit.

Jesus was saying, "*The world cannot receive Him because it does not see Him. It does not perceive Him. The eyes of their understanding are not awakened to God. They do not know Him. However, you know Him, for He dwells with you and shall be in you. You know Him because He's here in Me!*" Ever since that day, people that are full of the Holy Ghost have been introducing Him to others.

Painting a Portrait

Jesus said, "*But you know Him because He is with you.*" He was getting ready to leave. He was preparing the disciples for His departure. In doing so, He told them about the Comforter so that they would not miss Him. They would know exactly what to expect! They would be able to use their faith in the exact way to receive the exact Comforter. God would be able to produce in their life exactly what He had produced in the life of Jesus.

In the same way that the Old Testament prophets drew us a picture of Christ, Jesus drew us a picture of the Holy Ghost. The prophets told us where Jesus would be born. Jesus told us where the Spirit would come from. The prophets told us how Jesus would die. Jesus told us what kind of Spirit He is. The prophets told us how He would flow out of us. Jesus told us, "*Don't worry about getting another ghost! If you pray the Father for the Spirit of God, He won't give you a scorpion! He won't give you a snake! He won't give you anything else!*"

Jesus defeated fear with Truth. In the atmosphere of faith, the Holy Ghost is without limits. To come into the spirits of men, He would need a reception, or an invitation. He couldn't violate their will, so the believer had to be ready and receptive to His infilling.

Jesus painted a portrait of *who* the Holy Ghost is and *what* the Holy Ghost would do in them after they received Him. He was telling them, "*The world won't be able to receive Him because it doesn't see Him and doesn't know Him, but you know Him because He is with you and* shall be in you. Until now He's been with you in Me. However, now He's going to be in you, and I will be in you through Him."

Jesus said, "Listen! It is better for you that I go. I'm going to go, and I'm going to send you the Comforter. If you believe on Me, the same works that I do, you are going to do! And greater works than these will you do!"

Why is this Jesus? *"Because I'm going to go to my Father, and I'm going to send you the other Comforter."*

What is He going to do? *"He is going to empower you! The world can't receive Him because they can't discern Him."*

A bountiful supply of the Spirit—an overabundant supply of the Spirit—belongs to us daily!

Just Getting Started

Do you know of Christians who were baptized with the Holy Ghost but three months later were walking down in the dumps? Some of them continued to walk that way for twenty years!

They said, *"I'm going through a dry spell. It's the desert experience."* Their desert experience is the by-product of not discerning God's promise of the Spirit for *today*. They received a one-time shot of the Spirit and then began to walk like the world. They were not discerning Him because He's a Spirit. They were not knowing Him because they weren't spending any time in the realm where He can make Himself real to them. There are so many believers that think miracles are going to happen when God gets ready to perform them.

Miracles will start happening when the Christian gets so full of the anointing that a consistent manifestation of divine power will flow through them! *When are we going to see great and mighty works?* We will see this when we are so full of the reality of the Holy Spirit that His presence begins to influence our *daily* life!

We must *continue* to receive the promise of the Spirit through faith. The baptism of the Holy Ghost is just a *little* part of the promise of the Spirit! It's just the initial experience. The promise is that we can be baptized with the Holy Ghost, speak with other tongues, and live controlled, influenced, and charged by the anointing of the Holy Ghost *on a daily basis.*

What is salvation? It is being baptized into the Body of Christ. The Word baptizes you into the Holy Ghost. When we receive the baptism of the Holy Ghost, we are *immersed* into the person of the Spirit. Can you imagine being immersed into a person, yet knowing very little about Him? He is in you and you are in Him.

The Holy Spirit will not violate your will. He will say, *"If that's the way you want to live, go right ahead."* All over the world, people get themselves in a mess and start praying. They say, *"The Lord got my attention!"* No, the truth is that *you* got *your* own attention! You walked in the natural realm until you messed things up. It wasn't God! You did it yourself.

Faith in the Spirit's infilling has to be a daily practice. If not, we'll spend some days without an infilling. We'll talk words that aren't Spirit and life, and we'll walk steps that are not directed of the Lord. That's not God's best! This is the difference between carnality and maturity. It's the difference between a flesh-bound Christian and a Spirit-led Christian! *"For as many as are led by the Spirit of God, they are the sons of God"* (Romans 8:14).

You Will Not Be Orphans!

"...for He dwells with you and will be in you. I will not leave you orphans; I will come to you" (John 14:17b, 18). The Bible says that pure and undefiled religion before God is to visit the fatherless and the widows. *Why?* It's because the fatherless do not have a father to supply their need and to take care of them! Jesus was saying, *"I will not leave you without a provider! I'm going to send you the Holy Ghost!"*

Saints look up to Heaven and say, *"Why won't the Lord supply?"* God says, *"Why won't you pray in tongues?"* The power to perform Christ's results is in the ability of the Holy Ghost living on the inside of you. You are not an orphan! The anointing will pay your bills. The anointing will answer your questions. The anointing will solve your problems. The anointing will defeat your enemies.

Jesus had to tell the disciples, *"In that day you will ask Me nothing"*

He told them this because they were used to asking Him everything! *"What are we going to feed these people?" "What did you mean by the parable of the sower?" "How are we going to pay the taxes?" "Who sinned, this man or his parents, that he was born blind?"* They were asking Him everything!

They knew that He would answer all of their questions. He would meet their needs. He would solve their problems. They would ask, *"What should we do?"* and Jesus would tell them!

Now He's giving them new instructions, *"In that day you won't ask Me anything. You're going to have the same Spirit that gives Me the wisdom! You're going to have the same Spirit that gave Me the power to perform on your behalf! You're going to have this same spirit in you! You won't be an orphan anymore, and you won't need Me to personally be there. The other Comforter, who is the Spirit of Truth, will watch over you and take care of you."*

We have to allow the anointing to work in us. *"I'll pray the Father, and He'll give you another Comforter. He will abide with you forever. He will be in you!"* He is not only abiding with us, the Holy Spirit is living *in* us so that we will not be like orphans!

Meditation Brings Realization

If you ask anything in My name, I will do it. "If you love Me, keep My commandments. And I will pray the Father, and He will give you another Helper, that He may abide with you forever—the Spirit of truth, whom the world cannot receive, because it neither sees Him nor knows Him; but you know Him, for He dwells with you and will be in you. I will not leave you orphans; I will come to you. "A little while longer and the world will see Me no more, but you will see Me. Because I live, you will live also. At that day you will know that I am in My Father, and you in Me, and I in you. He who has My commandments and keeps them, it is

> he who loves Me. And he who loves Me will be loved by My Father, and I will love him and manifest Myself to him." Judas (not Iscariot) said to Him, "Lord, how is it that You will manifest Yourself to us, and not to the world?" Jesus answered and said to him, "If anyone loves Me, he will keep My word; and My Father will love him, and We will come to him and make Our home with him.
>
> John 14:21-23

The word *manifest* is the word *emphanizo*, meaning *to exhibit in person* or *disclose by words; appear; declare plainly; inform;* and *show*. Remember, the word *declare* means *to make plain*. So Jesus was saying, *"If you have My Words and keep them, you love Me. If you love Me, you'll be loved of My Father and I will love you and will manifest Myself to you. I will appear, declare plainly, inform, and show Myself to you."*

Jesus told them that they were going to get another Comforter. He's telling them that if they have His Words and do them, He will manifest Himself to them. The only way to do the Word is to meditate on the Word. The Bible says to meditate upon the Word until you learn to do all that is written in it. This book of the law, this Word, shall not depart out of your mouth. You will meditate on it day and night, and then you will make your way prosperous.

When will this happen?

You will learn to do what's written in it!

Under the New Testament, the key to doing the Word is to be what Jesus made you. It's impossible to do the New Testament religiously. Someone said, *"Well, we're just sinners."* You can never do the Word as a sinner. Someone said, *"Well, I'm weak."* You can never do the word as a weak person. The only way to be a doer of the Word is to actively remember what Jesus has made you—a new creation!

What does that make you?
A doer of the Word!

How do you participate in that revelation?
By meditating on the Word of God!

Meditation brings a realization. When you see who you are in the Word of God, you're going to do the Word! In the New Testament, God does not wait until you have *done* the Word to call you a doer of the Word. From the moment you *decide* that you are going to do the Word, God calls you a doer of the Word! If God waited until you performed, He would still be operating under the Law.

You say, *"But the Bible said that you have to be a doer of the Word, not a hearer only."* That's right! God knows who is hearing *to hear* and who is hearing *to do*! He is a discerner of the thoughts and the intents of the heart. From the moment you intend to be a doer, the Holy Ghost goes to work. You can't do it on your own. You need the Holy Ghost to help you do it. The moment you intend to do it, the Holy Ghost goes to work to produce the supernatural help you need to be a doer of the Word.

Loved By God

Jesus was saying, *"If you have My Words, keep them and do them."*

His Word says,
"You are a new creature!"
"As He is, so are you!"
"You can do all things."
"The joy of the Lord is your strength!"
"You are the righteousness of God in Christ Jesus!"

The moment you say, *"Yes!"* to God's Word, you've just done the Word. Then what happens? *"My Father will love you! The moment you intend to be everything that Calvary has made you to be, My Father will love you because you love me!"*

This is how you show that you love the Lord!

"My Father will love you, and We will come to you. And I will manifest Myself to you." Jesus is talking to the same disciples who have

been walking with Him for three and a half years.

Didn't they know Him better than anyone else?

"What do you mean you're going to manifest yourself to us?" He was saying, *"Now I've told you a lot of parables and I have spoken through the Old Testament prophets. I spoke scrolls of prophetic utterance through Isaiah and Jeremiah!"* From the beginning of the human race until today—the Scriptures have been spoken by men through the Spirit—the utterance of the Word of God has been released into the planet. It was Christ, the Word, that spoke through men and put Scripture down in writing.

Yet, the Pharisees, the Sadducees, and the Scribes did not understand what was written down! The disciples didn't understand much of what was written either. Peter told Jesus, *"You're not going to go to the cross!"* Even after Jesus died, they didn't understand that He was going to rise from the dead. They didn't understand! They didn't have the Holy Ghost—the Spirit of Truth—to lead them into the true interpretation of the Scriptures.

So what was Jesus saying? *"If you keep My Word, the one that I sowed in you, and you keep my commandments, then you're showing that you love Me. You are positioning yourself in a place where my Father and I will come to you through the Holy Ghost. I will manifest myself to you!"*

The Holy Ghost has come to give us a manifestation of the Word of God! *"I'm going to come to you, through the Spirit and I'm going to give you a revelation, a manifestation, of who I am. You have walked with me these three and a half years, but when the Holy Ghost comes, you are going to know Me better than you could have ever known me. You will know me better than when we walked with you on the shores of Galilee. The Spirit of Truth is going to cause My words to come to the forefront, and you will be able to see clearly what God has been saying throughout the history of mankind!"*

Inexhaustible Revelation

The Bible says, *"Study to show thyself approved, a workman that needs not to be ashamed, rightly dividing the Word of Truth"* (2 Timothy

2:15). You can't rightly divide the Word of Truth without the Holy Spirit. You can't do it! That is why there are so many *stupid* doctrines around! People leave the Holy Ghost behind and want to interpret the Scriptures in light of what someone has told them.

"If you keep My words, My Father will love you, and We will come to you and make Our abode, Our dwelling place, with you." That means the Holy Spirit is going to come and dwell in you. When the Holy Spirit comes and dwells in you, His job will be to manifest the Word of God to you. When He manifests it to you, you will see clearly! His job is to manifest or to exhibit, to disclose, to cause an appearance of, to declare plainly, to inform you of who Christ is so that the Word can live on the inside of you!

"But the Comforter, which is the Holy Ghost, whom the Father will send in My name, He shall teach you all things and bring all things to your remembrance, whatsoever I have said unto you" (John 14:26). Many times the Holy Ghost has taught me something and then, to back the Truth He was telling me, He would remind me of the Scripture. People have this process reversed! They want to look with their natural eyes, interpret Scripture, and *then* ask the Holy Ghost. That's not how it works. He is the Teacher!

Why do people dry up trying to study the Bible? The Holy Ghost is not in the study of it! If you get in the Spirit, the Holy Ghost will lead you into what He wants to teach you for that day. There won't be a bit of dryness in any of it!

Jesus said, *"When the Spirit of Truth is come, He will teach you all things (not some things!) and He will remind you of what I have said. The Holy Ghost will say, 'This is the way it is because the Word says....' He's going to remind you of what I said."*

Why is the Holy Ghost reminding them of what Jesus said? It's because He's not only teaching, He's manifesting Jesus to them! Jesus was saying, *"Listen! If you just keep My Word, then I will come and reveal Myself to you."* You could spend your whole life in the same text, and the Holy Spirit would just keep bringing more and more revelation out of it! It is impossible to exhaust the revelation that is available through Christ. All of this is available to us so that we can have His results and His power in our lives!

Jesus told them, *"The Father will send the Holy Ghost to you. He will teach you all things, and He will bring all that I have said to your remembrance."* The way the Holy Spirit brings the Scripture to remembrance is by causing Scripture to come to mind, in a relevant way for the day. If you *tried to remember* every Scripture that you know, you would just wear yourself out. You would spend your time quoting Scriptures that you didn't need to quote!

The Realm of Revelation

The Holy Ghost will teach you all things. He will begin to work with your spirit man and the life of the Word will begin to work in you. If you're not like the world—insensitive to the Spirit and not having a discernment of who He is—you will receive. If you know what to expect, then the moment the Holy Ghost begins to move, you will receive the promise of the Spirit through faith! That slight tugging—that subtle influence of the Spirit—will be met by an invitation from you. Then the Holy Ghost will move in and revelation will start operating in your life.

When the Word is preached, the Holy Ghost will take that Word and apply it to the specific situations that are represented among the people. A person can hear one Word that will lead them on a rabbit trail of revelation. They go off and start writing things down and looking at other Scriptures. *What is happening?* The anointing is leading them somewhere that is relevant to their individual circumstance. It is not to distract them from what the Spirit is saying, but to personalize it—to put a personal stamp on what He is saying to them. If we don't know about the realm of revelation, we will live our lives in the rational realm. We will live outside of the miracle realm.

The Holy Ghost becomes grieved when *you* are grieved in your spirit. If you are flowing in the anointing and then begin to waiver and go in another direction, your spirit will be grieved. You have missed it! You have to return again. You must go back to where the Spirit of Lord was moving. The only way to do that is to know Him by discernment. He is the Teacher. To know Him, you must spend time with Him.

There are people who get angry and say, *"They let women talk in their church! The Bible says, 'Let your women stay silent in the church!'"* A person like that doesn't know the Holy Ghost. They may speak in tongues, but it doesn't mean a thing. They are not receiving a constant, bountiful supply of the Spirit. They are not allowing the Holy Ghost to be their Teacher. The Holy Ghost knows how to interpret what He said through Paul! He wouldn't say through Peter, *"Your daughters shall prophesy,"* and then contradict it through Paul by saying, *"Let your women keep silent in the church!"*

One time a preacher came up to me after a service in amazement, saying, *"It was wild! You were ministering at the altar, and then went up and started praying in tongues. Then your team started praying in tongues and the people joined in. When everyone prayed in tongues, the anointing increased!"* I said, *"That's right!"*

The anointing shall destroy the yoke.

If a person can walk into the church and say, *"They're praying in tongues! It's out of order!"* they aren't letting the Holy Ghost do the teaching. The Bible says, *"What is it then? I will pray with the Spirit, and I will pray with the understanding. I will sing with the Spirit, and I will sing with the understanding"* (1 Corinthians 14:15). As a matter of fact, the Bible says that if love is behind all that you do, then everything you do is going to be for the sake of building up the Body.

Moved By Love

While ministering in London, I called out a woman to minister to her. After praying in tongues for some time, I laid hands on her. She went out under the power and that was it. A year later, I was in London again and that same woman was there. After the service, she walked up to me and said, *"You may not remember this, but I came up for prayer when you were here last year. You began to pray over me and you spoke in my native dialect. It's a Serbian dialect that very few people know, but it's in our family. You said, 'My daughter, I brought you out of bondage and brought you to this land to refresh you, to use you, and to anoint you.'"*

Her life was changed. However, some stupid person could have been sitting in that church service that day thinking in their heart, *"Well, I wasn't edified by that!"* They may have even thought, *"And she wasn't edified by that either!"*

Don't get so caught up in spiritual manifestations that you forget to prioritize the needs of another. Put someone else as your focal point. If you do that, then you'll be moved by love. If you're moved by love, God will make sure that the person is edified. Love is to edify another.

We have a Teacher who can teach us all things. All we have to do is *see Him by discernment* and *know Him by fellowship*. When we do these things, He will teach us! He will be the Provider in our lives, and we won't be like orphans! He will supply all of our need!

Chapter 9

The Words of This Life

---

*When they opened their mouth,
they preached Jesus Christ.
They didn't preach about Him!
They preached Him!*

Then said Jesus to them again, Peace be unto you; as my Father has sent me, even so send I you. And when he had said this, he breathed on them, and saith unto them, Receive ye the Holy Ghost; whosesoever sins ye remit, they are remitted unto them; and whosesoever sins ye retain, they are retained.

John 20:21-23 KJV

Jesus had just resurrected from the dead—the exact fulfillment of the promise He made to the disciples. This was the promise the Scriptures had spoken about. He appeared to His disciples, but a period of time had passed in which they had not been in contact with the anointing. The last time they saw the anointing was in the garden of Gethsemane, when Jesus said, *"I am He,"* and the people that had come out to get Him fell over backwards. When Peter took his sword and cut off the ear of the soldier, Jesus healed his ear. That was the last encounter they had with the power of God.

Remember, Jesus asked them again, *"Whom do you seek?"* They answered, *"Jesus of Nazareth."* He answered, *"I told you that I am He! Let these people go!"* In other words, He put the power of God and the demonstration of the Spirit to work to see to it that the disciples were not harmed. *That is authority!* The devil came to lay hold on Him, and although He went with them, He was in control all along. He said, *"I have the power to lay down My life, and I have the power to take it up again."*

That power was in His anointing. It was a commandment He received of the Father—a word God gave to Him, which He believed. He believed that no one could kill Him. Several times they tried to kill Him, but he walked right through the midst of them because it was not yet time. When the time came, He had to *willingly relinquish* His life to the hands of those who had come to take Him to die. That was the last time the disciples saw the anointing in action.

While Jesus was being tortured, beaten, and mocked, they did not have the ability to ask Him for anything. For three and a half years, Jesus had to meet their needs *("Cast your net on the other side...")* because they were under an Old Covenant. They were under the Law. Up until the day they met Jesus, they had never met the anointing of God—the provision of God—in everyday life.

As My Father Has Sent Me, So Send I You

The disciples were hiding out. They were afraid and they were totally confused. Then Jesus shows up saying, *"Peace be unto you! As my Father has sent me, so send I you!"*

How did His Father send Him? *"The Spirit of the Lord is upon me, because he hath anointed me to preach the Gospel to the poor; he hath sent me to heal the brokenhearted, to preach deliverance to the captives, and recovering of sight to the blind, to set at liberty them that are bruised, to preach the acceptable year of the Lord"* (Luke 4:18-19a KJV). That is how His Father sent Him!

"How God anointed Jesus of Nazareth with the Holy Ghost and with power; who went about doing good, and healing all that were oppressed of the devil; for God was with him" (Acts 10:38). God sent Jesus to heal the sick and to set the captives free. Nicodemus said, *"Rabbi, we know that thou art a teacher come from God; for no man can do these* [attesting] *miracles that thou doest, except God be with him"* (John 3:2 KJV). So we have enough Scriptural evidence to know that the way God sent Jesus was in an anointed way. The message He preached was, *"The Spirit of the Lord is upon Me."*

In Nazareth they did not believe it, so they could not benefit from the anointing that was upon Him. The Bible said that He could do there no mighty works because of their unbelief. He was just as anointed in Nazareth as He was anywhere else, but because they could not receive Him, they could not receive the benefit of His anointing. He told His disciples, *"He that receiveth you, receiveth me, and he that receiveth me receiveth him that sent me. He that receiveth a prophet in the name of a prophet shall receive a prophet's reward"* (Matthew 10:40-41 KJV).

You have to use your faith to believe the promise!

A preacher says, *"I've got an anointing to produce this in your life."* When you sense the anointing and hear the revelation in the Word, then you will know that the Spirit manifested Christ to that preacher. He is preaching truth to you so that you will have faith in the truth and receive the rewards of the anointing that is upon him.

Jesus told the disciples, *"As my Father has sent Me—with the same power, the same authority, the same anointing—I am sending you."* He gave them the right to go out and do what He had been doing! After He said these things, He breathed on them and said, *"Receive the Holy Ghost."* That was the provision of being born again! That was the provision of being saved. That represented the Holy Ghost within.

Two Experiences

Jesus told the woman at the well, *"If you drink of this natural water, you'll thirst again. But if you drink of the water I'll give you, you'll never thirst again. It will be in you a well springing up unto eternal life."* What is a well? The Bible says, *"With joy shall ye draw water out of the wells of salvation."* The well is relevant to salvation. Then He said of the Spirit, *"If you thirst, come and drink, (after you have been saved) and the Spirit will be in you as rivers of living water that will flow through your belly."* Your spirit is born of the Holy Ghost and it causes you to be alive to divine truth. *"That which is born of the Spirit is spirit."*

Then He told His disciples, *"You shall receive power after that the Holy Ghost has come upon you and you shall be witnesses unto Me."* John the Baptist said, *"I baptize you with water. But the one that's coming after me is mightier than I. He will baptize you with, or immerse you in, the*

Holy Ghost and fire." There is a power that comes to believers after they have been born again.

Not only did Jesus breathe on them and say, *"Receive ye the Holy Ghost,"* as a type of salvation, but He was giving them a visual contact for their faith. The Bible says that all Scripture is given by inspiration of God and is profitable. It also says that prophecy, or Scripture, came not in the past by the will of man, but holy men of God spoke as they were moved by the Holy Ghost (2 Peter 1:21).

Jesus is the Word. When He breathed upon the disciples and said, *"Receive the Holy Ghost,"* it must have left a visual impression upon them! The glorified Christ was breathing on them. The glorified Word—the resurrected Word—was breathing on them! He was providing an image of a living, inspirational Person who would come into their lives and cause them to be empowered by the supernatural.

The disciples had to relate their encounter with Thomas. Thomas hadn't been there and had a very hard time believing their story. He retorted, *"Unless I put my fingers in the nail prints and thrust my hand into his side, I will not believe."* When Jesus showed up later, Thomas immediately believed.

Jesus said, *"Receive ye the Holy Ghost. Whosoever sins you remit, they're remitted. Whosoever sins you retain, they are retained."* The Holy Spirit will give you the wisdom to know who *really* wants to follow God and who's just faking it. If that wasn't available, then Jesus would have never have left the remission of sins in the hands of believers! He told the disciples, *"I give you the Holy Ghost. Because you have the Holy Ghost, you're going to be able to tell who is truly coming to God. When they make Me Lord of their life, you will be able to tell them, 'God has forgiven you for all your sins.' As my representative, you will know who is playing games with God and who means business. You're going to be able to know by the Holy Spirit."*

If the Holy Ghost can give the disciples that kind of revelation, He can certainly convict *you* if you're playing games with God!

Receive the Holy Ghost

For these are not drunken, as ye suppose, seeing

it is but the third hour of the day, but this that which was spoken by the prophet Joel.

Acts 2:15, 16 KJV

Jesus had told them, *"The Spirit of Truth is going to teach you and remind you of what I said."* It was the Word of God—Christ—that was flowing through the prophet Joel. By the inspiration of the Spirit, he prophesied of the outpouring of the Holy Ghost at Pentecost. The Word became flesh before there was a New Testament. However, the same word was in the Old Testament being spoken through the lips of holy men as they were inspired by the Holy Ghost!

When the Holy Spirit came into the life of Peter, he began to teach him.

Jesus said to Peter, *"Before the cock crows you're going to deny Me. Satan has desired you. He wants to sift you, but I've been praying for you that your faith would not fail. When you are converted, strengthen your brethren."* Later He said, *"Watch and pray with Me,"* but the Bible said that Peter could not pray. Jesus was praying in the Spirit. He was agonizing, sweating great drops of blood. Peter, however, was incapable of stepping into that dimension of prayer. He fell asleep and then denied the Lord three times.

After three days, Jesus rose from the dead. He appeared to them and He restored Peter. Jesus told the disciples, *"Tarry in Jerusalem until you be endued with power from on high."* He stayed on Earth for forty days, appearing to His disciples and showing them things about Himself in the Scriptures.

> Then there were ten silent days.
> The disciples waited for the Promise.

As we study the New Covenant, we can see how Jesus prepared the disciples for the Holy Spirit. He was not only doing miracles, but He was depositing little nuggets in them about the Spirit. In the latter part of the book of John, He begins to pray and talk to the disciples, giving them some direct revelation about the Holy Spirit. He was preparing their faith so that they would be able to receive the promise of the Spirit through faith. He gave them the Word that would inspire faith.

Ten days went by and the disciples are gathered in the upper room.

Peter is there. Like the others, he has the Holy Ghost within. He was there when Jesus breathed on them and said, *"Receive ye the Holy Ghost."* He's born again and Scripture is coming alive to him. The same man who once said, *"Not you, Jesus! You're not going to the cross!"* is the one who understood Pentecost! Revelation is beginning to well up within him, and the Scriptures are starting to make some sense!

And there appeared unto them cloven tongues like as of fire, and it sat upon each of them.

Acts 2:3 KJV

Then the Holy Ghost came! The Bible said that the wind filled the upper room. All that were present were baptized with the Spirit and began to speak with other tongues as the Spirit gave them inspiration. Jesus had said, *"The world can't receive Him because it doesn't discern Him and doesn't know Him."* They had to *receive* Him.

You could now see the manifestation of the visual impression that He had left with them when He breathed on them. He had said, *"Receive the Holy Ghost."* This visual impression—this point of contact for their faith—was fully realized in the upper room.

He told them, *"Tarry in Jerusalem until you are endued with power."* Do you know what they had been doing for ten days? They had been waiting for the Holy Ghost! Do you know what they had been thinking about? *"When He has come, we won't be comfortless! We won't be orphans! When He has come, He's going to teach us! When He has come, He's going to remind us! When He has come, He's going to lead us!"* That's what they'd been meditating on!

These people had left everything. Now they're waiting in the upper room for the promise called the *Baptism with the Holy Ghost*. They knew that when the Holy Ghost came, they were going to do some things. They were going to be ready for this experience! They were going to wait with expectation! Come right on in! *"And suddenly there came a sound from heaven as of a rushing mighty wind…"* (Acts 2:2 KJV). They got baptized with power and began to speak with other tongues. It drew the whole city to them! What a commotion!

Prophetic Light

They took the only Man that carried an anointing and put Him on the cross. Demon spirits were saying, *"He saved others but couldn't save Himself. Come down off the cross, so we would believe in you!"* The devil was mocking Him because the devil knew, *"Cursed is everyone that hangs on a tree."* He knew that if you're cursed, you're not going to be doing any miracles. They think they have killed Him, but then He resurrects from the dead.

BANG!

All of a sudden, a hundred and twenty of them get anointed! They begin to pray with other tongues, and people come to see what's going on. They see them and say, *"They're drunk!"* When you get full, *things happen*. People don't mock you for being dead; they mock you for being drunk!

> **And they were all amazed, and were in doubt, saying one to another, What meaneth this? Others mocking said, "These men are full of new wine." But Peter, standing up with the eleven, lifted up his voice, and said unto them, "These are not drunken, as ye suppose, seeing it is but the third hour of the day. But this is that which was spoken by Joel."**
>
> **Acts 2:12-16 KJV**

The Holy Spirit immediately taught Peter what was relevant to the moment. He reminded him of what the Word of God said. He not only had revelation by the Spirit, but he had proof by the Word! He stood up boldly, without a theologian around to teach him. As a matter of fact, none of the theologians around would have known what was happening. There were probably some religious folks there who had spent their entire lives studying the Word of God saying, *"What meaneth this?"*

It's just like today! People spend their lives going to school to study about God. One time one of these students asked me, *"What is this phenomenon of people falling over backwards?"* I thought, *"My God! What have you been studying all these years?"* He was asking, *"What meaneth this?"* Without the Holy Ghost, you cannot know what God is doing.

Peter got up and he knew exactly what God was doing! He interpreted it in prophetic light.

What Proof Do You Have?

Therefore being by the right hand of God exalted, and having received of the Father the promise of the Holy Ghost, he hath shed forth this, which ye now see and hear.

Acts 2:33 KJV

He was saying, *"Now God has exalted Jesus. You killed him, but God has exalted Him. He's at the right hand of God. He received the promise of the Holy Ghost from the Father and has poured Him out on us."*

They had a dilemma. They said, *"Put Jesus in the grave and put a garrison around His grave because we don't want anybody to steal Him."* When He rose they said, *"Tell everyone that His disciples stole Him."* That would have probably worked, but the Holy Ghost came! That was their problem! The devil will always come up with a lie, but when the Holy Ghost comes, someone has to answer, *"What meaneth this?"*

Peter was saying, *"Listen! The same Jesus you killed is exalted!"*

What's your proof, Peter?
"Oh, Jesus just lives in my heart."

The proof of His resurrection is more than Him living in your heart! The proof of His resurrection is that He lives in your life with the same kind of power that He had when He walked the shores of Galilee! That's the proof that He's alive! *"If I by Beelzebub cast out devils, by whom do your children cast them out? Therefore, they shall be your judge"* (Matthew 12:27 KJV). Jesus was saying, *"Here is the proof that this thing is not going to end: when I leave, there will come a generation after Me producing the same things that I produced when I was walking in the Earth realm!"* That's the proof!

> **And they continued steadfastly in the apostles' doctrine and fellowship, and in breaking of bread, and in prayers. And fear came upon every soul: and many wonders and signs were done by the apostles.**
>
> **Acts 2:42-43 KJV**

Many wonders and signs were done by the apostles!

Christ Multiplied

Peter went on to tell them, *"You took Jesus and you killed him. But He rose again, is resurrected, and sits at the right hand of the Father. He received the promise of the Holy Ghost, and He shed on us the promise of the Holy Ghost. That's what you're seeing and hearing!"* So he was literally saying, *"From now on, you're going to have to deal with the resurrected Christ—multiplied!"*

The Bible said that the people were pricked in their hearts. They asked the apostles, *"What must we do?"*

Peter answered saying:

> **Repent, and be baptized every one of you in the name of Jesus Christ for the remission of sins, and ye shall receive the gift of the Holy Ghost. For the promise is unto you, and to your children, and to all that are afar off, even as many as the Lord our God shall call.**
>
> **Acts 2:38-39 KJV**

Suddenly, three thousand people joined the Church because *something* had happened to the disciples. Three disciples, Peter, James, and John, had been on the mount of Transfiguration with Jesus. They had been in the upper room. On the mountain Peter said, *"It's good for you that we are here. We can build you three tabernacles, one for you, one for Moses, and one for Elijah."* Then they saw the cloud, and God said, *"This is My beloved Son."*

Do you know what God was saying? *"No! You're not going to make ME three tabernacles! I'm going to make YOU three tabernacles!"* Not only three, but one hundred and twenty *instantly* became the houses of God!

This is the key doctrine of the New Testament: Christ did not die in vain. Neither was He the only one who would personalize God in the Earth realm. He was the forerunner! When the Holy Ghost would come, all who would believe on Jesus would become members of the Body—tabernacles full of the glory—housing the power of the Most High God!

They received the baptism and immediately things began to happen. When Peter got up and spoke, his words were so full of conviction that three thousand people joined the Church! The Bible said that they continued in breaking bread and fellowshiping, and many wonders and signs were done by the apostles.

What impact do you think that revival had?

Christ's Results

During the three and a half years of Jesus' ministry, He was the only one with supernatural power. When the disciples went out praying for the sick and casting out devils, they did it in His name. He was the only one with the anointing! No one had ever done what He did. Even when the disciples went out in His name, they weren't getting the kind of results Jesus got.

Jesus Himself said, *"If I had not done among them the works which none other man did they had not had sin."* None other man included the twelve and it included the seventy. That means even when they went out in those days, they didn't go in the fullness of what He had. It wasn't available to them. He told them, *"If I go away, I'll send you the Comforter. If you believe on me, the works that I do, and greater works than these, will you do, because I go to my Father."* There was a greater anointing coming! They killed Jesus—the *one* miracle worker—but all of a sudden, the apostles were doing great and powerful miracles for the Lord!

> **And they continuing daily with one accord in the temple, and breaking bread from house to house, did eat their meat with gladness and singleness of heart, praising God and having favour with all the people. And the Lord added to the Church daily such as should be saved.**
>
> **Acts 2:46-47 KJV**

> *Do you think that belongs to us today?*
> *Do you think God can rock a city?*
> *Do you think He can rock a nation?*

To achieve this, He has to get people's attention through the preached Word. He has to get His own focused on the greatest Teacher in the universe—the Holy Spirit. When He moves into your life in the way He wants to, you will begin to live your life in the super abundance of His presence! The desire to see God's will done will burn in you stronger than ever before. You will have a greater desire for the will of God than for your own needs or your own wants!

As this happens, God will begin to add to the Church. It will multiply. It will increase. We will have the kind of supernatural demonstrations that we should have—because He is alive. Jesus is alive, and there are witnesses providing proof that He's alive!

Who are those witnesses?

"You shall receive power after that the Holy Ghost is come upon you, and you shall be witnesses!" Everyone who receives power when the Holy Ghost comes upon them is a witness. These disciples were so convinced of His resurrection that they allowed the Holy Ghost to demonstrate His resurrection life through them! They were counteracting the curse with a supernatural act of blessing!

Such as I Have

And when Peter saw it, he answered unto the people, "Ye men of Israel, why marvel ye at this? Or why look ye so earnestly on us, as though by our own power or holiness we had made this man to walk. The God of Abraham, and of Isaac, and of Jacob, the God of our fathers, hath glorified his Son Jesus; whom you delivered up, and denied him in the presence of Pilate when he was determined to let him go. But ye denied the Holy One and the Just, and desired a murderer to be granted unto you."

Acts 3:12-14 KJV

Peter and John are at the gate, Beautiful. A man, lame from his mothers womb, is crying, *"Alms! Alms!"* They fasten their eyes on him, and Peter says, *"Look on us!"* Why did he say, *"Look on us!"*? He said that because he was a tabernacle. God was in him! *"Silver and gold have I none; but such as I have give I thee; in the name of Jesus of Nazareth rise up and walk"* (Acts 3:6 KJV). At once, he grabbed the man and lifted him up. The man went running and leaping and praising God!

This draws some attention! People from everywhere are coming to see what the commotion is. Peter sees them and says, *"Why are you marveling, as if we did this thing by our own power?"*

Today, religion has distorted what happened in the book of Acts and in the Gospels. People use this distortion to resist the expectation to receive. Religion has twisted what Peter said. He wasn't saying, *"Such as I do not have, I give thee."* He was saying, *"What I have and what I prioritize in my life—does not come from my own ability. It's not my own power. If it were my own power, me being the source, then it would be limited. Neither is it my own holiness. Such as I have, I give you."*

Do you think Peter was living holy at that time? We know that he was living holy for the forty days before he went to the upper room. During those ten days that he was actually living in the upper room, he was holy. When he got filled with the Holy Ghost and started preaching, he was living holy. The Bible recorded that they were *daily* breaking bread and fellowshiping—he was in church every day! Peter was walking holy!

What was Peter saying? *"It's not the work of the law—it wasn't my own performance—that gained me this power. Neither was it my own will that conjured up this power."* Powerless Christians will say, *"Oh, whatever the Lord wants."* The Lord wants *you* to get anointed and do miracles! Peter was saying, *"It is not what I desired; it is the will of God. We didn't do it by our own power. We didn't do it by our own holiness. Those things are not what caused this man to walk!"*

Repent and Be Refreshed

"God glorified his Son Jesus, the One you denied. You denied Him. You killed Him and desired a murderer to be granted to you." The same Peter, who denied Jesus three times, is saying this! Now Peter is full of a message.

Peter denied the Lord three times. After the third incident, the Bible records the following:

> **And immediately, while he yet spake, the cock crew. And the Lord turned, and looked upon Peter. And Peter remembered the word of the Lord, how he had said unto him, Before the cock crows, thou shalt deny me thrice. And Peter went out, and wept bitterly.**
>
> **Luke 22:61-62 KJV**

Why did Peter deny Jesus? His prayer life was insufficient. He couldn't pray like he ought to. He didn't have the same Holy Spirit that gave Jesus the boldness to say in Gethsemane, *"I am He! Take Me."* He didn't have that, and he denied the Lord three times. After the resurrection, he came to the realization that there is a place in God for repentance. Once he repented and got filled with the Holy Ghost, he became a completely different man!

"Don't look on us as if we did this miracle by our own holiness! Let me tell you something. You crucified Jesus and wanted Barabbas released. You killed the Just One and asked for a murderer to be released to you, but the God of Abraham, Isaac, and Jacob has glorified His Son. His Son received the promise of the Spirit and shed it upon me! His Spirit came upon me and that's how I'm doing exactly what He did—by the same Spirit! I didn't do it by my own power! I did it because He is exalted, and the Holy Ghost came!"

You denied the Lord! What are you going to preach, Peter? *"I'm going to preach repentance because I have a revelation of how to repent! Peter's best message was, 'Repent and be baptized, and you will receive the gift of the Holy Ghost!'"* The Gospel is simple, isn't it?

> **And his name through faith in his name hath made this man strong, whom ye see and know; yea, the faith which is by him hath given him this perfect soundness in the presence of you all. And now, brethren, I wot that through ignorance ye did it, as did also your rulers. Repent ye therefore, and be converted, that your sins may be blotted out, when the times of refreshing shall come from the presence of the Lord.**

Acts 3:16-17, 19 KJV

The original language reads, "… and times of refreshing shall come." How did Peter know that times of refreshing would come after repentance? He knew it because it happened to him! He repented, was converted, and times of refreshing came. That was the Holy Ghost!

Peter and the rest of the disciples were preaching everywhere in order to get people saved and filled with the Holy Ghost. *What was their mission?* To gain as many tabernacles for God as they could! The more people who have God living in them, the more the world will know that Jesus is alive! The proof that He is alive is the Church, His Body, doing His work and living by His power. Times of refreshing will come from the presence of the Lord.

Pursue the Power

> And as they spake unto the people, the priests and the captain of the temple, and the Sadducees came upon them, being grieved that they taught the people, and preached *through Jesus* the resurrection from the dead. And they laid hands on them, and put them in hold unto the next day; for it was now eventide.
>
> Acts 4:1-3 KJV

Not only did they preach that the dead are resurrected "through Jesus," but they were preaching "through Jesus" because it was Jesus living in them. It was Jesus doing the preaching!

"Howbeit many of them which heard the word believed; and the number of the men was about five thousand" (Acts 4:4 KJV). Five thousand people had just been saved as a result of Peter and the disciples ministering! *Do you know what set the stage for that?* The healing of the man that was lame! *Do you know what enabled Peter to minister to the lame man?* He knew he had something! He said, *"Such as I have I give you,"* and he administered the resurrection power of the Holy Spirit to him. Peter must have been *full* of the Spirit!

Peter and John were going to pray because it was the hour of prayer. Later, Peter told the Church, *"We should not leave the Word of God and wait on tables. We will give ourselves to prayer and the teaching of the Word."* So the disciples maintained an anointed position in God by pursuing a fresh touch of the Spirit. They pursued it!

Divine Invasion

> Then the high priest rose up, and all they that were with him, (which is the sect of the Sadducees) and were filled with indignation and laid their hands on the apostles, and put

> them in the common prison. But the angel of the Lord by night opened the prison doors, and brought them forth, and said, Go, stand and speak in the temple to the people all the words of this life.

Acts 5:17-20 KJV

This is awesome because this is the same chapter where Peter ministers to Ananias and Sapphira. Fear falls on everyone, and the greatest revival the city has ever known comes to pass!

> By the hands of the apostles were many signs and wonders wrought among the people; (And they were all with one accord in Solomon's porch and of the rest of them durst no man join himself to them; but the people magnified them. And believers were the more added to the Lord, multitudes both of men and women.) insomuch that they brought forth the sick into the streets, and laid them on beds and couches, that at the least the shadow of Peter passing by might over shadow some of them. There came also a multitude out of the cities round about unto Jerusalem, bringing sick folks, and them which were vexed with unclean spirits; and they were healed every one.

Acts 5:12-16 KJV

This is Jerusalem. The revival did not diminish when Jesus died. This revival escalated and went beyond the point of containment. This was a divine invasion! This was a divine attack by Heaven through the Spirit! All of a sudden, people are bringing the sick from everywhere! They are laying them in the streets. The apostles are laying hands on them, and they are healed. Peter is walking by sick people on beds and couches, and even his shadow cast over them is causing them to get up and walk! This thing is beyond containment!

This is happening in Jerusalem! The Bible said that Jesus suffered outside this city. He carried His cross outside the gate and said that we should go outside and bear His reproach with Him. This is the city that did not receive Him. He died on the outside, but through the disciples, He began to rule on the inside!

People were getting healed left and right because the apostles were doing what Jesus told them to do. They were not sitting around saying, *"Yes, I know that."* No! They knew *exactly* what the Holy Ghost was for, and they were *full* of that revelation. Everyone was healed! Three thousand were added! Five thousand were added! Multitudes! Multitudes! It could not be contained!

The religious leaders were *filled* with indignation. The Bible is full of statements about being filled!

> *"Why has Satan filled your heart*
> *to lie to the Holy Ghost?"*
> *"They were filled with indignation."*
> *"They were full of the Holy Ghost."*
> *"They were all filled with the Spirit."*
> *"The fullness of Him that fills all in all."*

Do you know what the Bible is saying? You're going to be a tabernacle, *one way or the other!* You're going to be a house, and you'll either be a house for God or a house for the enemy.

Putting Angels to Work

"But the angel of the Lord by night opened the prison doors." When you get baptized with the Holy Ghost it opens the door to angels.

Who is the most powerful Spirit in the universe? The Holy Ghost.

What are angels? "Are they not all ministering spirits sent forth to minister for them which would be heirs of salvation?"

What are demon spirits? They are fallen spirits. Now when you have the most powerful Spirit living in your life, He will lead you. He will put Words of power in your mouth. His faith in you will open an invitation to God's power.

The Bible said, *"Whosoever shall call on the name of the Lord shall be saved."* That word means *delivered, rescued, preserved, provided for, healthy and saved.* Why don't we see all of the provisions of that word fulfilled? It's not automatic. It's according to the power that works in you.

What power is working in you? Holy Ghost power is working in you!

What does Holy Ghost power do? It enables you to *expect* beyond what you can think or ask! So when the Holy Spirit is working in your life, the greatest Spirit in the universe is filling your life. He opens the door for all of Heaven's power to go to work.

The Bible says that we don't know how to pray like we ought, but the Spirit helps our infirmities with groanings, which cannot be uttered. We know that all things work together for good (Romans 8:26). *"All things"* is not referring to tumors or sickness! It doesn't mean, *"He got run over by a train, but the Lord said, 'All things work together for good.'"* Wake up! That's not what the Word is talking about! All things work together for good to those people who know how to pray like they should! They're allowing the Spirit to bear their infirmities, and they're praying in the Holy Ghost. Those are the people who have all things working together for good for them!

What kind of things are working together? All things within God's influence are working together, including angelic beings. They go to work for our good. When we get anointed, our angels go to work! *"The angel of the Lord by night opened the prison doors."* These are natural prison doors, but this was a spiritual angel!

"But the angel of the Lord by night opened the prison doors, and brought them forth, and said, 'Go, stand and speak in the temple to the people all the words of this life.'" The officers came the next day and couldn't find them in the prison. *"Where in the world are they?"* they wondered. Then someone came and said, *"They're over there, standing in the temple and teaching the people!"* When we get anointed, we will be terrorists to the Kingdom of darkness! The devil couldn't even keep them in jail effectively!

A Three-Point Sermon

And when they had brought them, they set them before the council; and the high priest asked them, saying, Did not we straitly command you that ye should not teach in this name? And behold, ye have filled Jerusalem with your doctrine, and intend to bring this man's blood upon us.

Acts 5:27-28 KJV

These were the same people that said, *"His blood be on us, and on our children!"*? It's easy to say that if you think that He is going to die and stay dead! However, Jesus doesn't. He resurrects from the dead, sprinkles people with His Blood, and anoints them by His Spirit!

They said, *"You have filled this city with your doctrine!"* What doctrine was it? *"Repent! Repent, be baptized, and you'll be filled with the Holy Ghost!"* The doctrine is, *"Don't look at us! You can do the same thing! He is alive! He is the first fruit! He is the forerunner!"*

Jesus came to make people like Him! Anyone who will come to Him will be changed into His likeness. That's the doctrine. It's straight from the Bible! I don't know what people have been teaching in our churches today, but this is the doctrine: *YOU can be just like Jesus!*

The world hasn't seen anything yet. They're about to run into men and women who look like Jesus, talk like Jesus, act like Jesus, and have Christ's results! It will be the greatest invasion the world has ever seen—and it's going to be an invitation for souls. *Whosoever will can come!* This is the central doctrine of the Bible: Believe on the Lord, and you will be saved. Then, the works He did, you will do!

They said, *"You filled Jerusalem with your teaching! Do you want to bring this man's blood on us!"* Then Peter and the other apostles answered and said, *"We ought to obey God rather than men. The God of our fathers raised up Jesus, whom ye slew and hanged on a tree"* (Acts 5:30 KJV).

If we had nothing to say but, *"He's alive! My bills are paid! I'm blessed! The devil's defeated! The Holy Ghost is for me! You can be delivered! You can be saved!"* We'd have people *flocking* to the Church! His resurrection, however, doesn't hold the same significance to the one who is *not* maintaining a Spirit-filled life. The more you get full of the Holy Ghost, the closer you get to God! You will get full of the comfort of knowing He is on the throne.

> **The God of our fathers raised up Jesus, whom ye slew and hanged on a tree. Him has God exalted with his right hand to be a Prince and a Saviour, for to give repentance to Israel, and forgiveness of sins. And we are his witnesses of these things; and so is also the Holy Ghost, whom God has given to them that obey him.**
>
> **Acts 5:30-32 KJV**

It's not enough just to say, *"I'm a witness."* We *are* witnesses and so is the Holy Ghost. Peter, however, is saying, *"Do you know why you can't keep me in jail? Do you know why the lame man is walking? Do you know why we're multiplying so quickly? Do you know why the whole city is full of our doctrine? It's because He's alive! We are witnesses, and so is the Holy Ghost!"* That's a three-point sermon! Peter is saying, *"Jesus rose, and I believe it. Therefore, I am promising—through the anointing—what He promised to others. And the Holy Ghost is bearing witness that Jesus is alive by doing what He promised to do for all who believe!"* That's good news!

"When they heard that, they were cut to the heart, and took counsel to slay them" (Acts 5:33 KJV). The devil is so stupid! You'd think he would have learned! He had said, *"Let's kill Jesus!"* Now, there are three thousand, five thousand, and a multitude! The whole city is hearing the doctrine because he killed *one*. Now he is saying, *"Let's kill all of them!"* He is stupid!

The Church is Winning

> **Then stood there up one in the council, a Pharisee, named Gamaliel, a doctor of the**

> law, had in reputation among all the people, and commanded to put the apostles forth a little space. …And now I say unto you, refrain from these men, and let them alone; for if this council or this work be of men, it will come to nought; but if it be of God, ye cannot overthrow it; lest haply ye be found even to fight against God. And to him they agreed; and when they had called the apostles, and beaten them, they commanded that they should not speak in the name of Jesus, and let them go. And they departed from the presence of the council, rejoicing that they were counted worthy to suffer shame for his name. And daily in the temple, and in every house, they ceased not to teach and preach Jesus Christ.
>
> **Acts 5:34,38-42 KJV**

Gamaliel is a doctor of the law and a man of reputation. He is Saul's teacher. Saul sat at the feet of Gamaliel and was taught by him. They said, *"Let's kill them!"* Gamaliel stood up and said, *"No, let's not kill them because if this work is of men, it won't go anywhere. But if this work is of God, then let's not fight against God!"*

Christianity has painted a picture of the disciples persecuted, driven out, martyred and lamenting, *"This world is not my home; I'm just passing through."* When I look at the book of Acts, however, I see the devil frantic. He's saying, *"How are we going to stop these people! They're a multitude! We can't do anything about them!"* The devil says, *"I've got an idea! Kill them! Kill them all!"*

Do you know why the devil is saying this? He is afraid! The devil is so afraid that someone is going to get a hold of the fact that Jesus is on the throne and that the power is for today. He is afraid! When we preach, *"Revival is coming!"* immediately he goes to work telling people, *"It's not going to happen! It's not that easy!"* He's afraid that people are going to see it, get a hold of it, and *do* it!

Gamaliel stood up and spoke his peace. The others in the council decided, *"Alright. We won't kill them."* So instead, they beat them.

They beat them, and then they threatened them: *"Don't teach in that name again!"* The devil said, *"I can't just leave them alone! I've got to put some pressure on them! I've got to pressurize them so that they will back off from the power that they're exercising toward us!"*

The devil is afraid of *you*! He wants you to stop!

The Bible shows us a totally different picture of the early Church than we have heard preached. I see the Church *winning* in the book of Acts! Someone said, *"But they beat them!"* Yes, and Herod was eaten by worms! He didn't give God glory, and the angel of the Lord smote him!

Angels were having fun in the early Church!

Astonishing Doctrine

When they departed from the presence of the council, they were rejoicing! They were happy that they were counted worthy to suffer shame! *"And daily in the temple, and in every house, they ceased not to teach and preach Jesus Christ"* (Acts 5:42 KJV). They ceased not to preach and teach Jesus Christ! *"Then Philip opened his mouth, and began at the same scripture, and preached unto him Jesus"* (Acts 8:35 KJV).

Jesus told them, *"I will manifest myself to you."* So what was the early Church preaching? They were teaching and preaching Jesus Christ! What did they teach about Jesus? *"Christ in you, the hope of glory!"* They taught, *"He is alive! He is living in Heaven, but the Holy Ghost is here and can live in you. When He does, He will be living in you with all of His power."* People asked, *"Who will be living in me?"* They answered, *"Jesus Christ, the Anointed One, the Miracle Worker! You'll be just like Him! If you'll turn yourself over to God, He will make your body the temple of the Holy Ghost, and He will live in you!"* Everything they preached, every doctrine they had, was Jesus Christ in you.

Then Saul, (who also is called Paul,) filled with the Holy Ghost, set his eyes on him, and said, O full of all subtilty and all mischief, thou child

of the devil, thou enemy of all righteousness, wilt thou not cease to pervert the right ways of the Lord? And now, behold, the hand of the Lord is upon thee, and thou shalt be blind, not seeing the sun for a season. And immediately there fell on him a mist and a darkness; and he went about seeking some to lead him by the hand. Then the deputy, when he saw what was done, believed, being *astonished at the doctrine of the Lord.*

Acts 13:9-12 KJV

Astonished at the doctrine! *What doctrine was he astonished at?* He was astonished that the Lord is still living in people! He was shocked that His power is so great in them that they can talk to a sorcerer and strike him blind for a season!

This is the life story of Saul. He had been Gamaliel's student. When Gamaliel stood up and told the council not to kill the early disciples, Saul irritably mused, *"Never mind. I'll kill them!"* He then killed Stephen, consenting to his death. However, on his way to Damascus, the Holy Ghost got a hold of him. *BANG!* All of a sudden, Paul became the premier weapon against the kingdom of darkness.

The devil said, *"Kill them all,"* but Gamaliel said, *"Now, wait a minute! If this thing is of God, then we don't want to fight God."* So the devil said, *"I'll just use Saul. I'll fill him with anger. I'll fill him with religious zeal. I'll make him a temple full of anger, hatred, and murder and send him out!"* So Saul went on his way, but he was interrupted. *BANG!* Jesus asked, *"Saul, why are you persecuting Me?"* Saul said, *"Lord!"* Ananias came and laid hands on him, and he was filled with the Holy Ghost.

The devil has been hitting himself in the head ever since saying, *"Why did I send Saul?"* Paul went on to write two thirds of the New Testament. He wrote, *"To make all men see my knowledge in the mystery of Christ: Christ in you, the hope of glory!"*

The central doctrine of the New Testament is the doctrine of the Lord. When they opened their mouth, they preached Jesus Christ. They didn't preach *about* Him! They preached *Him!* They preached

Him living in them *now* to do what He did yesterday. They promised others that He can live in them *now* too! This is the Good News!

CHAPTER 10

HEARING GOD

A child of God is not led by God's audible voice. If you were, you'd need to hear it every day! That's not hearing God! That's having a supernatural experience with God!

"But ye have an unction from the Holy One, and ye know all things"

1 John 2:20 KJV

I am going to teach you about power demonstrations and the still, small voice. As a believer, God has granted you the ability to hear His voice in your inner man.

The Bible says that the spirit of man is the candle, or the lamp of the Lord. If I want the light of God, I must connect my spirit with His Spirit. That is where the wellspring of life is.

"Keep (guard) *thy heart with all diligence; for out of it are the issues of life"* (Proverbs 4:23 KJV). In this text, the word *heart* is used interchangeably with the word *spirit*. Guard your spirit with all diligence! If the Bible is commissioning you to guard your spirit, that means there is a danger of it being affected and influenced by something that is hostile to it. Certain natural thought patterns, certain demonic influences, certain natural realm dictates, can affect your spirit man.

God wants you to diligently guard your spirit because out of it will come the issues of life. Your spirit is a wellspring of life. God is the source of that wellspring. Through your connection with the Spirit, rivers of life will come out of your spirit man.

There is a great and mighty Spirit living in your spirit. The Holy Ghost lives, contacts, and touches your spirit man in order to cause the life of God to flow into your spirit. In turn, God is counting on what *you* do with that revelation. *What will you do with the nature of God that flows from His Spirit into your spirit?* His desire is that you would put that nature to work—put that nature in motion so that it will influence your mind and influence your physical body.

When we speak of power demonstrations and the still, small voice, we are really majoring on the Holy Ghost. *"How God anointed Jesus of Nazareth with the Holy Ghost and with power"* (Acts 10:38). *"But you shall receive power after that the Holy Ghost has come upon you"* (Acts 1:8). *"But tarry ye in the city of Jerusalem until ye be endued* (or anointed) *with power from on high"* (Luke 24:49 KJV).

"Not by might, nor by power, but by My spirit..." (Zechariah 4:6 KJV). It's not by man's power or might but by the anointing. God's power is the by-product of God's anointing. The anointing is the dunamis. *It's the miracle working power of God!*

Say this out loud:

> *God will do exceeding abundantly above all that I can ask or think according to the anointing that is working in me.*

The Anointing Within

Two types of anointing belong to every child of God. One is the anointing *within.* Jesus, when speaking to the woman at the well, said, *"Whosoever drinketh of this water* (drink of natural gratification, drink of natural solutions, drink of natural priorities) *shall thirst again. But whosoever drinketh of the water that I shall give him* (salvation, deliverance, the provisions of the supernatural of God through the cross) *shall never thirst; but the water that I shall give him shall be in him a well of water springing up into everlasting life"* (John 4:13-14 KJV). That is the anointing within!

"But ye have an unction from the Holy One, and ye know all things" (1 John 2:20 KJV). In the Kenneth S. Wuest translation it says, *"But as for you (in contradistinction to the Antichrists), an anointing you have from the Holy One, and all of you have the capacity to know (spiritual truth.)"* The Bible is very clear. As a believer, you have an anointing within.

The Bible says that Jesus is the Christ. We believe that He is the *one* and the *only* Christ. There are not many *Christs*, and there is no such thing as an impersonal Christ. Christ is Jesus of Nazareth. He's the only one. That word *Christ* means *Anointed One*. When you have Jesus living in you, you have the Anointed One living in you. If you have the Anointed One living in you, then you have the anointing living in you!

You stand in contradistinction to the Antichrists. The Antichrists are the ones who do not have the Anointed One living in them. Now, of course, we believe a day will come when the Antichrist or the literal manifestation of Satan in the Earth, will come. However, the spirit of Antichrist is already at work today.

The Antichrist is anti-anointing!

Have you ever wondered why you don't have a hard time believing God when the anointing is flowing? How about when the message of faith is being preached? However, you cannot spend any length of time living in this natural world without having your faith and anointing wane. This is only because you have come up against the spirit known as "anti-anointing!" The devil hates the anointing and he majors in lies that will short-circuit the anointing in the life of the believer.

The devil is afraid of the anointing because the anointing will destroy the yoke. The devil believes in yokes. He believes in bondage. He hates anything that breaks bondage because it brings deliverance.

Does this mean that we are not to spend any time in the world? Absolutely not! However, it does mean that we need to guard ourselves so that we do not allow the world to *infiltrate us* in our thought life or in our attitudes. Jesus said, *"Let not your heart be troubled"* (John 14:27 KJV). When a person is troubled, it affects their attitude. In other words, *"Don't let your heart be troubled by the world! Be of good courage; I have overcome the world!"*

While we live in the world we must guard our spirit from the influence of the world. The influence of the world is anti-anointing. Once the world influences you, the anointing within you dissipates. This is why it is so important to get into the presence of God. God will use that time to recharge and reignite the anointing in you. It doesn't come through the natural, but it comes through fellowship with God.

The anointing lives in you. It's called the anointing within. Do you know that the Bible says that as many as are led by the Spirit of

God, they are the sons of God? It's not referring to the Spirit of God upon you. It's referring to the Spirit of God within you.

The Anointing Upon

The Spirit of God *upon* you is the baptism of the Holy Ghost. To those who are called into the five-fold ministry, it's the mantle that comes to equip the ministry gift for their mission. Not everyone is called to be an apostle, but if you are, a special mantle will come upon you to equip you to be an apostle. Not everyone is called to be an evangelist. However, *every believer* is called to *evangelize* and every believer will have the mantle to evangelize. Every believer is called to lay hands on the sick, but not every believer is called to lay hands on the sick as an apostle or a prophet.

There will be a greater measure of anointing upon those who are in the five-fold ministry than upon lay people. Regardless of where you fit in, you will have signs following you as a believer. There is a mantle that the believer receives. It comes upon you when you receive the Holy Ghost.

What did Jesus say about the Holy Spirit? He said that if you thirst, you can drink, and out of your belly will flow rivers of living water.

The anointing within is a well springing up.
The anointing upon is rivers flowing out!

One type of anointing is a well springing up. If you have a well, you can't just turn on a faucet and get water out. You have to go out and pump the well. You have to lower the bucket and draw water out of the well. If you don't, you'll remain thirsty. By the same token, Jesus said to the woman at the well, *"If you drink of this water you'll never thirst again,"* meaning that the potential to never be dissatisfied, never be dry, never be hard or parched in your Christianity is available!

You have that water in the well of salvation within you. The only way to draw it out is to give it priority in your life. I have the well of salvation living in me. I have the anointing of God living in me. That anointing will give me unction and an ability to know all things. Even though I have that in me, I can choose to walk according to the natural realm. If I chose, I can be overcome by the influence of the natural realm and the Antichrist spirit. I can be dry. I can be cold. I can be confused because of the things I have prioritized. All that aside, there remains a well of life living on the inside of me and on the inside of you.

Man Cannot Live by the Gifts Alone

The Church stands in contradistinction to Antichrists. *Why is this?* It's because the Church has an unction—the anointing—living in it. The Church has the capacity to know all the spiritual truths that it needs to know to live victoriously.

The Bible says that God gave you and me all things that pertain to life and godliness. That did not come to you through the anointing of God *upon* you. It came to you through the anointing of God *within* you. In other words, every one of us will experience supernatural power demonstrations. Every one of us will see the Spirit of God manifest Himself through us in *several* of the nine gifts of the Spirit.

Have you ever prophesied under the anointing of God?
Have you ever given a message with other
tongues as the Spirit gave utterance?
Have you ever had a word of knowledge?
Have you ever had the gift of healing
operate through your hands?

All of these things are wonderful, and they have come into our lives by the Spirit of God to enable us to do the job. However, we cannot be Spirit-led by the gifts of the Spirit. We must be Spirit-led by the *indwelling* Spirit!

The Bible doesn't say, *"As many as are led by the word of knowledge..."* or *"As many as are led by the word of wisdom..."* or *"As many as are led by the gift of prophecy...."* It says, *"For as many as are led by the Spirit of God, they are the sons of God"* (Romans 8:14). The Word of God says that the steps of the righteous are ordered of the Lord. What is God saying? He is saying that twenty-four hours a day, we can maintain a camaraderie and a communion with the Holy Ghost within us. This is the true meaning of being Spirit-led.

While being led by the Spirit, we will encounter situations that demand a supernatural manifestation of power. As you learned earlier, this manifestation is the by-product of the anointing of God upon us. As believers, we must make sure that our relationship with the Holy Ghost—the Spirit who lives in us—is in tune, is in harmony and is in faith. We must make sure that we have not allowed our heart to be infiltrated by doubt and unbelief, but that we are standing in faith, and in union with the Spirit. In doing this, our steps will continue to be directed by the Lord. We will have consistency in our daily walk with God.

People miss it in trying to live their life off the anointing that they experience in a corporate meeting. When we come together, the anointing in the corporate meeting will set us free. You can walk in bound, and the anointing will immediately deliver you. Thank God for the corporate anointing! You can walk in sick, and the corporate anointing will heal you. You can walk in discouraged, and the anointing will break the power of discouragement. The Word of God will impart faith, and courage will come.

Nevertheless, we are not to rely on the corporate anointing for our daily walk because that anointing is sporadic. That anointing is available when we come together and is manifested when the gifts of the Spirit are in motion. The anointing within us, which we have of Him, will operate in the form of relationship, fellowship, communion, friendship, and guidance twenty-four hours a day, three hundred and sixty-five days a year!

People miss it when they leave the corporate presence—with the manifestations of the Holy Ghost—and then get away from walking with the Spirit in their heart. When that happens, they come down.

Spirit-Led People vs. Flesh-Led People

Say this:

> *There is an anointing IN me, and there is an anointing UPON me! The anointing upon my life equips me to do what I'm called to do, but the anointing in me helps me to live the way I'm called to live.*

You can go anywhere, and the gifts of the Spirit may operate. However, if you are not following the guidance of the Holy Spirit in you, you'll end up in the wrong place at the wrong time, but still operating in the gifts. Please understand this: If you are not led by the Spirit of God, you can be at the wrong place *but still operate in the gifts.*

God wants you to be Spirit-led. If you are Spirit-led, then God calls you a son. If you are a son, you are mature. *"For as many as are led by the Spirit of God, they are the sons of God."*

We all know Spirit-filled Christians who aren't Spirit-led Christians. People have said, *"Oh, they're just barely born again! They shouldn't be allowed to flow in the gifts of the Spirit!"* That is completely wrong! Yes, they are baby Christians, but they were baptized with the Holy Ghost from day one. They're baby Christians, but they can flow in the gifts of the Spirit! Now, they shouldn't be allowed to hold an office just because they can operate in the gifts! The anointing *within* them has not yet been developed, so they can easily fall into the condemnation of the devil and be pulled down.

It's important to encourage a baby Christian to understand spiritual gifts and to flow in the anointing of God that flows through them. It is also important to realize that in our daily life, there is an anointing *living in us* that gives us the potential to know all spiritual things.

Say this:

> *I can know, by the anointing in me, everything that I need to know regarding life and godliness!*

There aren't a lot of Christian people living by that strength. Most believers are asking a lot of questions! *"Why is this happening to me?"* Have you ever asked that? Have you ever heard someone say, *"Well, if God is in control then why am I in the mess that I'm in?"*

There are Spirit-led people and there are flesh-led people. If you are walking in the flesh realm and letting the flesh realm lead you, then you're going to run into problems. You're going to get sick, but then you'll come to the corporate anointing and get healed. You're going to get bound, but then you'll come to the corporate anointing and get delivered.

There's a better place in God. There's a place where you don't have to get sick and you don't have to be bound. That *place* is called being *Spirit-led!* The anointing within you will take you to the place where your steps are directed by God. The Holy Ghost will lead you into God's perfect will for your life! It's going to take the development of a relationship with the Lord, but you have that potential. You have the unction and you know all things!

The Anointing Will Teach You

> **But the anointing which ye have received of him abideth in you, and ye need not that any man teach you; but as the same anointing teacheth you of all things and is truth, and is no lie, and even as it hath taught you, ye shall abide in him.**
>
> **1 John 2:27 KJV**

The Apostle John uses the words *Him* and *the anointing* interchangeably in this text because He (Christ) and the anointing are one and the same.

So what is John saying?

He's *not* saying that you and I should refrain from being taught by teachers! If he was, he would be contradicting the Apostle Paul in

Ephesians. *"And he gave some, apostles; and some, prophets; and some, evangelists; and some, pastors and teachers...."* (Ephesians 4:11 KJV). As a matter of fact, do you know that a teacher needs to be anointed to teach? Furthermore, just because the anointing is in us doesn't mean that the anointing upon the teacher does not benefit us.

He's *not* saying, "Do away with teachers in the Body of Christ!" He's saying, "The anointing on the inside of you has the ability to bear witness with the truth!" Sometimes you can receive one statement of truth that will come from the pulpit, and the anointing in you, will grab that statement and run off with it! The anointing within you will get a hold of that truth, run off with it, and begin to reveal to you certain things.

Here is another place where people have missed it. Some people have thought they were prophets just because the anointing in them was allowed to teach them the truth. I want you to see this. Every believer should know the truth because of the anointing in them, but a prophet will have a higher level of revelation knowledge operating. It will be revelation knowledge for the purpose of equipping the Saints for the work of the ministry. A prophet is *not* someone who can find out about people's lives by the Holy Ghost. A prophet is someone who can get revelation from God to help people rise up to be what God has called them to be!

As a believer, the anointing in you will get a hold of one statement that's anointed and run off with it. The anointing within you will start showing you things. When the anointing is flowing, you have the capacity to follow the Holy Ghost through a myriad of personal revelation. The anointing that is in you is teaching you!

Then why do we need a teacher? You need a teacher because it was the anointing upon the teacher that sparked the anointing within you to receive that download of revelation.

The Anointing That Leads

It's important to know how to put the anointing to work. Without the anointing, we cannot know all the things that we need to know about life and godliness.

I've heard people say, *"Well, I don't receive that."* or, *"I don't agree* with that." or, *"I just don't understand that!"* They will argue about something for *years* until one day a teacher explains the very thing they've been disagreeing with for a decade. *POW!* In an instant, that revelation hits their spirit! Perhaps that ministry gift said it a little bit differently than what they had heard before. They'll say, *"Finally, somebody explained it right! I can see it now!"*

No, it's not *"Finally, somebody said it right!"* It's *"Finally, it hit the right place! That revelation has been bouncing off their head; it's been bouncing off the natural; it's been bouncing right off! Finally, God was able to get that truth over to their spirit man, and that truth became a revelation!"*

If you *know that you know* that you're learning the Word of God, don't get discouraged! If you don't get a certain truth, don't give up! If you just don't understand it and don't quite know how to flow in it, don't let the devil lie to you and tell you that you're not getting it! Keep on hearing, and keep on sitting. One day, that thing is going to explode inside of you, and you may become an authority on the very revelation that you did not understand before! The anointing in you has the capacity to lead you into truth. You can know all things by that anointing.

Living In God

The Bible says that you've received of Him (of Jesus) the anointing, and it lives in you. The anointing teaches you and it is not a lie. It's divine truth! As the anointing teaches you, you can continue to abide in Him. You can continue in the anointing.

Say this:

> *The anointing lives in me, and I will live in the anointing!*

The anointing is in you! The anointing, however, can be in you, and you can choose to abide in the flesh. The anointing can be in you, and you can abide in unbelief. The anointing can be in you, and you can abide in confusion.

The things of the natural can distract you from the anointing within. If the anointing dwells in you, then you can abide in that anointing.

Say this:

> *In order for me to live in the anointing, I must listen to the anointing that lives in me! It's not enough that the anointing lives in you. If He's in you, and you don't listen to Him or give Him time, then you won't live in Him.*

If you're listening to the anointing, then you will live in the anointing! You will be led by the Spirit of God! You will walk into your high places! You will see a lifestyle of faith begin to develop, and then periodically, as the Spirit wills, you will see manifestations or demonstrations, of power in your life. The Spirit of God will bear witness to you with signs following.

Growing Up In God

"When I was a child, I spake as a child, I understood as a child, I thought as a child; but when I became a man, I put away childish things" (1 Corinthians 13:11 KJV). Paul said that he spoke like a child, understood like a child, and thought like a child when he was a child. As a child, you have childish speech. You have a childish form of understanding and a childish thought life.

"But when I became a man, I put away childish things."

An adult is smarter than a child. The adult has had years to develop their intellect, years to develop their body, and years to develop the way they speak. A child has not had that time to practice the things that are important to their natural growth. However, as they begin to think differently, they will begin to talk differently. As they grow up, they will begin to act differently. That is the natural process of growth.

What must you develop in order to put away childish things? The born again child of God must develop their spirit man! You don't grow up in the Spirit by developing your intellect. You don't grow up in the

Spirit by developing your body. In order to grow up into the salvation you've received, you're going to have to experience *spiritually* what a child experiences *naturally* in the growing up process.

What do you do to enable a child to grow up to be smart? You send them to school and fill their head with information.

What do you do to enable a child to grow up strong and not under nourished? You feed them. You educate their mind and feed their body because you want that child to grow! In the Kingdom of God, when you're born again, the only way to grow in God is to invest in your spirit man.

"When I was a child, I spake as a child, I understood as a child, I thought as a child; but when I became a man, I put away childish things." When we grow up in the Lord, we begin to separate ourselves from the thought-life and self-image of a child.

A child does not understand all of the things that an adult understands. As you grow up in God, you will begin to see who you are in the Lord. You will begin to understand what you stand for in God. As you grow, you will be able to walk away from childish things.

A child cannot be trusted with responsibility, but a grown-up can. The grown-up has practiced and demonstrated responsibility in the natural realm. Likewise, in the Kingdom of God, when we are grown up, we begin to demonstrate responsibility in the Spirit realm.

Responsibility In The Spirit Realm

God sees when our responsible spiritual posture is steadfast in Him. He knows when we have invested thoroughly in our spirit man. He can see when we have invested in our spirit by the anointing within.

Say this out loud:

The anointing teaches me how to be an adult and put away childish things!

When you're a child, your immune system is low. If you go out in the cold, you can get sick. Once you become an adult, your immune system has grown strong. When you're a child, you may fall and bruise your knee. When you're a grown up, if you fall as much as you did as a child, there's something wrong with you!

Spiritually speaking, when you first get saved, you get sick a lot. People will lay hands on you, and you will get healed. I have heard Christians say, *"I used to get healed right away when people would pray for me. Now, when people pray for me and lay hands on me, I just can't seem to get healed!"* That's because they were children and didn't have responsibility! God had allowed those who were stronger to bear their weaknesses. God will allow the strong to bear the burdens of the weak. The anointing that is in you must be given place, so that He can teach you how to grow up to be mature.

A mature child of God does not need the constant care that a child must have! *You* know your rights. *You* can stand on the Word. *You* can ask the Father and receive those things that you need!

A child needs an allowance, and their father gives it to them. They don't know what money is all about. They put it in their pocket, but their pocket has a hole in it, and they lose the money. The have no clue what happened to it! It's gone! They're irresponsible. They're a child.

When a child grows up, they become aware of the importance of money. They become someone who is responsible enough to take care of others.

How do you become a spiritually responsible person? The anointing within has to be given the opportunity to teach you how to be what God has called you to be.

The Sincere Milk of the Word

The problem in the Church world is that Saints have been told where they're going to go, but they haven't been taught what they should grow up to be.

The *anointing within* gives us an amazing potential in God. Very few people take the time to teach the fact that the anointing is working in us to make us like Jesus—in character, in nature and in thought life. They haven't told us that the mind of Christ is in the anointing within us! They haven't told us that the nature of Christ is in the anointing within us! They haven't told us that exceeding great and precious promises have been given so that we can have the divine nature of

God!

Once we know these things, we're on our way! We desire the sincere milk of the Word that we may grow thereby. We are growing by the anointing!

> *What is the milk of the Word?*
> The anointing!
>
> *What is the meat of the Word?*
> It is an anointed Word that carries a commission
> and a responsibility for the hearer.

When a newly saved baby Christian hears that they are supposed to live victoriously, the enemy will try to come in and bring condemnation because they're not able to do it. When a baby Christian hears that they're supposed to live above the circumstances of life, they will get mad because they're not able to live above the circumstances yet! If their pastor is the one that is preaching this to them, they will get mad at their pastor! When a baby Christian hears that their body is the temple of the Holy Ghost and that they can live without habits and bondages, they get condemned because they're still smoking cigarettes or marijuana. They get prayed for in church, but then they go out and do it again. Condemnation tries to come in.

Why does this happen? This happens because that baby is trying to run ahead of God! That baby is trying to eat meat! Meat is an anointed message that carries responsibility.

When babies use their diapers, you don't say to them, *"What's wrong with you kid? Don't you know that you're not supposed to do that?"* You simply change their diapers for them. They are babies! You give them milk and expect absolutely no responsibility on their part. The sincere milk of the Word is an anointed Word, free of charge, given to a child to grow thereby. It carries with it no responsibility for the hearer.

The Word That Carries Responsibility

When you begin to feed a child meat, you are giving that child an anointed Word that contains strength and nourishment. That word carries a responsibility with it. This is where the enemy tries to come in. He wants to give adults milk and feed babies meat.

A lady came to me one day and told me that I had laid hands on her and prayed for her. She had been addicted to cigarettes, but the power of God delivered her instantaneously. She said that she's never had a cigarette since!

Later, a man came to me and said, *"You laid hands on me and prayed for me to be delivered from cigarettes. I went home, but I began coming under condemnation because I couldn't quit smoking."* He told me that he prayed, *"God, you've helped me with my problem with drinking and my problems with dope and other things. Why can't you help me with cigarettes?"* In response, this is what he heard (the still, small voice), *"Who told you that I can't help you with cigarettes?"* He said that he's never had a cigarette since!

God had helped this man and delivered him when he was a baby Christian. As he grew, God gave him steak and said *"Eat! Eat and claim your deliverance through the Word of God!"* He didn't know how to do it, but the still, small voice—the anointing within—taught him. He discovered a revelation! When God said, *"Who told you I can't help you?"* He got a revelation. *"Well, of course! I'm a new creature in Christ and shouldn't be bound by anything!"* Immediately, the power of that thing broke off his life!

A Child Weaned

Milk is the anointing. It refreshes. It blesses, but it carries no responsibility to the hearer.

When we began our church, there was a great intensity, and excitement—a momentum that still continues today. After a time, the Spirit of the Lord spoke to me and said, *"There's going to be some sifting."*

The Lord told me ahead of time that there was going to be some sifting, and there was. We started out preaching the milk of the Word, saying, *"This is what God's going to do! This is where you're going in God! This is what is going to happen!"* There were absolutely no strings attached to that message. It was like a trumpet sounding, *"Let's go to war!"* It was a deep Word, and like the people following after Gideon, everyone joined in. However, when the battle came, suddenly people said, *"You mean there is a responsibility that I have to take?!"*

Once God told me about the sifting, I began to see Him shift what we needed to teach and preach. We didn't change our theological viewpoint; we just emphasized certain things a little more than others. *"We know God is going to do this, but if you don't do your part, God isn't going to do anything!"* All of a sudden, the babies said, *"Wait a minute! I want my bottle back!"*

It is abnormal for a baby to continue to be a baby. It's abnormal! It's also abnormal for an adult to live on a diet of milk! We must have more than milk. We must have meat with responsibility!

Connected To Purpose

We cannot learn to work with the Holy Ghost unless we learn to work with one another. We've got to fit as a hand in a glove. We've got to be fitly framed and joined together. This is part of doing the work of the ministry on behalf of God.

We are planted in the Church, *God's garden.* We fit in for a specific reason and we are supposed to unite with others in a complementary way. Our life is not independent from each other. You are not an island! We are all supposed to be a blessing to the work of God and to one another. Until we learn this and submit to it, we really cannot be Spirit-led in our individual lives.

The anointing that is in us will teach us two things:

1. To seek first the Kingdom of God and His righteousness *corporately*.
2. To seek first the Kingdom of God and His righteousness *individually*.

Why do people hop from church to church? In some cases, it's because they are searching for a place where God is moving. In other cases, it's because people will go where they are being told the good news. However, once the good news is followed by the responsibility, they shrink back. They don't understand the importance of taking responsibility for the Word that they hear. Instead, they get offended and march off to another church.

Say this:

> *Lord, tell me what you're going to do, and teach me what you want me to do about it. I am a responsible hearer of the Word.*

Without both parts, there's no covenant! Without a covenant, there's no reward or return on that covenant!

The Body of Christ is being led by the Spirit into God's Kingdom (God's will) *corporately* and *individually*. Both of these things are done by the Holy Spirit within.

The Part We Know

> **For now we see through a glass, darkly; but then face to face: now I know in part; but then shall I know even as also I am known. And now abideth faith, hope, charity, these three; but the greatest of these is charity.**
>
> **1 Corinthians 13:12-13 KJV**

When we get to Heaven we will see face-to-face. The Scripture is saying, *"Right now, in this earthly life, we have a limited measure of the unlimited gift that God will manifest in the next life."*

The Church has used this Scripture negatively. It's been used as an excuse. We've used it when we *didn't* know. We've said, *"Well, brother, we know in part,"* but what we really meant was, *"Don't ask me, because I don't know!"*

This Scripture is really saying, *"Almighty God knows everything, but in this life we will only know a part of that everything!"* If we knew everything, we wouldn't need to be introduced to one another. We'd know the name, the age, and the background of every person the way

God does. Now we know in part and prophesy in part, but there is a *part* we know.

How did we come to know the part we know? After we hear the truth, the anointing *within* will teach us the part that we need to know!

The anointing specializes in teaching you all things that pertain to life and godliness. It will teach you everything that you need to know in order to live victoriously! The Holy Ghost is committed to leading you into all truth.

Say this:

> *I believe that every revelation necessary to live for God, to prosper for God, and to succeed in God's Kingdom is laid out in the Word of God!*

We can live all of our life on Earth and not find out about what God has promised. The only way to get those promises out of our Bible and into our spirit, is to allow the anointing within to teach us what the Word of God is saying. The Spirit will teach us how to hear His voice.

Jesus said, *"My sheep hear my voice"* (John 10:27). This does not refer to the anointing *upon*. The moment you're born again, you have the ability to hear God's voice. The anointing *within* you will cause His voice to be heard by you. However, there are certain influences that will stop you from hearing God.

Have you ever been through spells when you couldn't hear God?

People wonder, *"How do you hear God? Why can't I hear God?"* There are very few teachers or preachers who will teach you how to hear God. Once in a while you'll hear a preacher share that one instance when they heard God's audible voice. A child of God, however, is not led by God's audible voice. If you were, you'd need to hear it every day! That's not hearing God! That's having a supernatural experience with God!

You can't live off your supernatural experiences with God. Rather, you must live off of the supernatural deposit that God has put in you by the anointing within. When you live off of that, you can hear God and be Spirit-led every day of your life!

The Bible says, *"For we walk by faith, not by sight"* (2 Corinthians 5:7). There are certain things, however, that will short-circuit or sever your spirit from the Spirit of God. There are things that will separate the two from flowing together. If this happens, you will have a hard time communicating with the Spirit of God.

"For now we see through a glass, darkly."
How do you see? We see by the anointing within.

What do you do when you are seeing through a glass darkly? You try your best to get a good glimpse of what's in that glass. You do that in your spiritual walk by syncing your spirit with the Spirit of God. You tune into God and tune out contrary influences.

Some people can't remember what they hear without writing it down. They should have their pens ready—not intellectually, but *spiritually*—to write down what God said. Some people can't write and listen at the same time. Instead, they should get their spirits so attentive that when they hear something, it gets deposited in them. There are even some people who can't remember what they heard after hearing it. If that's the case, they should buy the CD and continue putting it in their spirit!

Why do this? *"For now we see through a glass, darkly."*

If we saw the right way, then every time we would look in the mirror (the Word), we'd see something we hadn't seen before. Even if we are looking at the same Scripture, we would continue to see something we hadn't seen before.

As a matter of fact, the moment somebody becomes convinced that they're smarter than the Word, revelation knowledge stops flowing. The moment somebody believes that they know it already, then they are no longer looking. They're not even listening!

Have you ever tried to have a conversation with someone who wouldn't stop interrupting you? You couldn't even take a breath because they were ready to interrupt and tell you what they thought! A lot of times, you can get in a mode where you feel like you know it all. When this happens, you stop listening. Kenneth Hagin said it like this, *"After all, I know everything that I know."*

In other words, if I want to learn what I don't know, I've got to listen! I've got to listen to the Holy Ghost! Yet we pray, *"God, I'm going through this. God, I'm going through that."* He knows all that, and so do you! The moment a person forgets that God speaks by revelation knowledge through the anointing within, they hinder the anointing in their own lives.

God's Method For Victory

One time a preacher was talking to me about another preacher, saying, *"I think he's discouraged, because he's been pastoring that church for eighteen years. I think he's preached everything he knows about five times already, and it's time for him to go to another church."*

I just remained quiet, but on the inside I was thinking, *"My God! How can you preach everything you know?"* If I preached everything I knew, I'd go to where I got everything from and get a little more!" The Spirit of Wisdom and Revelation will reveal things to you!

We see through a glass darkly, *but we do see!*

Who is showing us? The anointing! The anointing will show you what you need to do in your life, but the anointing will not show you every little detail that you will go on in your life. If He did, you wouldn't walk by faith! You wouldn't need faith in the Earth realm because you would already know everything.

You need faith in the earth realm. It is the way you accomplish victories in God! You know what He accomplished for you and you receive it. Then you allow the anointing within you to show you the way.

Hath God Said?

People ask, *"If God is in control, then why am I going through this?"* They don't understand. You have to *know that you know* that you're walking with God.

I have heard people say, *"I had a vision, and God said this."* A month later, they're doing exactly the opposite of what they claimed that God said!

Of course, there are some things that are dependent upon decisions. For example, God can put two people together. He can speak to a young man and speak to a young girl and tell them to get married. He can tell them that they are the right ones for each other. Now, in that situation, you have two wills involved and God is *not* in sovereign control. If He were, He would have to force people to make the right decision!

Once those two people know God's will, they have to fight the enemy over the truth they heard by the Spirit. The enemy will try to come and steal that thing. If it falls apart, we can't go to them and say, *"I thought you said that God said you were supposed to marry that person!"* There are two wills involved!

We need to know how to be led by the Spirit, and the only way to do that is to *begin*—step by step. When you *know that you know* that the still, small voice has called you to be in a certain place, has called you to be a certain way, has called you to do a certain thing, then you will never turn from it.

You must never let go of the relationship that you have with the Spirit of God. There is no way to walk away from the anointing unless you *break fellowship* with the anointing. Once you break fellowship with the anointing, you get confused. You forget what God said!

The Law of Love

"And now abideth faith, hope, charity, these three; but the greatest of these is charity." In Paul's letter to the Ephesians he prays that we would be rooted and grounded in love and that we will know the love of Christ, which passes knowledge.

Why?
That we might be filled with all the fullness of God.

What is the fullness of God?
The anointing!

The Bible says that the *agape* love of God (that's the same as charity) has been shed in our heart by the Holy Ghost. It's the anointing that brought the love of God into our hearts.

What does that love do?
Love operates by faith. Faith works by love!

The New Testament is called the *Law of Love*. As a matter of fact, there are really only two commandments, as far as God's concerned. One is to love the Lord your God, and the other is to love your neighbor as yourself. That's the Law of Love.

God says, *"If you love your neighbor as yourself, then you're not going to cheat your neighbor, you're not going to stab your neighbor, you're not going to rob your neighbor, you're not going to covet what belongs to your neighbor!"* There are only two ways to sin—against God and against man, which is why you only need two commandments! If you love God, you won't sin against God. If you love man, you won't sin against man!

Love gives you the ability to walk without ought. When you walk without ought, you walk without condemnation. *Why?* It is because you have forgiven! Once you have forgiven, you can be forgiven. When you walk without condemnation, you have boldness toward God. When you have boldness, you have faith. Now your faith is working – *by love*.

Consistently Victorious

For the Kingdom of God is not eating and drinking, but righteousness and peace and joy in the Holy Spirit.

Romans 14:17

When are you righteous? Twenty-four hours a day.
When do you have peace? Twenty-four hours a day.
When do you have joy? Twenty-four hours a day!

Joy isn't just there when you're laughing in the Spirit. That's just a manifestation, or a revealing, of a joy that abides in you. You can, however, lose touch with that joy. You can get depressed and cry, *"Where is the joy?"* The Bible says, *"The joy of the Lord is your strength"* (Nehemiah 8:10).

Years ago, I was interning as a pastor in an Assemblies of God church. One day the worship leader stood up and said, *"The joy of the Lord is our strength. If we lose our joy who gets it?"* The whole congregation answered, *"The devil!"* Shocked, I rose up and said, *"Wait a minute! First of all, the devil cannot have the joy of the Lord. What's wrong with you, folks? Throw away that hymnal!"*

Can you imagine the devil with the joy of the Lord?

It's righteousness, peace, and joy *in the Holy Ghost!* You cannot lose the Holy Ghost, so you cannot lose the joy! You can, however, lose touch with the joy. When you lose touch with the joy, you lose touch with the strength. You lose touch with the anointing. You lose touch with the Holy Ghost within.

When the anointing comes upon a Church, some will respond to the anointing. They may weep, they may laugh, and they may begin to pray in tongues. The anointing that came upon them touched their spirit and released the anointing that is within them. Wells began to spring up and rivers began to flow out. The city of God was made glad by streams from the river of the Lord! They responded to the anointing that came upon them, *and a release came.*

Another type of person has seen it over and over again. They've become discouraged. They don't even care if they get delivered because they know that it won't stick. They come to church, and the anointing comes upon them. They're touched, but they don't respond to the anointing. They bask in it, it's touching them, it's affecting them, but for whatever reason, they don't respond to the anointing and allow the release to come.

Why is that? There may be condemnation in the background. There may be unforgiveness that has prevented them from having a permanent release. If they would allow the anointing in them to teach them, then they would walk in victory. They would walk in the liberty wherewith Christ has made them free!

The anointing within you will eventually make you a consistent victor if you never give up on it or become a victim of condemnation.

You'll become *consistently* victorious!

The God-Kind of Love

You can't give in the offering two times and say, *"I've given, and God hasn't blessed me."* You can't pray two times and say, *"I believed God, and God hasn't healed me."* You're trying to live off of the gift. You can't live like that!

The good news is this: you are growing up! Now God is saying to you, *"I'm not going to take that corporate anointing from you. Keep that—it should increase! I want you to not only let it bless you, but for you to keep it!"*

"That good thing which was committed unto thee," Paul said, *"keep by the Holy Ghost which dwelleth in us"* (2 Timothy 1:14 KJV). He's talking about the anointing within.

How did you receive that good thing? Through the corporate anointing.

How do you keep it? By the anointing within.

Faith, hope, and charity—the greatest of these is charity. Faith works by love. When you understand the love of Christ which passes knowledge and you're rooted and grounded in love, you will be filled with all of the fullness of God. As you operate in the love of God, you can operate in the faith of God.

I want you to say this:

> *I cannot manufacture the love of God. The Holy Ghost, the anointing, indwells me with the love of God. I cannot manufacture the faith of God, but the anointing within me, provides me with that faith!*

When the love of God has its way, it never fails. Without exception, love always causes faith to work! The God-kind of love will cause the God-kind of faith to spring into action.

Paul knew how it worked, and Paul was *highly* anointed. *"God wrought special miracles by the hands of Paul"* (Acts 19:11 KJV).

So what's the key, Paul? *"I am crucified with Christ."*

How often are you crucified, Paul? *"Daily!"*

If you say, *"Well, I'm crucified when that anointing comes upon me in church,"* then you're in trouble! If the corporate anointing is what brings you to your decisions, you're in trouble!

"No! I'm crucified daily!"

How do you do it, Paul? *"I reckon myself dead"* (Romans 6).

In other words, I'm not carrying some cross of treacherous hurts and wounds. I'm not going through the land talking about how I'm "suffering for the Lord." I die daily by simply saying, *"I'm crucified!"* I make a decision: *"I am crucified with Christ; nevertheless I live; yet not I, but Christ liveth in me".*

What does Christ mean? *"Nevertheless I live. Yet not I, but the Anointed One, or the anointing, lives in me. And the life that I now live in the body, I live by the faith of the Son of God who loved me and gave Himself for me" (Galatians 2:20).*

When you're dead to sin and you have a revelation of that truth, *you love God*. When you're dead to sin and you know it's the truth, *you love man*. When you know it's the Anointed One living in you, you cash in on the love of the Anointed One. The love of the Anointed One causes the faith of the Anointed One to work!

It is no wonder that Jesus said, *"Have the God-kind of faith!"* and then went on to say, *"Whosoever shall say unto this mountain, 'Be thou removed and be thou cast into the sea;' and shall not doubt in his heart..."* (Mark 11:22-23 KJV).

Who is it that does not doubt?
The one who is filled with all the fullness of God!

Who is filled with all the fullness of God?
The one who is rooted and grounded in love.

What would bring doubt?
Violating the Law of Love.

You will know if you've been walking with the Lord. You will know if you've been putting the anointing to work. You will know if you've been forgiving others. Jesus said, *"When you stand praying, forgive! Forgive so that your Father will forgive you your trespasses also."*

Do you want to be highly anointed and move mountains? There

are certain miracles that will not happen unless a person meets God's spiritual criteria.

What did Paul do? He died daily. He let the Anointed One live in him, and as he did this, he was Spirit-led. Paul learned to be content in whatever state he was in. He knew what was of the devil and he didn't let it overcome him. He resisted the thing—*he stood firm*—he did what he needed to do as a mature Christian. As a result of his obedience, the anointing within him had His perfect work. That anointing increased to bear witness to his Christ-like lifestyle.

The anointing will bear witness of the Word: *"...the Lord working with them, and confirming the Word with signs following"* (Mark 16:20 KJV). We tend to assume that this Scripture only refers to the preaching of the Word. To a certain extent it means that, but it also includes the Word living in the person preaching the Word! The Holy Ghost is bearing witness that Jesus is living in that person and that it's the anointing teaching through him.

Fear Stops Faith

If our spirits are developed by the Holy Ghost, we won't have to worry about being seduced by a cult leader. It's *amazing* to me how much fear is in the Church world, especially in this area! We know that people think like that because they're bound up and don't know the first thing about the Spirit of God.

Think about it: the fear of Satan doing miracles. *Fear of Satan doing miracles!* It would take someone who is spiritually dead on the inside not to recognize the difference between a Holy Ghost miracle, a Holy Ghost manifestation, and a demonic manifestation!

In order for me to start mistaking the devil for God, I would have to spite to the Spirit of grace. I would have to consider the blood of the covenant that I was washed with as an unholy thing! I would have to walk *so far away* from the cross, the Holy Ghost, and the Word of God, that I would have frustrated the Spirit of Grace. If that had been the case, I would have been given over to a reprobate mind before I—a child of the Living God, full of the Holy Ghost—could mistake the devil for God!

Why would the devil spread that lie? The moment you have fear or doubt operating in your life, your faith is short-circuited. It's stopped and the anointing is limited from teaching you what the anointing wants to teach you!

Living in the Supernatural

> **Not that we are sufficient of ourselves to think any thing as of ourselves; but our sufficiency is of God who also hath made us able ministers of the new testament; not of the letter, but of the Spirit; for the letter killeth, but the Spirit giveth life. But if the ministration of death, written and engraven in stones, was glorious, so that the children of Israel could not steadfastly behold the face of Moses for the glory of his countenance; which glory was to be done away. How shall not the ministration of the spirit be rather glorious? For if the ministration of condemnation be glory, much more doth the ministration of righteousness exceed in glory.**
>
> **2 Corinthians 3:5-9 KJV**

You are a minister in your own right. You are called to do some service for the Lord. As a matter of fact, your life on Earth is a service to God, and your identity through Christ is to give honor and glory to God. When people see who you are in Christ, it ought to bring God glory!

The Apostle Paul says we have *not* received the ministry of the letter. We're not called to teach people simple principles or religious principles. We're called to be ministers of the new covenant. The Bible calls it ministers of the Spirit—*ministers of the anointing*. It's not of the letter, we're ministers of the Spirit!

In order for you and I to do service unto God, we must be acquainted with the deposit He put in our spirit man. We must let it have its full and total reign. As believers, we have to develop this spiritual deposit and serve God through it. Once we do, then the supernatural will be a natural part of our daily lives!

Miracles come and go. Miracles are here and there, but the supernatural never goes away! You can live above the circumstances of life all of the time. That's supernatural! No one could do it under the Old Covenant, but you can keep the devil out of your life every day. No one could do that under the law, but you can live by faith, not by sight, every day. That's a provision of the New Covenant.

It's a supernatural union with God! The Bible calls it, *"Walking in the light as He is in the light."* No one could do that under the Old Covenant, but today through the anointing, we can walk in the light as He is in the light!

Say this:

> *I need to develop my spirit man. Only the anointing, which teaches me all things, will reveal the message of the Word to my spirit and develop my spirit.*

What about praying in tongues? The Bible teaches, *"He that speaketh in an unknown tongue edifieth himself"* (1 Corinthians 14:4 KJV).

Somebody reading this book may have thought, *"You keep quoting that same Scripture! I already know that one."* Yes, but *you're* not praying in tongues! You see, until you are praying in tongues, you don't *know* that Scripture! Knowing the Word is an *experiential knowledge.* Until you catch yourself talking under your breath in tongues or waking up at night praying in tongues, then you don't *know* that Scripture!

Paul said, *"My spirit prayeth, but my understanding is unfruitful"* (1 Corinthians 14:14 KJV). His *spirit* prayeth!

Have you heard the statement, *"I gave him a piece of my mind?"* How does someone do that? It's easy: their mind talked out of their mouth. Have you heard the saying, *"The first thing on my mind?"* The first thing on your mind *speaks* out of your mouth. If your mind can speak out of your mouth, then *why don't we let our spirit speak out of our mouth?* When our spirit prays, both our understanding and our mind are unfruitful!

Lay hands on yourself and say this:

The anointing in me will teach me, in my spirit, how to grow and how to know the things of the Spirit of God. When the anointing within grows, the anointing upon will function! I won't be in victory only when there is a manifestation or when there's a corporate anointing, but twenty-four hours a day I'll be in victory, in Jesus' name. Thank you, Jesus!

Chapter 11

Yielding to the Anointing

As we invest in the anointing that is in us, yield to Him, listen to Him, let Him teach us—our spirit man will grow, prosper and shine.

I want to teach you how to be yielded to the anointing on the inside so that you can be Spirit led in your Christian life.

> **Who also hath made us able ministers of the New Testament; not of the letter, but of the Spirit; for the letter killeth, but the Spirit giveth life.**
>
> **2 Corinthians 3:6 KJV**

Paul said that we are ministers of the Spirit. This New Covenant is a spiritual covenant. We're not ministers of the dead letter that kills. We are ministers of a Spirit that gives life! Jesus said, *"The words I speak unto you, they are spirit, and they are life"* (John 6:63).

The anointing of God is in our spirit. Therefore, we need to be diligent about guarding our spirit because it's going to spring forth with life. It is a wellspring of life. It's where the issues of life come from. This life is the divine life of God.

The Bible said that our spirit man is the lamp of the Lord. The Holy Ghost brings the light of God's Word to us. The power of God's Spirit, the anointing, the provisions of God through Christ, come into our spirit by the Holy Ghost. Jesus said, *"The Words that I speak unto you are life."* As we put God's living Word in our heart (our spirit) then the Spirit of God (the life of God) will be alive in our spirit man!

We can be filled with God's living Word!
We can be sensitive to the Spirit of God in our spirit!

Let There Be Light!

The Bible said that there is a glory to the Old Testament and there is a glory to the New Testament. It teaches that the Old Testament is the ministration of death. The Old Testament told us what to do. It laid down the law and outlined what we were guilty of. Under the Law, we were all worthy of death. The letter kills because it proves that you cannot do what you're called to do!

Say this:

Not by might, or by power, but it's by the Spirit of the Lord!

Religious people today will put condemnation on you because of the letter, when in reality, keeping the letter condemns you to die! If legalism could save you, everyone in the Old Testament would have gotten saved. Only the Spirit of God and the residency of the Lord Jesus Christ can redeem you from the curse of the law.

The Old Testament was written on stones, (the Ten Commandments) and it was glorious. The children of Israel couldn't look at the countenance of Moses because of the glory.

> **But if the ministration of death, written and engraven in stones, was glorious, so that the children of Israel could not steadfastly behold the face of Moses for the glory of his countenance; which glory was to be done away.**
>
> **2 Corinthians 3:7 KJV**

In other words, from the beginning, God planned that the Old Testament would be a temporary shadow of things to come.

Then it continues,

> **How shall not the ministration of the spirit be rather glorious? For if the ministration of condemnation be glory, much more doth the ministration of righteousness exceed in glory.**
>
> 2 Corinthians 3:9 KJV

Do you know any New Testament believers that don't have the glory? It's not a mental glory. It's not a natural glory. This glory is only dependent upon *you* walking in the anointing *within*. It's dependent upon you walking in the spirit. That walk will bring the glory, the light, the life, and the power into your spirit man. Your spirit man is the lamp of the Lord!

The House of God's Glory

Some of our lamps are lit up a lot stronger than others! When you pray in an unknown tongue, your spirit prays, and you are edified (built up). Paul prayed that God would strengthen you with might by His Spirit in your inner man. *That means there were some Christians who could have used more strength in their spirit man by the Spirit of God.* As we invest in the anointing that is in us, yield to Him, listen to Him, let Him teach us—our spirit man will grow, prosper and shine. It will be the house of God's glory in us!

The New Testament reveals that there are measures of the anointing that are available to us. Some New Testament believers are living under Old Testament principles. They have been told that once you get saved, *that's it.*

You have to grow in that anointing! People wonder, *"What's wrong with me? Why can't I think right? Why can't I do what's right? Why can't I make the right decisions? Something must be wrong with me!"* No, there's nothing wrong with you mentally. There's nothing wrong with you physically. There is, however, something temporarily wrong with the strength of your spirit man. That situation will be rectified the moment you yield your spirit to *the anointing in you* and begin to pray!

Your spirit is born again, but the strength available to your spirit is made available by the Holy Ghost or the anointing of God. God wants you to develop your spiritual strength. Praying with an unknown tongue—which causes your spirit to pray—will build you up. It will strengthen you spiritually. If there is a lot of light in your spirit, there will be a lot of revelation. God brings revelation to your spirit man because it's pertinent to life and godliness. It's pertinent to spiritual things.

The anointing has the capacity to teach you spiritual things. It will teach you. You are going to hear God about direction in life. You are going to hear God about godliness. You are going to hear God about the life you should live in Christ Jesus. The Word of God and the mind of Christ are going to live to you by revelation knowledge in your spirit. Through the agency of the anointing, the wisdom of God will come alive to you.

Say this:

> *The wisdom of God doesn't live in my head; it lives in my spirit by the Spirit of God.*

Seeing Past the Veil

> **Seeing then that we have such hope, we use great plainness of speech; and not as Moses, which put a veil over his face, that the children of Israel could not steadfastly look to the end of that which is abolished.**
>
> **2 Corinthians 3:12-13 KJV**

In other words, even that which was abolished, that which was to be done away with, was so glorious that it scared the children of Israel.

They were afraid to look at it! Through the New Covenant, we have a kind of hope that gives us great plainness of speech, or boldness in our supernatural speech.

> **But their minds were blinded; for until this day remaineth the same veil untaken away in the reading of the Old Testament; which veil is done away in Christ.**
>
> **2 Corinthians 3:14 KJV**

The Bible said that their minds are still blinded because the same veil operates on their spiritual perception. It covers their mind and stops them from seeing clearly. It blinds them every time they read the New Testament.

This doesn't mean that when you read the Old Testament there's a veil on *your* mind. When you read the Old Testament, you read it from a position of already being a partaker of Christ. Christ is already with you. The Spirit of wisdom and revelation will enable you to see the Old Testament through the light of God's glory. The anointing within you will rightly divide what the Word is saying to you. The people referenced in the Scripture above don't have Christ. They don't have the mind of Christ. When they looked at the Old Testament, instead of recognizing it as a shadow of things to come, they staggered at the letter of the Word. They didn't have that Holy Ghost relationship available to them. They didn't have the Holy Ghost supernaturally enabling the Word to live in them.

"*…Which veil is done away in Christ.*" It didn't say, "*Which veil is done away in Christianity.*" I know a lot of Christians with a veil, but the veil is done away in Christ. Christ is the Anointed One and the anointing. The only way for the veil to be taken away is when the anointing, causes the things of God to live. Then your spirit is no longer blinded. It sees. Your spirit perceives and your spirit gets a hold of exactly what the Lord Jesus is all about. Jesus said, "*When the Spirit of truth is come, He will take of Mine and show it unto you.*" The veil is done away in Christ.

Blinded By the Shadow

When they looked to the Old Covenant there was a veil and they were blinded.

What were they blinded by? They were blinded by the shadow of things to come. Instead of recognizing their Redeemer, they were blinded by their attempts to try to do the law. Once a person receives the Redeemer, the anointing in Jesus will take away the veil! It will remove the shadow.

Someone said, *"I don't agree with that; I just think that when you become a Christian there isn't a veil on you anymore."* That's not true. There are Christians who read the Bible, but don't see that it is God's will to heal. There are Christians who don't believe that a Christian is the righteousness of God in Christ Jesus. There are Christians who don't believe that they are holy. There are Christians who don't even believe that God's will is to prosper the believer.

What's wrong with them? They have a veil upon their heart regarding these subjects.

Who put the veil over them? The god of this world blinds the minds of those who don't believe. Once they believe, the bondage is broken.

They cannot believe what they cannot see, and they cannot see a thing without the anointing! Neither can you! They should take a Bible School course at the International Miracle Institute and allow the Holy Ghost to show them some of the things they're blinded to! Like a friend of mine says, *"Not only do the believers need equipping, but the preachers need equipping!"* We don't have it all, but we are on a divine pursuit to allow the Holy Ghost and the anointing to teach us about everything that we do not see, as of yet, in the Word of God!

In order for someone to become a Christian, they need to have a revelation of salvation. In order for them to become Spirit-filled, they need to have a revelation of the Holy Ghost. Someone could live twenty years saying, *"The Holy Ghost is not for today,"* and then look at the Bible one day and say, *"My God! It's in there! How did I miss it?"* The veil was taken away because the anointing in them went to work. They listened to the Word and the anointing in them brought a right division of the Word. The Word lived, they believed God, and they got filled with the Holy Ghost.

What if someone was sick for twenty years and was dying, and didn't believe healing was for them? What if one day they read, *"What things soever you desire when you pray, believe that you receive, and you shall have them"* (Mark 11:23-24 KJV). For two decades that had been taught that it's not the will of God to heal them, but suddenly, the anointing in them causes the veil to be taken away. They receive the revelation and live!

When the anointing is in motion, and received into your heart, then revelation knowledge will come. Otherwise you will try to get the answer *intellectually*. You will try to get the answer naturally, but you won't get a thing because it's by the Spirit of the Lord. The Bible didn't say, *"When they turned to Christianity, the veil was done away."* No, the veil is done away *in* Christ!

Qualifying For Greatness

"But even unto this day, when Moses is read, the veil is upon their heart" (2 Corinthians 3:15 KJV).

What is their heart? It's their spirit.

There is not an anointing available in Moses to take the veil away. You can read the New Testament through eyes of legalism, through eyes of self-righteousness, through eyes of religious tradition, through eyes of unbelief, and it will not take the veil away. The only way for the veil to be removed is for the anointing to have its way in the lives of people. As a matter of fact, no one can even come to Jesus without the anointing.

Jesus told the Pharisees, *"Don't murmur among yourselves! No man can come to Me except the Father draw him."* How does God draw people? By the Holy Ghost! You cannot even come to Jesus without the Holy Ghost. You cannot be chosen by God without developing a relationship with the Holy Ghost. I didn't say that you cannot be *called* by God. I said that you can't be *chosen* until you develop that dependency upon the Spirit.

Many are called, but few are chosen.

Why are few chosen? The answer is simply that few will do what

Elisha did with Elijah. Now Elisha was *called* when Elijah threw his mantle on him. Elisha, however, wasn't *chosen* until he continued to walk with the anointing, learn from the anointing, and observe the anointing. His consistency and faithfulness qualified him to have his own mantle (or his own anointing) for service. God is looking for a person that can qualify for responsibility.

How many of you would hire a babysitter that had been arrested nine times for kidnapping children? That person may be called to be a babysitter, but they won't be chosen to be a babysitter by anyone in their right mind! By the same token, God may *call* you to the ministry, but if you develop a consistent pattern of doing it your way rather than the Holy Ghost's way, you won't be *chosen*. You are going to have to start all over again and develop a relationship with the Holy Spirit. God is not trying to hold something back from us! He wants us to realize the fullness of our call, but if we're not Spirit-led, we will become a casualty.

You can't be Spirit-led by the *gift*. I know people that can have a word of knowledge so accurate it would boggle your mind. The power of God operates in them strongly. However, they have *not* chosen to allow the Spirit of God to cause the Word of God to live to them. They have *not* chosen to be *led* by the anointing. They have the power demonstration, they have the manifestation of the Spirit, *but they have not developed that qualifying element for responsibility in their life.* They're not responsibly walking the Spirit-led lifestyle.

What is the Spirit-led lifestyle? It's walking by faith. It's walking in communion with the Spirit of God in you. It's walking attentive to the voice of the Lord, the anointing of the Lord, and the power of God. When it's time to forgive someone, you forgive them. When you're tempted to have ought against someone, you resist. When you want to say, *"I'll never have anything to do with them again!"* you don't. Instead, you sit down and take a deep breath, and the anointing will talk to you. Then you will change your mind because you are yielded to that anointing. You cannot walk on your own and qualify for greatness in the Kingdom of God.

Seeing Through the Light

The veil is done away in Christ.

Nevertheless when it shall turn to the Lord (speaking of Israel). the veil shall be taken away. Now the Lord is that Spirit.

2 Corinthians 3:4

This Scripture is saying, *"When Israel turns to the Spirit...."*

It takes hard work to be an unbeliever in the cross of Calvary. He's ready to move! If there has been a seed sown in someone's life, the Holy Ghost will move to convict them and turn them to Christ. After Jesus died, the Holy Spirit moved into the earth realm to lead people to Christ! In reading Moses, there was a veil. There was no anointing. The veil, however, is done away with in Christ. When Israel turns to the Lord, the veil will be taken away.

Now the Lord is that Spirit, the Lord is that anointing, and where the Spirit of the Lord is there is liberty. *Where there's a veil, there's bondage.* Some people can't get over the veil of women cutting their hair. They see a woman on the platform with short hair and say, *"You're going to Hell! Everybody here is Hell bound!"* That person may have gifts operating in their ministry. They may have manifestations of the Holy Ghost, and some may say, *"They're anointed!"*

There may be an anointing *upon* their life, but the anointing *within*, which they ought to live by, is being neglected. No one could read the New Testament and get that messed up unless they were ignoring the person that was sent to reveal the New Testament. They are doing their own interpreting! They think they are smart; but they're not. You cannot understand the Word of God without the light that the Lord sent to reveal the Word. That light is the Spirit of God.

Some people can't get over the veil of women in the ministry. They say, *"Well, I just don't believe women should be in the ministry!"*

Have they asked the Holy Ghost what He thinks about it?

One time Jesus knelt down and wrote on the ground. When He was finished He looked up and said, *"I have no problem with you stoning her. I just want the person without sin to throw the first stone."*

Jesus spoke by the anointing. The Holy Ghost went to work.

Bondage in the Veil

When there's a veil, there's bondage. There's no liberty. *How do you know when someone is not operating in the liberty of Christ?* They have no joy. I've seen whole congregations like that. When there is bondage, the anointing is hindered. Not only is the anointing *within* not free, but the anointing *among* is not welcomed. Jesus said, *"You will go into some cities, and they won't receive you. They won't receive you! If you go into a house and they receive you, then go ahead and do what God has called you to do!"*

What causes people to reject the anointing? The veil! If they are blinded to a truth, they'll misinterpret that truth. One time I was in a meeting, and my wife, Robin, got drunk in the Spirit. She started laughing hysterically. People all over the church were getting drunk in the Spirit. After the service, a man came up to her (I wasn't there) and said, *"I just believe we should be reverent when we're in the presence of God. I don't think this laughter should be allowed!"*

She just laughed at him. That man had a veil.

What does the veil do? The veil causes the letter to live and the anointing to wane, or to become unimportant. When the letter lives, religion says, *"Bless God! We're going to have order in this church!"* You can have order but end up in Hell! However, if the Holy Ghost is flowing in the church, even if you have a service out of order, you will still leave *free*! The Church has had the whole thing mixed up! Christians have thought that if one day there was just *too* much anointing, that God would be mad. That lying doctrine has produced dead churches where the anointing is not free to do anything. They are thinking, *"We're safe now."* Meanwhile, the people are in bondage.

The veil comes as a by-product of breaking fellowship with the Lord. It comes when a Christian ignores the anointing on the inside.

They ignore prayer and they ignore the mind of Christ. The veil comes when a Christian takes the helm of their life and begins to do it on their own. Traditions of men blind them to spiritual truth. When the veil comes upon a heart, there comes sorrow. Joy leaves and the anointing is not free to work. Bondage operates, and the Christian can't be Spirit-led. Confusion comes, but the Bible said that God is not the author of confusion. You cannot operate in union with the Spirit of God and be in confusion.

Liberated From Spiritual Blindness

> **Now the Lord is that Spirit (the Spirit of God's anointing); and where the Spirit of the Lord is, there is liberty.**
>
> **2 Corinthians 3:17 KJV**

This can also be interpreted, *"Where the Spirit is Lord, there is liberty."* He is in you, and if you let Him be *Lord*, then there is liberty. There will be liberty in your heart and liberty in your life. There is liberty to say, *"Yes, Lord."* There is liberty to be led by the Spirit. There is liberty to see clearly. You are liberated from spiritual blindness. You are liberated from not knowing and from being ignorant.

Why? The anointing in you teaches you all the things that you need to know!

You are liberated from a limited, human mind-set. You are liberated by the supernatural mind-set of Christ. This miracle takes place through the anointing. Where the Spirit is Lord, the veil is taken away! In your heart there is liberty. That liberty is liberation from striving to do it yourself and then miserably failing. Now, *you can believe it and do it.* It's liberation from not seeing the truth. Now, you see the truth by the anointing. The anointing will take your *humanity* and link it with His *divinity!* The anointing will provide you with the element that you can't manufacture.

If divine wisdom was attainable by man, then unregenerate man would have had divine wisdom long ago. Man, however, can't obtain divine wisdom. We can only have the wisdom of God through the anointing! The Bible said, *"If any man lack wisdom, let him ask of God and not doubt, and God will give it to him"* (James 1:5). How is this done? *By the anointing!*

You could not attain this wisdom on your own. This wisdom *only* comes by the anointing. Through the anointing, God will show you things that you would have never dreamed of knowing. He's going to show them to you, and you're going to know them! It's that easy! Wherever the Spirit is Lord, the veil is removed! When I look at the Word in faith, it's going to leap off of the page! That Word is going to talk to me because there is no veil! The Spirit of God is going to speak to me and I am going to be changed!

Fearless Heart, Open Face

> **Now the Lord is that Spirit; and where the Spirit of the Lord is, there is liberty. But we all, with open face beholding as in a glass the glory of the Lord, are changed into the same image from glory to glory, even as by the Spirit of the Lord. Therefore seeing we have this ministry, as we have received mercy, we faint not.**
>
> **2 Corinthians 3:17-18, 4:1 KJV**

What is an open face? This is not our physical or our natural face. This is the face of the heart.

Where's the veil? The veil is on the heart. It's anywhere that there is a letter that kills rather than a Spirit that gives life. It is everywhere the Spirit is *not* Lord. It is where there is no liberty. Remember: Where the Spirit is Lord, there is liberty. When the veil is taken away, we have an open face and our heart is absolutely unafraid. There is no veil to cover us from the glory because of fear. We're not afraid of the glory.

The Spirit giveth life. When the anointing goes to work in our heart, there is therefore now no condemnation for those who are in Christ Jesus. There is no condemnation for those who walk, not after the flesh, but after the Spirit. There's no condemnation because there's no veil. There's no fear. It's taken away. Our heart is in communion with God, *face-to-face*. Without fear, our heart is saying, *"Show me a little more!"*

The religious mind looks at us and says, *"Heretics! Hyper-faith! Cult!"* The religious mind is stupid because it can never know truth! It's trying to, but it can't know the truth without the anointing. With an open face, we are beholding the truth. Our heart is open. Our heart is beholding as in a mirror the glory, or the light, of the Lord. I'm not afraid of the light because the light of God's Word is going to shine on the tablets of my heart. It's going to change me from glory to glory by the Spirit of the Lord—by the anointing within.

The anointing *within* will set you free so that you can see the Word. Then the anointing *within* will change you into what God has called you to be!

The Veil of Condemnation

When the veil is taken away from your heart, *you can see!* The veil stops your heart from beholding the glory of the Lord with an open face.

Let me give you an example. A person was in prayer one day and decided, *"God, I'm just going to wait on You. I'm not going to be moved by the circumstance. I believe You are with me. I believe You'll never leave me and now I believe you're going to reveal to me what I need to know. I'm not going to make any moves in the natural until I have the witness of the Spirit."* They prayed, but then anxiety came because the situation demanded, *"You had better do something about me now!"* They responded to the pressure by saying, *"Alright! I'll move on it now!"* and subconsciously, *they put up a veil.*

Why did they put up a veil? A veil went up because their heart condemned them! They knew *subconsciously* that they were messing up. As a result, they don't even want to hear God. They are afraid that God will say, *"Stop doing what you're doing to solve the problem."* They put up a veil of separation between themselves and the anointing. God didn't tell them to go that direction in the first place. Anxiety brought the veil. It's easier to correct a situation like that in the beginning, than to try to pick up the pieces later. If a person keeps going on like that, they will end up far away from the will of God.

Jesus said, *"Take no anxious thought,"* and, *"Let not your heart be troubled."* What was He talking about? Your spirit man will not benefit from the anointing of God within when anxiety begins to infiltrate your heart. *Why?* The anointing cannot be Lord when anxiety is being lord. *Whatever you're moved by is who you're listening to.*

You are learning about the still, small voice. *Whatever you're moved by is what you're listening to.*

Living Off of the Anointing Within

Now where the Spirit of God is Lord, there is total liberty. Where the anointing is having its way, there is freedom. Anxiety, doubt, and fear are reasons that the veil comes. Hurts and wounds are others. People get hurt, and they put up a veil on their heart. You go to minister to them, but they never open up to you. You go to lay hands on them, but they never let the anointing come in. It just bounces off of them.

They do the same thing with God. They won't open up to God because, if they do, the anointing will set them free. The anointing will deliver them. They're afraid to open up because they won't have a wall. If they don't have a wall, they won't have defenses. They are carnal Christians with absolutely none of the benefits that come to a spiritual being. Their spirit man is weak and emaciated because he has come under the siege of the bondage of the veil! They won't look in, and they're not going to let anyone else look in either. *The veil has separated them from the anointing within.*

If they are a minister, they may flow in the gifts of the Spirit, and the power of God may fall. However, after ministering in the pulpit, they *come down* from that anointing *upon*. When the anointing upon them is not in operation, they will go back into daily life and succumb to depression. There's no consistency in their lives. A lot of preachers have a strong anointing in the pulpit, but they don't have a strong anointing in their daily life. In daily life, people have to live off of the anointing *within*.

You get high in the pulpit during services! I'm sure the worship team does, too! The anointing will even get the congregation high!

You'll feel really good for a day or two. However, if you don't develop your spirit man, you're liable to come down and be depressed. You'll wonder what is wrong. The enemy tells people, *"The reason why you're depressed is because you're in that church!"* He'll take them to a dead church, and of course, they don't get high while they're in the service, so they don't come down in their daily life! They think that everything is solved, but in reality, they just hit ground zero.

What's the solution? Build up your spirit man and the anointing within! Then when you come down off the high of the corporate anointing, you can click right into the anointing that's on the inside of you. There will be no dive; you'll just shift sources! You'll let the anointing within go to work because the anointing *within* is for your daily life. The anointing *upon* is equipment so that you can do what you're called to do!

Glory: The Source of Strength

"Therefore seeing we have this ministry, as we have received mercy, we faint not" (2 Corinthians 4:1 KJV). That means we don't faint!

Wait a minute, Paul! Aren't you the man who said, *"Everybody sinned. The letter killeth. No one does good, no not one. All have sinned and come short of the glory of God. All our righteous is as filthy rags?"*

How do you receive mercy? When the anointing reveals to you that mercy is available, then you receive mercy. You receive pardon. Paul was saying, *"We know how we received pardon. Now we're going to keep the pardon we received through the power that provided the pardon for us!"* We keep from fainting by keeping the anointing within us—*working!"*

When does a person faint? A person will only faint when he tries to do it himself. He won't faint when he does it in the anointing! We've received mercy, and we faint not. That means we keep the anointing that's in us flowing. We look to God with a heart that is open and are changed from glory to glory. We keep flowing in that. We keep the source of strength, the liberty that's in us, in the right perspective.

People who didn't have an understanding of the whole counsel of God have said, *"We can't do anything. We're not holy. We're not righteous. We're incapable."* They have misinterpreted the Word to mean something that it doesn't.

The anointing is provided, through Christ in us, to give us something that we can't manufacture. We can't produce the wisdom of God! If we think hard, we can come up with some clever ideas. However, as long as we are coming up with them, it's not the wisdom of God!

If you let the anointing flow, you will come up with things! You'll see things and know things that you could have never imagined. That's the anointing flowing through you.

What are those things for? So that you can be what you could have never been. In other words, even when we try our best to be like Jesus, we can't. If we yield to the Holy Ghost, we will! That nature is only available to us through the anointing that Jesus sent to live in our spirit. When we say, *"We can do all things!"* we're talking about *through the anointing* because it's Christ who strengthens us. The Church is not a group of failures! The Church is a group of winners! We win by the anointing! Glory is our strength.

When Paul said, *"We faint not,"* he was saying, *"We don't try to do it without the anointing."* We can't earn mercy. We receive mercy. If we receive mercy, and mercy is unmerited favor, then why can't we receive transformation into Christ-likeness? The Bible says that God predestined us to it—so it's available! We can't earn it, but we can receive it by grace through faith.

Considering Him: The Rest Dimension

"...As we have received mercy, we faint not." Where do you faint? In your mind, or in your heart. We're going to use them interchangeably. *"For consider him who endured such contradiction of sinners against himself, lest ye be wearied and faint in your minds"* (Hebrews 12:3 KJV).

Why would your mind faint? It will faint if the veil creeps back in and separates you from seeing with an open face. When that happens, it will hinder the Word from talking to you through the anointing. Weariness will come into your life and you will faint.

How did this start? It started in your *mind*. It started in your *heart*. It started in your *soul realm*, because the Spirit was not able to bring the light of God's Word to it. The Spirit was not able to bring the light into your mind so that strength would come.

The anointing was short-circuited somewhere.

How? By not considering Him!

Who is He? The Word. He is the anointing. When you stop considering Him, you cut yourself off from the source of strength. You become weary.

> **Even the youths shall faint and be weary, And the young men shall utterly fall, But those who wait on the Lord shall renew their strength; They shall mount up with wings like eagles, They shall run and not be weary, They shall walk and not faint.**
>
> **Isaiah 40:30-31**

How do you wait on the Lord? With an open face. The Spirit of God in your spirit renews your strength by the anointing. You mount up spiritually like an eagle, and you are able to run and not be weary. You're able to walk and not faint. It is something that belongs to every believer, and every one of us has the ability to walk into it.

The problem is that many of us are trying to do it right, but we're failing. The Bible tells us to enter into His rest. *Enter into His rest.* When you get into it, suddenly, things are easy! The glory flows, the faith abides, and the goodness of God lives in you by the anointing! *That's the rest dimension.*

When I preach, I know that the Lord is talking to people's spirits. I also know that there will be people in the congregation who will try to get a hold of it in their head, but their mind will resist the wisdom of God! They are trying to get a hold of God *intellectually*.

Entering into His rest is coming to a place in God, in the Spirit, in the anointing, where you can receive what you are trying to get a hold of. You know that your flesh can't manufacture it, that your mind can't dream it up and that you can't earn it. However, you know that it's done and that it belongs to you! So you just lift your heart, lift your hands and receive it! You *receive* mercy!

What happens then? You don't faint! You *keep* knowing that you didn't earn it, that you can't manufacture it, and that you can't perform it. Then you keep receiving it and continue operating in it.

Peace That Passes Understanding

> **Be careful for nothing; but in everything by prayer and supplication with thanksgiving let your request be made known unto God. And the peace of God, which passeth all understanding, shall keep your hearts and minds through Christ Jesus.**
>
> **Philippians 4:6-7 KJV**

Don't be anxious. Be careful, or full of anxiety, about *nothing—nothing at all!*

The Word says, *"Trust in the Lord with all thine heart; and lean not unto thine own understanding. In all thy ways acknowledge him, and he shall direct your path"* (Proverbs 3:5-6 KJV). When it said, *"Trust in the Lord with all of your heart,"* it wasn't saying, *"Trust in the Lord in Heaven, who is sovereignly moving people like puppets."* No, it was saying, *"Trust in the Lord in here with all your heart, and lean not unto your own natural, human understanding—but in all your spiritual ways acknowledge Him."*

What will He do when you do this?

"He will direct your paths."

How is He going to direct your paths? Are you going to hear a booming voice from Heaven? No—He's going to speak by the still, small voice. He's going to guide you in your spirit! He's going to direct your paths! That is His covenant with you, and He will do it because He lives in you. However, you are going to have to do some things—one of them is to be anxious, or full of anxiety, *about nothing!*

"Consider him who endured…lest ye be wearied." Weariness is the product of anxiety. Weariness is the product of fear. *"Let us not be weary in well doing"* (Galatians 6:9). Weariness is the by-product of

looking at what you've been doing and getting tired of doing it! You may be tired of doing it because you've been doing it without the refreshing of the Holy Spirit. You may have been doing it without the leading, without the witness, without *knowing* that it's a spiritual service. Anxiety will wear you out. Spiritually speaking, it will cause you to faint. However, if we have received mercy, we do one thing: we faint not. *We don't faint!*

Paul is saying, *"Listen! Do not be full of anxiety about anything, but in everything, with prayer and supplication with thanksgiving, let your request be made known to God."* The Wuest translation says it like this: *"Stop worrying about even one thing, but in everything by prayer whose essence is that of worship and devotion..."*

Do you know what prayer is? Prayer has its essence in worship and devotion! *How did Jesus say we should worship?* He said, *"God is Spirit. They that worship Him must worship Him in Spirit and in Truth."*

Chapter 12

Power for the Hour

In this final bow, when we die to the natural ways, it is going to create more damage in the kingdom of darkness than all of the preceding generations of Church history.

This is an hour of opportunity. God has not called us to be passive. God has not called us to be inactive. God has called us to shine. God has called us to glow. God has called us to reach out and touch the environment, touch the people around us, and touch the world with the power of the Good News of Jesus Christ.

I believe that the Church should be the head and not the tail. I believe that the Church should be going over and not going under. I believe that, as a believer in these times, God has placed before you an open door. Only pessimism, doubt, unbelief, and inconsistency can keep you out of the blessings and the rewards that God has placed in you.

Those who have dared to rise up and embrace the Word of God like never before are going to see the blessing of God unfold in their life. Others around you will become envious of what the Spirit of the Lord is doing in you and through you.

You can plug into a time table in God that will forever remove you from an inconsistent walk. You don't have to be a yoyo for Jesus. You don't have to ride a roller coaster in God. You don't have to zigzag in the Holy Ghost. You can be on your way somewhere in God and maintain consistency and victory everyday of your life.

The Countdown Has Started

There is power for this hour. You don't need power yesterday. You don't need power tomorrow. Tomorrow will take care of itself. You need power for *today*! God is calling us to maintain our God given ability to have the anointing of the Lord present in our lives.

The line of separation between the mediocre believer and the tenacious believer is going to become clearer. It's going to be visible for all to see. *Brother Couldn't-Care-Less* and *Sister Half-Committed* are going to be revealed for who they are. I believe that God is going to raise up an army that is ready to run the race set before them—*ready* to take Jesus at His Word. This is an army of those who are fed up with religion, fed up with tradition and fed up with unbelief. They are fed up with allowing the devil to steal their rights and privileges in God. God is raising up an army who will speak the Word of God with boldness. God, in turn, will hasten over His Word to perform it.

There are many people in the world who become envious and angry when they see a child of God overwhelmed with divine blessings. They stand and wait, hoping for something bad to happen to me—but it doesn't matter what happens to me. No weapon formed against me shall prosper, and every tongue that rises against me in judgment will *I* condemn! I'm blessed in my going out and blessed in my coming in. This is *your* confession.

The only thing that I care about is pleasing and magnifying God. I'm not going to be slack about His promises. I'm not going to wake up one day and say, *"I was anointed last night."* No! I need power for the hour, and so do you. We're not going to be able to cruise along the way some people did in previous decades. The countdown has begun. Soon, and very soon, Jesus is going to blow that trumpet!

Before He does this, His enemies will be made His footstool. I believe that the Church is going to demonstrate to everyone that it's not a conservative party that's going to do it. It's not a religious order that's going to do it. It's not grandma or grandpa that's going to do it. It's not some narrow-minded bigot that's going to do it. It's not going to be a black person. It's not going to be a white person. It's going to be a Holy Ghost person—anointed by God to heal the sick, raise the dead and cast out devils!

God has called us to raise you up. However, you have a responsibility. You have a role to play in order that you might fulfill your divine call. You cannot forget your responsibility! You need to press in for the power for the hour!

Rights and Responsibilities

"But my horn shalt thou exalt like the horn of an unicorn; I shall be anointed with fresh oil" (Psalm 92:10). The horn is the word *qeren*, which means *strength, honor, victory*. The fresh oil is dunamis. It's the anointing. It's the power of the Holy Ghost fresh on you for today. The horn is a symbol of position. It shows the type of an animal and the strength of that animal.

Jesus gave us *exousia*, which is authority. Authority is not dependent upon how you feel. You can get up feeling as if you've been run over by a truck, but that doesn't mean you don't have authority. You're still a believer. You're still on top. You're still a winner. You're saved, even when you don't feel saved. You're full of the Holy Ghost, even when you don't feel like praying in the Holy Ghost. You're more than a conqueror, even when you don't feel like a conqueror. Your victory is not dependent upon your achievement! Your victory is dependent upon what Jesus has already accomplished on your behalf!

Exousia is the right, the privilege, and the jurisdiction to do something and to be someone. It is within your jurisdiction to prosper. It is your right to walk in divine health. It is your right to walk in victory. It is your right to see your husband or your wife saved, your children grow up to serve God, and your life to continue to magnify Jesus. These things are your God given right. However, just because you have rights and privileges does not mean you're enforcing them. There is a thief that goes about to steal what you have.

The psalmist said, *"You're going to take my horn, and you're going to exalt it."* Jesus has exalted you and me. The Bible said that He has glorified us. He has exalted us. He has caused us to sit with Him in heavenly places. We are authoritative, Word-believing men and women who cannot fail if we hold on to the helm of Calvary.

Anointed With Fresh Oil

The psalmist spoke of something *beyond* authority. In your daily life you're going to need something more than the exousia. Jesus told the disciples to tarry in the city of Jerusalem until they were endued with *dunamis*—the power, the fresh oil, the anointing. The Bible says that you are filled with the Spirit. He gave you His Holy Ghost when you believed in Jesus, and then the promise of the Spirit became yours. It became within your jurisdiction, it became your right to receive the Holy Spirit. You believed and you received, and you began to speak with other tongues as the Spirit of God gave you utterance. That is the baptism with the Holy Ghost, with the evidence of speaking with other tongues.

God says:

> *Don't just live relying on memory. I want you to be anointed with fresh oil every day. I want you to have power for the hour! I don't want you to walk down and out one day and up and coming another. I don't want you to come to Church and shout on Sunday and go home and weep on Monday. I want you to be consistent. I want you to be tenacious. I want you to be mobile, active, strong and bold, and the only way to do it is to be anointed with fresh oil!*

The psalmist said that it's within our jurisdiction to be anointed with fresh oil. Fresh oil is the Spirit of the Lord coming upon a person. The book of Acts tells us that when they whipped the Church, when they beat the believer, when they rebuked them and told them, *"Don't preach in Jesus' name!"* the Church rallied together. It didn't talk about how to leave town; it talked about how it was going to preach *more* boldly! They said, *"God, grant that, in the name of your Son Jesus, signs and wonders would be wrought. Give us the ability to articulate with boldness—the goodness you've given to us!"* and the Holy Ghost came upon them. Fresh oil came, and the building they were in shook. Men and women were filled with the Holy Ghost and spoke the Word of God with boldness!

Holy Ghost Energy

In the Old Testament there was a judge whom God raised up,

by the name of Samson. The Spirit of the Lord came upon Samson consistently and enabled him to do certain things that a natural, human person is not capable of doing. When you're full of the Holy Ghost and walking with fresh oil, you'll be able to do things natural humans can't do. You're liable to run on Holy Ghost energy!

At eighty years old, Dr. Lester Sumrall was burning out at least four young men every year! He would hire them, and they'd burn out because they couldn't keep up with the man! He was running on Holy Ghost energy! He wasn't relying on yesterday's power. He was living in the now! *Today* is the day that the Lord has made! He rejoiced and was glad in it, and fresh oil came upon him and enabled him to do what God had called him to do.

If you're going to be what God has called you to be, you are going to have to tune into and plug into the superhuman ability that the Holy Ghost makes available. That means you're going to have to pray a little bit stronger than, *"Yabba dabba doo. Amen. I'm filled with the Holy Ghost. Shaka taka…zzzzzz…,"* and fall asleep praying. A person like that doesn't only need fresh oil, they need a change of oil!

Sanctified Unto God

Samson was a judge called to govern in the house of the Lord. He was raised up by God. As a matter of fact, the angel of the Lord went to his mother and told her, *"You're going to have a son. He will be a Nazarite, born unto God. Don't cut his hair; don't let a blade touch his hair. He's going to grow up, and he won't touch the unclean things. He won't touch a dead body. He won't drink the fruit of the vine. He's going to be separated unto the Lord. He is called to be sanctified, to work and to minister."*

I believe that *you* have been called to be sanctified! I don't believe sanctification belongs to the preacher only. People point the finger at preachers and say, *"What about preacher 'So and So' who fell into adultery?"* I say, *"What about YOU?"* Sanctification belongs in the pulpit and in the pew. It belongs in every Christian's life.

It's not a religious sanctification. That's an ugly sanctification! When religion tries to sanctify you, it just makes you ugly! When God sanctifies you, He beautifies you! He beautifies the meek with salvation. Religion will try to take away your deodorant, take away your cologne, take away your makeup (that's just for the women!), but none of that will sanctify you. Furthermore, it *definitely* won't make people more receptive to the message that you have to offer! When Jesus Christ anoints you with fresh oil from Heaven, you don't have to dress a certain way. You don't have to act in a certain religious mode. The Holy Ghost enables you to have fun in Jesus and live right for God! Your steps are directed by the Lord.

You're called to be sanctified and separated. In this day that we're living in, we're going to realize more and more that you can't be separated without Holy Ghost power. It doesn't matter what you know intellectually. It doesn't matter who you knew growing up or what kind of upbringing you had.

The world itself has become an open door to satanic forces. The medium of television, the medium of radio, and the advertisement industry, by and large, are dominated by satanic forces. These forces try to infiltrate the minds of people and even try to turn the believer away from the path that is straight and the gate that is narrow.

The Bible says, *"Be not conformed to this world; but be ye transformed by the renewing of your mind"* (Romans 12:2). This is not talking about an intellectual renewing. It's talking about a Holy Ghost affirmation, a Holy Ghost remembrance, a Holy Ghost activation, a Holy Ghost washing *every day* in God. When you stir up the gift of God in you, the Holy Ghost comes upon you, and your mind is changed. You become a Nazarite unto God. People will tempt you saying, *"You can do that and get away with it,"* but you will say, *"Yes, I know I can, but I don't want to because the Holy Ghost has called me to live a life that is pleasing unto the Lord."*

The Lion's Last Roar

The Bible says that Samson began to grow. He grew up into the kind of man that made God happy and blessed people. However, there were certain things that began to manifest in his life. Some of those very things are manifesting today in the lives of contemporary believers.

Samson was out walking one day, and a young lion roared at him.

The Bible said that the Spirit of the Lord came upon him. It didn't say, *"The concordance fell on his head."* No! The Spirit of the Lord came upon him!

You need the Spirit of the Lord in your life. You need the Spirit of the Lord to come upon you to give you the ability to answer questions the right way. When you visit your relatives, you need the Holy Ghost to come upon you and put a Word in your mouth that will go beyond their barriers and reach into their hearts to touch them. You need the Holy Ghost! Religion is not going to help you; only God can.

The Holy Ghost came upon Samson, and do you know what he did? He grabbed that young lion, without a weapon, and ripped it apart! He tore the lion and killed it! He did this with his bare hands.

The Bible says, *"Be sober, be vigilant; because your adversary the devil, as a roaring lion, walketh about, seeking whom he may devour"* (1 Peter 5:8). Most Christians run from the devil. They cry tearfully, *"You don't understand! We're getting evicted! Oh, we're going to go to jail! We're going to die sick!"* Somebody has been roaring at them, and they believed it!

You need the Spirit of the Lord to come upon you! When the devil says, *"You're going to die and not live,"* you need the anointing to come upon you so that you can say, *"I've got power for the hour, devil! I'm not planning to die. I'm not planning to live in failure. I'm not planning to backslide. I'm not planning to quit. I'm not planning to starve. I've got the Holy Ghost!"*

The Spirit of the Lord came upon Samson, and he grabbed that lion! You can imagine the last thought that lion had. You're a lion. You're used to people responding to you in a particular way. Normally, you roar and they run! That's the natural order. This time, you roar, and he grabs you! You think, *"Is this my last roar?"* Samson ripped that lion in half and killed him!

The devil is seeking whom he may devour. He ought to avoid you and he will, on the days you're anointed. The solution is, *stay anointed!* Walk in the Spirit, and you won't fulfill the lusts of the flesh. Walk in the Spirit! You'll stay strong. You'll stay bold. You'll stay powerful. You'll stay on top.

One Foot in Compromise

Samson went over to the Philistines. He said, *"Dad, I want to marry a Philistine."* He wanted one foot in Holy Ghost power and one foot in compromise. That's like some powerless Christians today: *"Well, you know, Brother, I read two verses yesterday."* That person might be able to rip a *kitty* in half—*if they meet it in daytime!* God forbid that it meows at them at night!

Samson said, *"I want to marry a Philistine girl."* They brought thirty Philistines to him, and he put forth a riddle to them. Why? It's because he had walked back to the carcass of the lion he had killed and found bees in the carcass making honey. He said to himself, *"I know I'm a Nazarite. I know I'm not supposed to touch a dead thing—but there's honey!"* Then he reached in and got some honey. He also brought some to his mother and father. He brought them honey from the carcass of the dead animal, which typified sin.

"Well, Brother, you don't understand," they say. *"It's sanctified money!"* and they're dealing drugs! It's drug money! *"But I'm tithing on it,"* they explain. (You'd be surprised the way the mind works when it's not washed with the Word of God!)

Samson gave his mother and father the honey but didn't tell them where it came from. He was thinking that he was very smart. So he went to some Philistines and gave them a riddle. *"Thirty changes of garment if you can tell me what this means: 'Out of the eater came forth food.'"* They didn't know what it meant. They wondered, *"What in the world is he talking about? He's crazy!"* They went to his wife (she was called his wife, but they were just engaged) and said, *"You'd better find out what he's talking about!"* So his wife asked him the meaning of the riddle. He told her the answer, and she then went and revealed the answer to the Philistines.

Christians think that they will always be able to get away with compromise. *"But I'm still anointed,"* they think. Likewise, the Spirit of the Lord was *still* coming on Samson, and he was testifying.

When he saw the men again, they were able to tell him the meaning of his riddle. He got mad and went out and killed thirty Philistines! He took their garments and gave them to the men who had answered his riddle.

You can begin to see a pattern developing in Samson's life. It's as if he's *playing* with the anointing. He was thinking, *"I've got the anointing. It's working. Now, let's forget about the things that I'm commanded to be separated from."*

Let me break it down to you.

Christians say, *"I know I ought to be in prayer, but the Lord understands. I know I ought to be in the Word, but the Lord knows. I know I ought not to lose my temper and cuss my wife (or my husband) out, but the Lord knows. I know I shouldn't lie but it's just a little white lie. Besides, I come to Church and I'm anointed!"*

You can see these patterns in Samson's life.

Superhuman Strength

Samson's father-in-law took Samson's wife to be and gave her to somebody else. Samson went down to Gaza and found a harlot and stayed with her. Then the Philistines from Gaza came out and waited for him at midnight, and to spite them, Samson rose up and ran off with the city gates! Do you think the Spirit of the Lord had come upon him? Power for the hour was working with this man, even though he was messing up! Aren't you glad God is gracious?

Has God been gracious to you?

Samson got up at midnight, came out of the harlot's house, and grabbed the city gates. He picked them up, post and all, and ran off with them! That was superhuman. That's not natural; that's abnormal! When you're anointed by the Holy Ghost, you're abnormal! Where everyone else gives out, when everyone else gives in, *you pick up!* There ought to be certain elements working in your life that are superhuman! God will give you the ability to make the right business decisions. He will give you wisdom. He will give you the supernatural knowledge to be able to detect who's who in the Kingdom of God. You ought to know who the wolves are and who the sheep are. You should not be a gullible. You should not be easily deceived.

When the Spirit of the Lord comes on you, you will have power for the hour! God will begin to reveal things to you. The power gifts will work in you. The revelation gifts will work in you. The utterance gifts will work in you. When you are anointed by the Holy Ghost, you won't say, *"Oh, I don't know."* You won't avoid answering someone because you're intimidated. The power of God will come on you, and you'll tell people the truth in love. It will convict them. It will convert them. It will deliver them.

There will be a power working in you *for today*. Your witness will never be a memory. You'll never have to rely on the testimony of two days ago or of two months ago. People come to me all the time saying things like, *"I remember…,"* or *"Years ago, I had this wonderful encounter with Jesus…,"* or *"Things used to be better, a while back."* You don't have to live like that when the Spirit of the Lord is available to you now!

You can have power for the hour!

Grace Period

Samson got up in a time of compromise. It was a grace period.

Aren't you glad there's a grace period?

This is where the devil gets people. They think, *"Well, I'm still anointed."* What they don't realize is it's a grace period. The Spirit of the Lord came upon him, and he got up and ran off with the city gates. Then he found a woman named Delilah, and fell in love with her. The Philistines came to Delilah and said, *"We're going to give you silver—a lot of it—if you will find out from this man what the source of his power is."*

Today, when you find Christians blessed and ask them, *"Why are you so rich? What is the source of your wealth?"* many will answer, *"Well, you know, I'm intelligent. I'm educated. I made the right business moves."* As a believer in God, there is something you need to know—the sooner you know it, the happier you'll be. If you are going to get anything in God, it should be the result of the power of God coming upon you and enabling you. You need to cherish that and know that it's the reason for your anointing.

The reason for Samson's anointing, the symbol of his separation, was that he had never cut his hair. In other words, his identity was determined since childhood. He was a Nazarite.

Do you know that God predestined you to be confirmed to the image of his dear Son? When you were born again your identity was set in motion. You became a believer. You became heaven bound. It's a birthright you received, just as Samson the Nazarite received a birthright. Up until that time he had not tampered with his identity, but He tampered with his function.

Have you ever said, *"Well, I know I'm not what I ought to be."* In other words, you haven't tampered with your identity; you've tampered with your function. Your function has come short of your identity.

Thank God for the grace! As long as you are believing, as long as you are striving, as long as you are not intending to blatantly violate your function, God will enable you to live the way He called you to live. You'll be the good example that you should be for the Lord Jesus Christ.

Tampering With Identity

Delilah came to him and asked, *"Samson, what's the secret of your power?"* He answered, *"Tie me with some thread that has never been used, green thread, and I'll be weak, like any other man."*

Say this out loud, *"I'm not like any body else!"* There was one thing that would have made Samson like any other man: *tampering with his identity.* It would have made him weak. When a Christian tampers with their identity, they let go of their authority.

If a Christian says, *"I'm a sinner,"* when the Bible says that they're a Saint, they're tampering with their identity. If a Christian says, *"I'm sick,"* when the Bible says that they're healed, they're tampering with their identity. If a Christian says, *"I can't,"* when the Bible says that they can do all things through Christ, they're tampering with their identity. If a Christian says, *"I'm poor,"* when the Bible says that they're rich, they're tampering with their identity. Through their own confession, they take the source of strength out of their life. They become weak, like anybody else. Show me a Christian who is murmuring and complaining, and I'll show you someone who is living just like the world without the power of God.

So she tied him up with green cords, and he went to sleep. At night, she said, *"The Philistines are upon you, Samson!"* Samson shook himself, and the thread broke. Then she said, *"You deceived me! You lied to me! What's the secret?"* He said, *"Tie me with ropes that have never been used."* She tied him again and said to him, *"The Philistines are upon you, Samson!"* and he shook himself and broke the ropes. The Spirit of the Lord was upon him! He had power for the hour. However, do you know what Samson was doing? He was flirting with danger. He was seeing how far he could go. The issue, the thing that the devil was after, was the very identity he possessed as a Nazarite.

The Bible said, *"You gave My Nazarite wine to drink and commanded My prophets, saying, 'Prophesy not!'"*

When we came to this city we realized we had met a religious devil. It was as if that religious spirit in the atmosphere was saying, *"Shut up! Leave us alone! We've had a nice little religion going for us."* The devil did not *just* start commanding the prophets to shut up and to not prophesy. He's been doing it for many, many years! However, Jesus Christ defeated him two thousand years ago!

We're going to prophesy over this city, this nation and the world! We're going to prophesy over the churches! We're going to prophesy over the Christians! Revival is going to hit like a whirlwind! There will be a fire of revival in the land! Schools will be caught up with rapture, when men, women, and young children walk in there full of the anointing of God! God is going to raise up an army of believers that know their identity in God. Now, you may be part of that army, or you may be a bystander. The choice is yours.

Do you want to be part of it?

Flirting With Danger

"Tie me!" he said. The Spirit of the Lord came on Samson, and he ripped those ropes, like putting fire to dry twigs.

Superhuman!
Anointed!

People have been telling us for years now, *"Slow down, my brother!*

There's no way humanly possible for someone to do what you are doing!" That's right, but we're not trying to do it in a human way! We believe for power of the hour! We walk in it, we contend for it, and we thank God for it!

He broke the ropes. Delilah said, *"You lied to me again, didn't you? Tell me, please, the secret of your power!"* So he said, *"If you tie my hair...."* (It's getting closer to the truth, isn't it?)

The Bible tells us to be doers of the Word and not hearers only, deceiving ourselves. You're not deceiving Delilah! You're not deceiving the Philistines! If you're *not* a doer of the Word, it doesn't matter how much you act like you are. You're deceiving no one but *yourself!* Samson got into self-deception. He thought, *"I'll never tell. I'll never backslide!"* Christians say, *"I'll never leave Church! I'll never fall away!"*

"Just tie the seven locks of my hair," he told her. She tied them and hooked them to the beam. He was asleep. She said that the Philistines were upon him. Samson woke up, and the Spirit of the Lord came on him. He still hadn't tampered with his identity, but he was very close to it. Fresh oil came on him, and he shook himself, jumped up, and the beam was ripped! There was nothing wrong with the man. He was full of strength.

Once again Delilah said, *"Tell me! Tell me! You've been lying to me!"*

Samson answered, *"If you shave my hair I'll become weak, like any other man."*

Church, you should know what makes you weak like any other man. Don't allow it! You should know! You don't have to go down to the level of the *human*, the *mere mortal*, gossiping, fighting, and splitting up. You don't have to get on the level of griping, complaining, and talking against the promises of God. You don't have to get on the pessimistic level that the world lives on. You ought to know what makes you weak. You are called to separate yourself from it in order to maintain fresh oil.

I want you to lay hands on yourself right now and say this:

> *I need fresh oil! I need power for the hour! I know I have the Holy Ghost, but I need a stirring! I need an infilling! I need a refill in my life daily to maintain strength for victorious living!*

The Day When You Pay

You know the story. Samson said, *"I have never touched my identity. I have never shaved my head."* The Philistines brought in a barber and gave Samson a haircut! Delilah said, *"The Philistines are upon you!"* He woke up, and out of the mouth of God's champion, you heard the words of presumption spoken. At no other time did you hear it.

He said, *"I will go out and shake myself as before."*

And she said, "The Philistines are upon you, Samson!" So he awoke from his sleep, and said, "I will go out as before, at other times, and shake myself free!" But he did not know that the Lord had departed from him.

Judges 16:20

You come to Church. You get used to a routine. You lift your hands, like you did before. You sing the nice little charismatic song, like you did before. You think, *"That's good,"* and you think, *"That's okay,"* but you did not know that the Spirit of the Lord had departed. You're not aware of the fact that yesterday's anointing was fresh, but today your heart is somewhere else, your mind is somewhere else, and you're just going through the motions! It's easy to get into that rut, isn't it?

"I'll go out and shake myself as before!"

Presumption! He went out only to realize one thing: *there's a day when you have to pay.*

Do you hear?

The Bible says that we wrestle not against flesh and blood but against principalities and powers. If anybody is to be embarrassed, it should be the devil. It shouldn't be an embarrassed Christian saying, "I'm sorry! I didn't live the way I know I'm empowered to live!"

The devil should be embarrassed because he cannot penetrate the shield of fresh anointing that the Christian is maintaining in their life daily! You can do that easily. You can do that easily if you let the Word of God live in your life! The Bible says that you will keep yourself, and that wicked one will not be able to touch you!

Death at Delilah's House

They took Samson.
They blinded him.
They bound him up.

Do you think the devil wants you bound?

They bound up Samson and put him to work, spinning around a mill. The devil is a taskmaster. He doesn't want the Christian working for God. He wants the Christian working for him. He wants the Christian bound up, spinning around a mill, going nowhere in life, wandering in the desert, never getting to the promise land. That's what the devil can do when the anointing lifts off of a person's life.

Why would a person walk dry and parched?
Why would their life have no anointing?

Some people go to dead churches and won't leave the dead church! They say, *"Auntie Bertha goes there. My friends are all there."* That's a high price to pay for a nice haircut! *"But, you know, I just can't leave because everyone there is depending on me."* It's social-level Christianity. For some people, it's their friends: *"Well, I'm trying to minister to them. I'm trying bring them up to my level."* (Samson was trying to minister to Delilah!) They end up reaping something they are not called to reap.

Somebody said, *"But you're too intense! You don't understand! What danger could there be in going to the wrong church?"* It could mean life or death when you're dealing with principalities and powers. When you get sick and people tell you, *"It might be God's will, in order to teach you something,"* you're not going to be able to run to me and get a "nice little sermon from Dr. Christian Harfouche" as an antidote for *all* of the unbelief you've been fed from the pulpit. No, if you stick it out at a dead church, you will pay a big price and get nothing in return.

What in the world did Samson gain that could have been equivalent to what he lost when he got that haircut? He got embarrassed. He got defeated. He got bound up. He got put where he didn't want to be. Imagine a man, who ripped a lion in half and ran off with the city gates, coming out there to shake himself! All he did was shake.

People come to church and shake a little, but there's nothing in it. They left the power at Delilah's house! Got a haircut in the wrong barber shop!

Samson: A Type of the Church

> **Then Samson called to the Lord, saying, "O Lord God, remember me, I pray! Strengthen me, I pray, just this once, O God, that I may with one blow take vengeance on the Philistines for my two eyes!" And Samson took hold of the two middle pillars which supported the temple, and he braced himself against them, one on his right and the other on his left. Then Samson said, "Let me die with the Philistines!" And he pushed with all his might, and the temple fell on the lords and all the people who were in it. So the dead that he killed at his death were more than he had killed in his life.**
>
> **Judges 16:28-30**

They took Samson, put him in the house of Dagon, their god, and were going to mock him. The Bible says in verse twenty-two, *"Howbeit the hair of his head began to grow again after he was shaven."* They went to mock Samson, but his identity was coming back to him. The only thing they were able to take away from him was his natural sight. In a way, they did him a favor, because he could no longer see Delilah, the harlot. He couldn't see the Philistines. As his hair began to grow, His identity began to return. His mind began to focus on things that were primary, that were significant, that were priority, and his heart began to turn to God and to cry out. He turned to the throne of God and said, *"God, strengthen your servant once more."*

The name *Samson* means *sunlight*. The name *Delilah* means *languishing, lacking alertness, melancholy*. The Holy Ghost spoke to me out of the book of Judges about Samson. He said that he is a type of the church. The way Samson was prophesied about, the Church was prophesied about. Samson was foretold about by an angel; the Church was foretold about by prophets. Samson was born to be separated to God; the Church was born to be separated unto God, sanctified and ready for His use. Samson grew up ready to do what God had called him to do; the Church was born into the Kingdom for such an hour as this.

The lion—the devil—roared against the early Church, but it grabbed it and ripped it in half. The Philistines—the hosts of darkness—came against the early Church, but the Church, by the Holy Ghost, picked up the jawbone of an ass and killed the Philistines left and right. It won Jerusalem. It reached the nations of the Earth. They put the Church in jail, but instead of it staying bound, the Church shook itself. Paul and Silas began to pray and sing praises unto God. The Holy Ghost came upon them, and the thing that had bound them broke right off. The Church had not violated its identity—its hair was uncut. It had not violated its separation and sanctification unto the Lord. It walked in victory. The Church walked in the anointing!

Delilah, the Harlot of Religion

All of a sudden, the sunlight—the Church called to shine the light of the Son—met the melancholy Delilah. *Who's Delilah?* Delilah is the harlot of religion. When the devil could not stop the anointing of the believer, he said, *"Let's do this. Let's take the statues, the idols, of the goddess Diana. Let's take the idols of the Greeks, the idols of the heathen, and let's give them saints' names."* The Church fell in love with recognition. The Church said, *"We've been on the wrong side of the tracks too long. We need to be recognized! We need the right kind of bride."* The Church got together with Delilah. The Church got together with religion. We call it the "Dark Ages." Samson went through some dark ages, too. They took both of his eyes!

What was so dark about the Dark Ages? They took the Word of God, the Bible, and shut it in libraries. They shut it in vaults, and the average believer could not see. They took the eyes away from the Church! Delilah was the one that was responsible. She even has some churches around the world today. If *you* go to one of them, you need to get out of there! Delilah is still in business.

They took the eyes away from believers. They couldn't read the Word of God. They bound up the believer. They couldn't quote Scripture and didn't know their authority. They tampered with the believer's identity.

However, one day, Martin Luther read a Scripture, *"The just shall live by faith."* When he read it became, *"Howbeit the hair of his head began to grow again after he was shaved."* Martin Luther read, *"The just shall live by faith,"* and the Church's identity—its shaven hair—started growing again! Its strength started coming back again!

The devil wants to put the Church of Jesus Christ in the house of Dagon. He wants to mock the Church. He wants to take away its ability to see the promises of God's Word. He wants to rob you from the ability to do what God has called you to do. However, the moment your hair begins to grow, the moment the Word begins to work, the moment your identity begins to return, your heart will turn to God.

The Final Blow

Samson, *the sunlight,* cried out to God.

Today the Church is crying out to God. Samson said, *"Let me die with the Philistines!"* When you die to Delilah, when you die to the Philistines, when you die to religion, when you die to the world, when you die to the human way, when you die to the flesh, when you die to the natural, you will kill *in that death* more of the enemy than you could have ever killed in your own ability or might! The Church of Jesus Christ is about to get a hold of the pillars that are holding up the house of Satan, and with one final blow, we're going to launch an attack on the kingdom of darkness.

I'm going to die to limits!
I'm going to die to mediocrity!
I'm going to die to doubt and unbelief!
I'm going to die to Delilah!
I'm going to die to religion!
I'm going to die to fear!
I'm going to die to intimidation!
I'm going to die to man's opinion!
I'm going to die to man's belief!
I'm going to die to man's tradition!
I'm going to die to what you think!
I'm going to die to what the world has to say!

In that death, the Philistines are going to die! When you die to your fear, that devil of lack in your life is going to be buried under the rubble! He's going to be buried!

Samson pushed those pillars down, and down came the house of Dagon. The Bible said, *"at his death."* You can't offend a dead man. Somebody said, *"Well, I would like Dr. Harfouche if he just stopped shouting."* Who cares who you like? Go down the road and have a conference with Delilah! I don't care what you think! I'm dead! Every day I am going to say, *"In my death today, strengthen your servant. Give me fresh oil, fresh anointing, fresh ability today!"*

We're going to reach out to the highways and the byways. We're going to break the power of the devil off the lives of people. We're going to set the captives free. We're going to see men and women rise up to be everything God has called them to be. We're not going to walk around a millstone! Our hair is growing!

God's Champions: The Final Bow

"Strengthen your servant once more," he prayed. Fresh oil came upon Samson, and that last embarrassment was erased forever. In the eleventh chapter of the book of Hebrews, Samson is mentioned among the champions of faith! He erased his embarrassment! He did more in that final act then he had ever done before. He killed

thirty Philistines—that was thirty-fold. He killed a thousand with the jawbone of an ass—that was sixty-fold, but in his death was the hundred-fold. At his death he erased *everything* that the devil had branded on his life.

That's what the Church is going to do! Every embarrassment the Church of Jesus Christ experienced in the Dark Ages because of a lack of knowledge is going to be erased in this final hour. Even in the last century, the Church was mocked because Pentecostals didn't know how to operate in the Holy Ghost. They rolled in the aisles, and people said that they were wigged out and crazy. The Church was mocked because Charismatics went overboard with the tambourines and the banners. The Church was mocked when preachers fell into sin and bowed the knee to the enemy. All of those things are going to be erased in this final hour.

God will take the early, and God will take the latter. He's the Alpha and the Omega. This thing started with power. Peter preached and thousands were added to the Church in one day. That was the early rain, and the latter rain is coming. When the latter rain comes, God will not only give us the latter rain. He'll give us the early rain and the latter rain in the first month. When we get to eternity, the Apostle Paul will say, *"Tell us your testimony!"*

We are in the final hour. We are at the closing part. We are the ones entrusted with holding the pillars that hold up the house. God said to Jesus, *"Sit down on my right hand until I make your enemies your footstool."*

How are you going to do it, Father?

I'm going to give them an identity. I'm going to grow their hair. I'm going to return their strength to them. They will know their authority. They will bind, and it will be bound. They will loose, and it will be loosed. They will resist the devil, and he will flee. They will stand, and nothing will prevail against them. They will get a hold of one pillar of the house of Dagon with their one side and the other pillar with their other side!

The Bible says that Samson bowed himself with all his might. We're going to bow! We're going to bow to the King of Kings and the Lord of Lords. We're going to bow with Holy Ghost power! Before, when we shouted and shook, there was nothing there. In this final bow, however, when we die to the natural ways, it is going to create more damage in the kingdom of darkness than all of the preceding generations of Church history.

Strengthen Your Servant Once More

You have a mission! You have a role to play in the destruction of the house of Dagon.

You are part of the Body of Christ! You are bone of His bone and flesh of His flesh! We're going to get a hold of that pillar, that traditional lukewarm Delilah. The Bible said that on the day of Pentecost, when they were all speaking with other tongues, Jews, Egyptians, Arabs, Greeks, and people from every nation came to see what was happening and asked, *"Aren't they all Galileans? How come they're acting and talking the way we do? They don't understand our culture."*

When you get full of the Holy Ghost, your culture goes out the window!

You need deliverance from melancholy Delilah. Religion is melancholy, but we are going to get a hold of that pillar. It holds up the house of the enemy, and we're going to say, *"God, strengthen your servant, once more. Strengthen us once a day."* That's power for the hour! Paul said, *"I die daily."* Everyday we're going to bow. Every day when we get up, the Dagon is going to wonder, *"Are they going to bow again today?"* Yes!

You will destroy more when you take your hands off of it than you did when you were trying to do it yourself. Just let go and let God; and you'll see the house of poverty fall. Let go and let God; and you'll see the house of sickness fall. Let go and let God; and you'll see the house of failure fall. *BOOM!* Just take a little bow!

Chapter 13

Possessing Supernatural Power

If you find yourself gravitating toward something because it has some kind of mysterious element about it, rebuke yourself! The supernatural of God is not mysterious!

Possessing supernatural power and putting it to work in my life is the fire that burns on the inside of me! I am tired of seeing the world delve into the occult. I am tired of seeing the world deceived by the enemy as if there is no *real* power in God.

As I travel around the world, I run into Christians everywhere who are living beneath their privileges. They are forfeiting their divine rights, leaving their responsibilities in the hands of God, and not being faithful to take up the blessings that God has given them to act upon.

God has sent me to change people! God never changes, but people change through God's power. That is my call! My call is to change the believer, through the power of the Word—from a child in God to a grown-up who knows how to operate by faith.

"*The just shall live by faith*" (Galatians 3:11).

Vessels of Gold

In the Church, God will separate the vessels of honor from the vessels of dishonor. He's going to separate them because those who want more in God will contend for more in God!

> **Therefore if anyone cleanses himself from the latter, he will be a vessel for honor, sanctified**

and useful for the Master, prepared for every good work.

2 Timothy 2:21

The Bible says that if you want to be a vessel of honor, separate yourself from the latter.

Separate yourself from what? Separate yourself from vessels of clay, vessels of straw, vessels of wood and vessels of silver. If you want to be a vessel of gold, then you have to separate yourself from these and begin to expect more in God. You have to begin to give God more of your time, more of your thoughts, and more of your commitment than any other vessel gives. You have to go for the gusto! You have to shoot for the gold! You have to press toward the mark if you want to be part of the remnant mightily used by God.

Do you have a divine call from the Lord?

Do you know that you'll never arrive there without discipline?

Don't let any man fool you. You can fold your hands, sit around, *and go nowhere in God.* You'll add wrinkles to your face and gray hair to your head. *The days that you lose will never be redeemed again.* You can live that way if you want to. God will not force you to be a vessel of gold.

This is the day that the Lord has made. I will rejoice and be glad in it! There's no reason to wait until tomorrow. We have to begin *now* to contend for the destiny that we have in Christ Jesus! To get there, we must understand that He gave us the power to do it.

But as many as received Him, to them He gave the right to become children of God, to those who believe in His name.

John 1:12

There's power available to those who receive Jesus. If you notice, He didn't make them sons of God immediately. They were children of God. They were babies in the Lord first, but they were desirous of the sincere milk of the Word. God gave them power to become sons.

The word *become* means to *grow up to be*. When you receive Jesus, you are a child, but you have the power *in you* to grow up and become a mature child or a mature believer in the Lord. Yet, you can have that power, and never put it to work in your life. You can have that power and never use it, never benefit from it, and stay a baby in the Lord all of your life! No one wants to be called a child. People get upset when you call them children, but the fact is—they are *still* spiritual babies. There's nothing wrong with being a baby, but there is something wrong with a baby that doesn't grow.

The Bible says, *"That we henceforth be no more children, tossed to and fro"* (Ephesians 4:14 KJV). A child is someone who can't make up his or her mind long-term. A child is someone who can't stand up. They can't pull their weight or begin to build anything for God.

If you can't see the progress of God in your life, it's not because God is sovereign and has chosen to withhold His blessing from you. It's because you've been double-minded. It's because you won't separate yourself from mediocre vessels. Anyone can become mediocre. Anyone can work for something that can be accomplished in a week. It is, however, a person of destiny who will go for something that is too big for them to perform in their own ability.

God gave us the power to become sons of God.

What is a son of God? A son of God is a person who is destroying the works of the devil! A son of God is not a believer who's just holding the fort. He's someone who is going after the adversary! He is not someone who loses his mind or has a nervous breakdown.

As ministers of the Gospel, we will minister to the weak, right along side with the strong. We will feed them, we will bless them, and we will minister to them. Those who are children today will become those who are mature in the Lord tomorrow—*if they are willing and obedient*.

Willing and Obedient

If you are willing and obedient, you shall eat the good of the land.
Isaiah 1:19

It's not enough to be obedient; you must be willing. You can be obedient to the Word and not be willing to be blessed. It takes faith to say *"Yes!"* to an invisible blessing that God has already granted you.

At one of our crusades, there was a woman in a wheelchair who came forward for healing.

I looked at her in that wheelchair and said, *"Are you ready to get up?"* She answered, *"Oh no, I can't walk!"*

I walked away from her and wouldn't let her say anymore. Someone may think that was cruel, but it wasn't. There were several hundred people there in need of a miracle. I didn't want to give her another opportunity to speak unbelief and rob someone else of their faith!

I walked away from her.

Then she had a thought, *"Well, maybe I can walk!"* She made a decision at that moment to get out of the wheelchair—and she began to walk! When we had an opportunity to talk to her later that night, we found out that all the pain in her body had left. Realizing that the pain was gone, she took the initiative to get up and walk.

What if she had never made the effort to get up? If she didn't *act*, she would have stayed in that wheelchair—even though God had healed her.

It's not enough to be obedient and say, *"I came to church. Pray for me!"* You have to be willing to act upon the Word of God, get up out of the rut you are in, and begin to contend for something better in the Lord!

The Bible tells us, *"For God hath not given us the spirit of fear; but of power (the Spirit of dunamis—miracle working power!), and of love, and of a sound mind"* (2 Timothy 1:7). It didn't say, *"God has given us the brain of power."* Most Christians want to lean on their own understanding. If they do, they're still children!

How do you know when you're mature? You're mature when you lean on your spirit, and in turn, your spirit leans on the Holy Ghost and on the Word of God. A grown-up in the Lord is a spiritual person in God.

The Source of Supernatural Power

The word *supernatural* means, *"existing or occurring through some agency beyond the known forces of nature."* It means, *"believed to be miraculous or caused by the immediate exercise of divine power."*

This is not a thorough description of the word *supernatural* because it does not only mean the exercise of *divine* power; it can also mean the exercise of *demonic* power. If you don't believe there are two supernatural sources of power, you'll fall right into the New Age, into spiritism, or into the occult. One source is God's Spirit; the other is a demon spirit. You must know the difference!

A Christian in their right mind will never blame God for what the devil is doing. They'll never say, *"The Lord is in control,"* when the psychic is doing the reading. They'll never say, *"The Lord is in control,"* when the witch is performing the sacrifice. They'll never say, *"The Lord is in control,"* when the coven is drinking the blood mixed with desecration. No—that is not the work of God! That is the work of demon spirits!

Man has a hunger in his life for the supernatural. A mature child of God will be able to discern between good and evil. They will be able to walk in harmony and in agreement with the power of the Holy Ghost.

A mature child of God will go against the grain, even in the Church world. They will be the object of criticism because they don't follow after the flesh. That's why Paul wrote to the Church and said, *"Walk in the Spirit, and ye shall not fulfill the lust* (the desires) *of the flesh"* (Galatians 5:16 KJV).

This key will help you—pay close attention: God's Word and God's will are *never* mysterious. If you find yourself gravitating toward something because it has some kind of mysterious element about it, rebuke yourself! Bring yourself back in line because the supernatural of God is not mysterious! It's not metaphysical! It's not weird! It's not flaky!

The supernatural of God is something available to every child of God. It is supernaturally *natural*. It seems as if there is no miracle working power in it, but there is. For instance, that woman in the wheelchair was healed, but nobody saw her do flips and land in the chair! Nobody saw the power that went into her. She didn't even know that she was healed!

Most of the time, God uses His Word to do something supernatural in the hearts of people. The natural person—the weak person, the child—doesn't perceive it because his concept of the miraculous is totally off base.

Possessing supernatural power is the will of God for the believer. Jesus said, *"But ye shall receive power"* (Acts 1:8 KJV). He said that you will receive *dunamis*—miracle working power—after that the Holy Ghost is come upon you. That means that you that you have been chosen by God to walk in the power of the Lord and to have it accompany you wherever we go!

Stability in God

Jesus said, *"And these signs shall follow them that believe; In my name shall they cast out devils"* (Mark 16:17). Devils are invisible forces. Most Christians can't detect devils, let alone cast out devils! Most Christians hold conversations with devils!

When I travel around the world people try to give me a "Word from the Lord." They tell me, *"The Lord said...,"* but it wasn't the Lord at all! *Who were they talking to?*

In My (Jesus') name shall they—*the believers who are walking in My name*—shall cast out devils. That means they will detect what is evil, resist what is evil, rebuke what is evil, reject what is evil, and stay free from what is evil! However, if a person doesn't understand the difference between good and evil, they will become victims of the lies of the enemy.

If they never turn back from the Lord, if they walk with God, if they trust God for their salvation, they will go to Heaven. However, they will live beneath their privileges on Earth because of the work of the devil. When they get to Heaven, they will find out that they had the power necessary to deal with the forces of darkness all of their lives—but they wouldn't learn.

Do you know that it is God's will for us to learn so that we are no longer children, tossed to and fro, and carried about with every wind of doctrine (Ephesians 4:14)?

That means stability!

People get mad at you *when you know what you believe.* They call you arrogant. They say, *"You faith people think you've got all the answers!"* We have one answer: *stability.* If that's all I learn through the Word of God, that's good enough for me!

People will call you arrogant because you refuse to blow with every wind. They attack you because you are a standard of conviction to them. People will criticize you for continuing to say the same thing you were saying years ago.

God is consistent. He is still saying the same thing He's always said. He hasn't changed the Word. He is the same today as He was yesterday.

You and I are supposed to have stability, too!

Miracle Working Power

> **But we preach Christ crucified, to the Jews a stumbling block and to the Greeks foolishness, but to those who are called, both Jews and Greeks, Christ the power of God and the wisdom of God.**
>
> **1 Corinthians 1:23-24**

The Bible tells us that Christ is the power of God.

Do you possess Christ?

Do you have Christ in your life?

You did not receive Him to keep Him silent. You did not receive Him to keep Him inactive. You did not receive Him to keep Him invisible in your life. You received Christ so that He can be seen in your life as a standard for a new creation born of God—a miracle working, devil defeating, mature child who is not tossed to and fro with the lies of the adversary! You received Christ, and when you did, you received a supernatural person into your life!

Yet, born again people are the most ridiculed, most avoided

people on Earth because the world sees absolutely no power in most Christians! The world sees weaklings when it sees Christians. The world sees foolish people when it sees Christians. They see foolishness because they see believers who talk doctrine of devils instead of the Word of God. The world says, *"I'm going after something that provides power!"* so they delve into the occult.

The average Christian doesn't have the backbone to say, *"Shut up, and listen to me! You don't know what you're talking about!"* The average Christian accuses someone with that kind of boldness of not having love, but *all they have* is the cliché, "Jesus loves you." When was the last time you got someone saved saying, "Jesus loves you?" If it's not working, you had better find out why!

This is the bottom line: when God called us, He did not leave us powerless. He told us that He gave us Christ! Of course, when you receive Jesus you are saved, but then He comes to *live* in your life! The Bible calls it, *"Christ in you, the hope of glory"* (Colossians 1:27).

Christ is the power. That word *power* in the original Greek is *dunamis*. It's the miracle working power of God. *Where does it live?* The miracle working power lives in us!

The word *Christ* is the Greek word *Christo*, which means "the Anointed One; the Messiah." It comes from the word *chrio*, which means, "to smear or rub with oil."

"And Jesus returned in the power of the Spirit into Galilee" (Luke 4:14). Jesus returned in the power of the Spirit. He didn't return in the power of the soul. He didn't return in the power of human ability. He didn't return in the power of the enticing words of man's wisdom. Jesus returned to Galilee in the power of the Holy Ghost.

When did Jesus of Nazareth receive the power-factor of the Holy Ghost into His life? When He was baptized in the river Jordan!

The Bible said that when Jesus went into Galilee He preached, *"The Spirit of the Lord is upon Me because he hath anointed Me..."* (Luke 4:18 KJV). In other words, Jesus was saying, *"He has chrio (anointed) Me, and that's what makes Me Christo (the Anointed One)!*

The Lord has anointed Me, and what does that anointing do? It gives me the ability to preach with power! It gives me the ability to preach people out of poverty and out of sickness. It gives me the authority to preach the acceptable year of the Lord!"

Then He said, *"This day is this scripture fulfilled in your ears"* (Luke

4:21 KJV). He was saying, *"Now this Scripture is a reality! There is an Anointed One among you who will do these things!"*

Sadly, the majority of the Church world seems to think the Anointed One is no longer among us! They say, *"He used to do it, but He doesn't do it anymore. He can do it, but you can't count on Him to do it."* The Church does not understand that Christ is the same yesterday, today, and forever (Hebrews 13:8).

Contending For Glory in the Earth

Christ is the power of God! If you have Christ, then you the *dunamis* power of God.

Why do believers see lack of power if God has given them power?

When it comes down to *God performing* in your life—sincerity won't help you. Fellowship and numerical agreement won't help you. The power will only work with the Word you *believe*. The Word you believe is the Word that you *know* and *utilize*. It's the revelation that you put into everyday practice.

We do not have a lack of power in the Church world. We have a lack of *knowledge* in the Church world! The Bible says, *"My people are destroyed* (perish) *for lack of knowledge"* (Hosea 4:6 KJV).

The Lord prophesied that in the last days, *"The earth shall be filled with the knowledge of the glory of the Lord, as the waters cover the sea"* (Habakkuk 2:14 KJV).

Why did He say, "The knowledge of the glory?" He said that because the glory will never cover the Earth unless someone gets knowledge of it! That's why the Lord has sent ministry gifts to teach this revelation on the anointing, the glory and the power and miracles. God is beginning to pour out of His vessels into other vessels. He is giving revelation knowledge so that we would all come to the place where we would benefit from the glory that's going to cover the Earth!

The Bible says that although the knowledge of the glory of the Lord will cover the Earth, darkness will still be in the world. The glory of the Lord can be on someone, yet their mind-set can separate them from its influence completely. Your mind-set can either separate you from the benefits of the power, or it can unite you with and cause you to receive the benefits of that power.

In these last days, sinners will hear the message, and some of them will believe that Christ is the power of God and be delivered. Miracles will take place, but the world will still have darkness in it.

I don't want to miss what God has for me! I'm not going to miss it. I'm receiving it; I'm growing in it; and I will not allow *anyone* to talk me out of it! No one will be able to talk me out of what God has for me.

What about you?

Partakers of the Divine Nature

Jesus returned in the power of the Spirit. The anointing made Jesus superhuman. *Superhuman* means *above the range of human power or skill; miraculous; divine.* Superhuman is beyond normal human ability or power. Jesus was anointed. The anointing will make you superhuman!

"Wait, wait, wait! Doesn't superhuman mean divine?"

Yes! The Bible says, *"Whereby are given unto us exceeding great and precious promises: that by these ye might be partakers of the divine nature"* (2 Peter 1:4 KJV). The divine nature is the anointed nature. The anointing is the presence of the third Person of the Trinity in the life of a believer. That's what made Jesus superhuman!

"No, no, no! Jesus was superhuman because Jesus was God!"

Yes, but He humbled himself and became a man! He emptied himself of the power of deity and became a natural human. Although He was incarnate (not born of man), He operated within the same limits that humans operate in.

What made Him superhuman?

The presence of the anointing, or the third Person of the Trinity, in His life gave Him the power to operate miraculously. The anointing will do the same thing for you! The divine nature is available to you through His exceeding great and precious promises.

It is God's nature to quicken the dead and call those things that are not as though they were. That's God's nature. He has no problem with that. God calls the things that are not as though they were because it is part of the divine nature.

"But that's God!"

Yes, but He's made His nature available to you through His Word. He wants to live in you and be more than a silent partner in your life. He wants to be more than an insurance policy in your life. He wants to be more than a religious icon in your life. He wants to be the Living One who lives in you!

> **Therefore "Come out from among them And be separate, says the Lord. Do not touch what is unclean, and I will receive you."**
>
> **2 Corinthians 6:17**

God says, *"I will be your God, and you will be my people. I will live My life in you and through you."*

What kind of life is God living?

A victorious life! A life that raises the dead! A life that calls the things that are not as though they were! God is always talking faith. His Word is *never* a fear word. It is always a faith word!

Releasing the Power

If Christ is the power of God, and you have Christ, then you have the power of God!

The Bible says, *"In the beginning was the Word, and the Word was with God, and the Word was God"* (John 1:1).

The power of God is released by the Word of God that you know. You have to *know* it! You have to have a revelation of the fact that you have Christ in you. You must have a revelation of what He stands for. He is the Word and He only stands for the Word of God!

Jesus does not stand for man-made traditions. If He did, many women would be going to Hell right now, and some churches would tell them that! You can cut your hair and still go to Heaven! You can go out without a veil on your head and still go to Heaven! You can break the code of being silent in the church, as a woman, and still go to Heaven!

You can have all the power of God available in the world, but not know how to shoot it into your life. A revelation of the Word of God triggers the power of God in your life. That's why the devil fights it so much! He does not want you releasing the power of the living Christ in your life through the spoken Word.

Christ is the power of God and Christ is the Word of God. If you words don't line up with *THE WORD*, then you are in rebellion against Christ. When your words are in line with His Word, then you're willing and obedient! When you do these things, God can begin to work in your life!

A Prophetic Prayer

In Psalm 22, the Spirit of God is prophetically speaking through the psalmist the very things Jesus will pray and think and say:

> **For dogs have compassed me: the assembly of the wicked have enclosed me: they pierced my hands and my feet. I may tell all my bones: they look and stare upon me. They part my garments among them, and cast lots upon my vesture. But be not thou far from me, O Lord: O my strength, haste thee to help me. Deliver my soul from the sword; my darling from the power of the dog.**
>
> **Psalm 22:16-20 KJV**

This is the Lord talking. The only one whose hands and feet were pierced and who had lots cast for His garment was the Lord. The Lord is praying to the Father, saying, *"Deliver my soul from the sword. Deliver my soul, my darling, from the power of the dog."*

In America, a dog is not the same as a dog was in Israel in those days. I have several dogs. They get groomed, they get bathed—they are part of the family, so to speak. However, dogs in those days just got whatever crumbs they could get. Dogs weren't a part of the family. A dog was considered a low thing.

Who is the dog in this verse? It's the devil! *Have you ever wanted to say that to him?* "Dog! Dog! Dog!" Some Christians say, *"Don't call the devil a dog—he might hear you!"*

Religion respects the devil foolishly.

Jesus was saying to the Father, *"Satan's power is getting ready to grip me. Deliver me from the power of the dog!"*

The Bible teaches us that the devil's power was death.

> **Forasmuch then as the children are partakers of flesh and blood, he (Jesus) also himself likewise took part of the same; that through death he might destroy him that had the power of death, that is, (the dog) the devil; and deliver them who through fear of death were all their lifetime subject to bondage.**
>
> **Hebrews 2:14-15 KJV**
> (parentheses added by author)

Sadly, bondage still operates in the lives of a lot of Christians.

Why is that? Where there is an absence of the anointing, there is the presence of bondage. The Bible says that the anointing shall destroy the yoke (Isaiah 10:27). The yoke shall be broken, smashed, and *annihilated* because of the anointing! That anointing comes through the Anointed One.

The Bible says that the heathens raged, and the people imagined a vain thing; they gathered themselves against the Lord and against His Anointed (Psalm 2:1-2; Acts 4:25-26).

They beat Him until the flesh was ripped right off his ribs. They parted his garment amongst them and cast lots for it. He was getting ready to go through the piercing of the sword, and He cried out,

"Deliver my soul from the sword, my darling, from the power of the dog." He was saying, *"I'm going to die, but, God, I know that your power is going to reach Me after I die and deliver Me out of the place that no one has ever permanently been delivered from! I know that I'm going to be buried, but I believe I'm coming up out of the grave again! I believe the power of God is bigger than the power of the dog! I'm putting my trust in you, God. I'm believing that Your power and Your anointing will rescue Me!"*

Know Your Rights!

It is *imperative* to understand that this world is in a conflict. There are two sources that have power: one is demonic; the other one is divine. The good news is this: when Jesus defeated the devil, the devil lost the power he had over those who believe on Jesus!

Of course, those who don't know any better are taken captive by the devil at his will. *Do you understand this?* They're taken *captive* by him! Even Christians who don't know any better are taken captive by him!

Christians think, *"If we don't talk about the devil, then he can't harm us."* They think, *"If we don't use faith against the devil, then he'll just leave us alone."* No! The security that you have in God is not dependent upon the ignorance you allow! You *must* understand that your security is dependent upon the knowledge you have of the Word! You have to know your divine rights in order to know that you are secure. Otherwise, the thief will get away with all kinds of things in your life.

Christians don't know their rights. They say, *"I'm trusting the Lord."*

For what?

"Well, I'm just trusting God."

For what?!

Jesus said, *"You're going to deliver me from the power of the dog—that's what I'm trusting!"*

Save me from the lion's mouth: for thou hast

heard me from the horns of the unicorns.

Psalm 22:21 KJV

What is the horn of the unicorn?

The Bible says, *"But my horn* (that's promotion and strength!) *shalt thou exalt like the horn of an unicorn: I shall be anointed with fresh oil"* (Psalm 92:10). A horn is what you put the anointing in. Symbolically, the horn is the house of the power of God.

"You have heard me from the horn of the unicorn. You have heard me from the power of your Spirit! You have heard me! You're going to deliver me from the power of the dog. You're going to deliver me from the sword. You're going to deliver me from the mouth of the lion!"

Verse 22 is prophetic:

I will declare thy name unto my brethren: in the midst of the congregation will I praise thee.

Psalm 22:22 KJV

Not only did Jesus pray, *"You're going to rescue me from death,"* but He started prophesying what He was going to do after He came out of the grave:

"I'm going to declare Your name to My brethren. I'm going to show up and say, 'All power in Heaven and Earth is given unto Me! I'm going to declare to them that God's divine right is in Me. I'm going to tell them, 'Tarry in Jerusalem until you be in endued, or cloaked, with power from on high.' I'm going to give them their rights and tell them, 'Whatever things you desire when you pray, believe that you receive them and you shall have them!' "I'm going to tell them, 'You've got the keys to the Kingdom! Whatever you bind on Earth will be bound in Heaven! Whatever you loose on Earth will be loosed in Heaven!'"

He prophesied it! Then he said, *"In the midst of the Church I'm going to sing praises unto You."*

> *How does Jesus sing praises unto the Father in the Church today?* He does it through the power of the Holy Ghost!

Alive for Evermore

Jesus died. He prayed that prayer, and He died. The dog thought he had Him. Then they took His body and put it in the grave.

He had already prophesied by His Spirit, through David, saying, *"For thou wilt not leave my soul in hell; neither wilt thou suffer thine Holy One to see corruption"* (Psalm 16:10 KJV). *"Even my body will not decompose and begin to stink because I'm the Holy One of God. Before it begins to decompose, You're going to claim it out of the grave again! I'm coming out of the grave!"* He prophesied it!

The Bible says that He was put to death in the flesh but quickened by the Spirit. (1 Peter 3:18-19). He went down to the lower parts of the Earth, delivered the captives, and rose from the dead (Ephesians 4:8)!

On the Isle of Patmos He appeared to John and said, *"I am he that liveth, and was dead; and, behold, I am alive for evermore, Amen; and have the keys of hell and of death"* (Revelation 1:18 KJV). That means the dog doesn't have the power any more!

The keys of death were in the hands of the dog. Death was the power of the dog, but Jesus had prayed, *"Deliver me from the power of the dog!"* So, on His way up He said to the dog, *"Give me that! You're not going to have that power any more!"* and He took it from him!

Do you know what He did then?

He went right back into His body! When He did, resurrection life hit His Spirit and He came up out of the grave! He appeared to the children of God and began to declare good news: *"From the time that I send you another Comforter, you will never again have to ask Me anything! You'll just ask in My name! In other words, you'll say, 'On behalf of Jesus… In the stead of Jesus…Christ in me is asking…The Spirit of Christ in me is crying, Abba Father.' And whatever you ask, you will receive!"*

Now, *that's* power!

Prerequisite for Power

> How God anointed Jesus of Nazareth with the Holy Ghost and with power: who went about doing good, and healing all that were oppressed of the devil; for God was with him.
>
> **Acts 10:38 KJV**

The only reason Jesus was able to heal all that were oppressed of the devil was because God had anointed Him!

Jesus said:

> **Verily, verily, I say unto you, He that believeth on me, the (same) works that I do shall he do also; and greater works than these shall he do; because I go unto my Father.**
>
> **John 14:12 KJV**

Believing on Him is a prerequisite for doing the works! The condition of the Church world today clearly reveals that "the believing on Jesus" that the Church has been doing, has not met biblical criteria for believing on Jesus.

Why? The works that Jesus did are not being done today, and greater works are *definitely* not being done! Of course, there are men and women of God doing the works today, but I'm talking about by and large, throughout the Church world. I'm talking about *you*! I'm talking about *your* life! In your life there is more in God!

Jesus said, *"He that believes on Me, the works that I do shall he do also."*

Do you believe on Jesus? Then, what's the problem?

The problem is the way Jesus has been portrayed and what you've been taught about Him. The problem is what people have told you from the pulpit. They have misrepresented Jesus! The gospel you heard regarding Jesus must not have been accurate. If it had been, you'd believe on Jesus the *right* way, and the works He did—you would be doing today!

The evidence is in the works—*or in the absence of them!* If you are not doing the works He did, then you do not believe on Jesus the way you are called to. Of course, you believe Jesus is the Savior, but would you dare let Jesus do the talking through you? Would you allow Him to live through you?

No one has taught us that this is the call of God on our lives! We've heard religious people separate us from Christ, making us two different entities. As a result, they have robbed us of what is available to us in God!

Jesus said, *"If you believe on me, the works that I do shall you do also!"* What works was Jesus doing? He was delivering those that were oppressed of the devil!

That word *oppressed* in Acts 10:38 is the Greek word *katadunasteuo*. It comes from the words *kata*, which means "down or under," and *dunastes*, which means *to hold power or lordship over*. Those who were oppressed, or *katadunasteuo*, were actually under the domination, or the lordship, of Satan!

Yet, what pastor would dare tell you that if you are putting up with sickness and disease in your life—you are under the domination of the devil! People would get angry and fight it because they don't understand that there are two sources of power active against one another.

Don't Let the Devil Dominate You

God has nothing in common with the devil! Sickness is a part of the curse of the law—which is enforced by demonic spirits. *Oppressed of the devil* means *pressed under by the devil* and *under the lordship, or the domination, of the devil.*

How does the devil oppress people?
The devil oppresses through sickness and disease.

"No! I'm saved! I'm not under the lordship of the devil!"

The Bible says that the tithe belongs to the Lord. If you are in debt, and you lower your Christian standards and stop tithing in order to pay your bills, *you are stealing from God*. Whose lordship are you under?

We have learned to believe that the moment we give our heart to the Lord, He is Lord. We say, *"Jesus is Lord in my life. I just believe the Lord is in control."* Well, if the Lord was totally in control, we would be healthy, wealthy, and strong! People would look at us and say, *"What is it about you?"* The world would want to be like *you*.

You would have a commitment to God that says, *"I won't let the devil dominate any area of my life!"*

In Acts 10:38 the *oppressed* were those who were oppressed of the devil and those who were under the lordship of Satan *physically*. It says that Jesus went about doing good, and healing all that were oppressed of the devil.

There are many who have said, *"I believe Jesus healed them spiritually."* However, the word *healed* in that text is the Greek word used for *physical* ailments—so there goes that theory! God anointed Jesus to deliver people from sickness and disease, and He made it clear that sickness and disease is the power of the devil.

What does the supernatural power of God do?

It dispels the power of the devil! It breaks the dominion of the devil off the life of the believer! Faith triggers the power of God, and the power of God drives the power of the devil out of your life!

You are no longer supposed to be under the domination, or the lordship of Satan.

Does that mean that when you get symptoms in your body you are under the domination of Satan? No, but if you say, *"I'm sick!"* then you are saying, *"Devil, give me a headlock!"* With your mouth you are getting out of agreement with what Calvary has provided for you! That is what the Church has not understood. The power of God is with us to work in our lives, but the power only works when we stay in agreement with the Word of God.

The View from Calvary

We've discovered that Christ is the power of God. We discovered that the anointing in Christ's life is the power of God. We discovered that the devil's power is oppression through sickness and disease, physical death, and, of course, sin. We know that Jesus has dealt with the sin issue in our lives.

> **For the preaching of the cross is to them that perish foolishness; but unto us which are saved it is the power of God.**
>
> **1 Corinthians 1:18 KJV**

The preaching of the cross benefits those who are *already* saved!

"I thought the preaching of the cross was for the sinner! I thought the preaching of the cross was to get the sinner saved!"

For so many Christians, Christ's power has been narrowed to the salvation of the soul. However, the Bible says, *"The preaching of the cross is foolishness to those that perish. They don't believe it! But to those which are saved it is the power of God!"*

What is the power of God in that text? The preaching of the cross!

This text doesn't just say, *"The cross is the power of God."* It says, *"To the believer, or the one who is saved, the preaching of the cross is the power of God."*

What does that mean to me? It means that you have to direct your speech in line with what the cross has provided! View everything from the victory of Calvary!

> What do I say to sickness and disease?
> *"At the cross, Jesus carried you away from my life!"*
>
> What do I say to poverty?
> *"Christ has redeemed me from the curse of the law when He was made a curse for me!"*
>
> What do I say to demons?
> *"You were defeated at the cross!"*

The Bible says that Jesus spoiled principalities and powers, and made a show of them openly, triumphing over them by the cross (Colossians 2:15).

The preaching of the cross is the power of God to the one who is saved already. The preaching of the cross is the power of God that leads us out of childhood and into maturity. It leads us out of being sickly into being healthy. It leads us out of being confused into being clear.

The cross has provided us with the mind of Christ! The cross has provided us with a new nature! The preaching of the cross in our life destroys the power of condemnation!

> **For what the law could not do, in that it was weak through the flesh, God sending his own Son in the likeness of sinful flesh, and for sin, condemned sin in the flesh.**
>
> **Romans 8:3 KJV**

Where did this happen? At the cross!

The law could not provide a new nature in your heart and mind, so everyone was guilty. The devil took advantage of the guilt of people and messed them up. Jesus, however, took the power of sin, guilt, and condemnation and nailed it to the cross! Through the act of the crucifixion I can have absolutely no condemnation in my life.

What does this do? It puts the devil out of your life!

When you see it like that, you will *declare* it like that, and the power of God for protection will work in your life.

The Salvation of the Saved

> **For I am not ashamed of the gospel of Christ: for it is the power (dunamis) of God unto salvation.**

Romans 1:16 KJV

The word *salvation* is the Greek word *soteria*, which means "salvation of the soul, healing of the body, divine health, prosperity, preservation, protection, and rescue." No wonder the Bible says, *"For the preaching of the cross to those who are saved is the power of God!"*

When I'm in a situation and the devil says, *"You're going to die!"* I say, *"Not according to the preaching of the cross! According to the preaching of the cross, I'm going to be rescued! I'm going to be protected! I'm going to be preserved! My God shall supply my need according to his riches in glory!"*

That puts the power of God to work in my life. I am narrow-minded in believing! Everything I see, I see from the cross! I don't want to join the masses on their way to mediocrity! I don't want to become like the majority! I'm not impressed by the majority. I'm impressed by the King of Kings and the Lord of Lords!

If the Gospel is the power of God to rescue and preserve the *saved* person, then the Gospel doesn't end when you get saved! The Gospel *begins* when you get saved! The reason we lack power in our lives is our failure to understand that the same gospel that saved us packs the power to keep us healed. It has the power to keep us on top and the power to give us clarity!

I don't understand why people spend their time running from person to person for counseling. They use the excuse: *"The Bible says that in a majority of counselors, there is safety."* They need to get in the anointing, regain clarity and begin to act in God's will.

There will, of course, be times when you need help. There will be times when you will need prayer, but if your life consists of nothing more than asking questions of others to see what they think, you'll never get anything done for God! That's why I don't consult people. If you do, you will start listening to contrary voices and let go of what God has called you to believe.

A baby Christian is afraid of persecution. A baby Christian cries, *"They're putting pressure on me!"* Put pressure on them! When you're mature, you're not afraid of persecution.

The Bible says that all who live godly in Christ Jesus will suffer persecution (2 Timothy 3:12). The Bible also says that when persecution arises for the Word's sake they are offended (Mark 4:17). Persecution arises for the *Word's sake*! They are offended at the Word because they are babies!

> **Great peace have they which love thy law (thy Word): and nothing shall offend them.**
>
> **Psalm 119:165 KJV**

Do you know how to tell if someone doesn't love the Word? They get offended by the first thing you say! Sometimes things will make you angry, but if you get offended and stay that way for three decades, there is something very wrong!

You will get persecuted when you are doing things right. When you start living according to the Word, you will be persecuted.

"*When men shall revile you, and persecute you, and shall say all manner of evil against you falsely, for my sake,*" Jesus said, "*Rejoice, and be exceeding glad*" (Matthew 5:11-12)! You ought to return to church saying, "*Ha, ha, ha! I want to testify! Look at me! They are saying lies about me!*" You'll be in good company!

The Greatest Show On Earth

Jesus was declared the Son of God with power by the resurrection from the dead (Romans 1:4). The greatest act of power God ever demonstrated was raising Christ from the dead.

The Bible also says that God is upholding all things by the Word of His power (Hebrews 1:3). That means His Word is His power.

Who is His Word? Christ! When you have Christ, you have the power!

What is the power of God doing right now? It is upholding the universe. The Word of God, the living Word of God, is holding the universe together!

> **That the God of our Lord Jesus Christ, the Father of glory, may give unto you the spirit of wisdom and revelation in the knowledge**

> of him: The eyes of your understanding being enlightened; that ye may know what is the hope of his calling, and what the riches of the glory of his inheritance in the saints, And what is the exceeding greatness of his power to usward who believe, according to the working of his mighty power, which he wrought in Christ, when he raised him from the dead, and set him at his own right hand in the heavenly places, Far above all principality, and power, and might, and dominion, and every name that is named, not only in this world, but also in that which is to come: And hath put all things under his feet, and gave him to be the head over all things to the church, Which is his body, the fullness of him that filleth all in all.
>
> **Ephesians 1:17-23 KJV**

Do you know what God said the Church should do? He didn't say, *"Wait for Me, Ephesian church, to pour out My power on you."* He didn't say, *"Ephesian church, travel to a special meeting to find My power."*

I am tired of people asking me, *"Where did you get this anointing?"* I didn't get it at somebody's meeting. I got it from the Living God! I got it from God, and God is everywhere. Wherever there is faith, God is there!

I have nothing against any place where God is moving. However, I do have something against Christians who have absolutely no stability—Christians who need to take trips to different parts of the world to get a "shot in the arm!"

I know people get mad at me for saying things like that, but what if your pastor had to run all over the world to come up with a sermon? You wouldn't understand—you would criticize. I'm not criticizing—I'm *correcting*. I believe in God's people more than they believe in themselves! I found out what God says about His people in His Word. *I believe in you!*

Now, I'm not against going to special meetings, but what I am saying is this: when you go somewhere, *go there full of God already!* Go there full of God, and what you experience there should either confirm what you believe or reaffirm by the still, small voice. Go with your guard up, ready to reject what's not of the Lord and ready to receive what is of the Lord. Don't live your life dependent on being revived by going to a special place—a shrine!

There's Power in the Church

Do you know that most Christians build a church and put a steeple on top? *Why the steeple?* It's because they have a religious concept of Church. The Church is *not* the building. We are the Church and we are not dependent upon a steeple or a sanctuary to pick us up. That does not define our identity in Christ! Greater is He that is in us than He that is in the world!

People have said about me, *"Well I just don't like the way he dresses."* I know I look different from the average pastor, but before God is finished, Christians will not look like they have looked in the past. Most Christians look like they stopped in 1950!

Let me explain some things to you. The Charismatic Movement was of God. The Healing Revival was of God. The Holiness Revival was of God, but if you go to a Holiness church, you will see people who look like they're still back in the Holiness Revival. If you go to a Charismatic church, you will see people who look like they're still back in the Charismatic Movement.

That's when they stopped thinking! When God moved forward with further revelation from the Word, instead of investigating it and proving it, they rejected it. They stopped utilizing the mind of Christ! They thought that the whole mind of Christ was involved in a certain practice or a particular song.

Paul said, *"I'm praying for you (Spirit-filled Ephesian church) that the eyes of your understanding would open up...so that you'd start understanding!"*

What are you going to understand?

Paul continued, *"You are going to have the Spirit of wisdom and revelation; your eyes are going to be enlightened; you're going to know the hope of His calling and the riches of the glory of His inheritance; and you're going to know what the exceeding greatness of His power toward you is."*

Toward you! You're going to know what His power is *toward you!* The only thing that stops the power from operating—is your lack of understanding of the exceeding greatness of the power that is toward you.

What kind of power is it?

It's the kind of power He wrought in Christ, or demonstrated in Christ, when He raised Him from the dead. It's the kind of power that He exercised, or demonstrated, in Christ when He took Him up to Heaven and sat Him down in heavenly places and put all things under His feet.

Whose feet?

Christ's feet! All things—thrones, dominions, principalities, powers—are put under His feet. Poverty, sickness, demons, trials, obstacles, battles—all power is under Christ's feet.

Do you know what put it there?

The power that raised Christ from the dead! The Bible says that God gave Christ to be the head over "all things." He gave Him power over the things that He had already put under His feet! He put *all things* under Christ's feet, and He gave Christ to be the head over those things. Christ is on top of all things under His feet!

Christians are walking around saying, *"I need to find the anointing!"* God says, *"No, you just need a revelation of the kind of power that is already on the inside of you! You need to find out that the devil is under your feet! You need to find out that your situation is not the same anymore! You need to find out that you can get up out of that spiritual wheelchair and walk around! You have been redeemed by the power of the Lord!"*

You've been redeemed! The glory is in you! You should have revival wherever you go! People should travel to *your* house! They should take trips to your house and say, *"Every time we go to that house something happens!"* You have glory on the inside of you! You have the anointing in you!

Tapping into Resurrection Life

Now the Lord is that Spirit: and where the Spirit of the Lord is, there is liberty.

2 Corinthians 3:17

We know that if Jesus was raised from the dead by the Spirit of God (and He was), and if Jesus was raised from the dead by the power of God (and He was), and if you and I are anointed with the Holy Ghost and with power (and we are), then the Spirit, the Lord, and the power of God are synonymous.

But if the Spirit of him that raised up Jesus from the dead dwell in you, he that raised up Christ from the dead shall also quicken your mortal bodies by his Spirit that dwelleth in you.

Romans 8:11

In an earlier verse it says, *"Now if any man have not the Spirit of Christ, he is none of his"* (Romans 8:9). We can conclude that if you're born again, you have the Spirit of Christ because you have the Lord. If you're born again you've got it! If you don't have that, you're not saved—you don't have Christ.

We know that the Spirit of God—the power of God—and the Lord are synonymous. The Lord is that Spirit; God raised Jesus from the dead by the power of God; the Spirit raised Jesus from the dead. They're synonymous.

How will your mortal body be quickened? Your mortal body is quickened by His Spirit that dwells in you. Do you have the Spirit of God living in you? He said that if He's living in you, He shall quicken you. *Quicken* is the Greek word *zoopoieo*. It comes from *zao*, meaning "live," and *poieo*, meaning "to make." It literally means, "To make live!"

Having seen the word *mortal* in that verse, some people read it and say, *"It's talking about the resurrection—if the Spirit of God lives in you,*

He'll quicken, or make alive, your mortal body after you die." However, in the original Greek, the word for *mortal* is a totally different word than the word for *dead*. As a matter of fact, it is the same word that Paul used when he said, *"Let not sin rule in your mortal body"* (Romans 6 KJV).

Now, if he were talking about a dead body, it wouldn't make any sense. *"Let not sin rule in your dead body."* After you die, you don't have a problem with sin, so he couldn't be talking about that. Greek is a very precise language. It is so specific, that when you look up the origin of the language and study it in context, you have to work hard to misinterpret Scripture—and most people do! The word *mortal* is the Greek word *thnetos*. It means "liable to, or subject to, death," but it never refers to a dead body.

So the Bible is saying that if the Spirit of God dwells in you, He will put life into your body (which is subject to death) or make life in your body (which is subject to death). It's talking about *supernatural resurrection life*. This is the *zoe* life of God that you can cash in on by faith because the Holy Ghost lives in your body (which is not dead but is subject to death)!

Although your body is subject to death, you can cash in on strength today because the Scripture says, *"As your days are, so shall your strength be"* (Deuteronomy 33:25)! That's why Dr. Lester Sumrall said, *"I command strength into my body every day!"*

When you know what the Bible says about you, and you get up in the morning feeling weak, you may think, *"In the natural I'm weak."* Don't then go on to say, *"Oh, I'm getting old; I must be getting old."* No! Remember that the power of God is in you by the Spirit of God! If the Spirit of Him that raised Jesus from the dead dwell in you, He will make life—*resurrection life*—in your physical body (which is subject to death).

Do you know what will happen then? Resurrection life will be in your body!

You can overcome a spirit of slumber.

Did you know that some people fall asleep in the anointing? When the service is over, they wake up saying, *"What are we going to do now?"* They're awake, they're ready, and they'll talk your ear off after the service! When the anointing was moving, however, they fell asleep.

They are not bad people, but that's something they can deal with by the anointing. They can put the anointing to work, and resurrection life will get on the inside of them! They can cash in on the power of God, possess that supernatural power, and put it to work in their life.

Yielding To the Spirit

Likewise the Spirit also helps in our weaknesses. For we do not know what we should pray for as we ought, but the Spirit Himself makes intercession for us with groanings which cannot be uttered.

Romans 8:26

Do you know what you have on the inside of you?

You have the Holy Ghost on the inside of you! You can't, however, yield to the Holy Ghost unless you practice what this verse says. If you don't practice it, you'll be very apprehensive, very shy, and very reserved about it—like most of the Church world! When you say, *"Let's pray in the Spirit,"* most people whisper in tongues or pray under their breath in tongues. They don't yield to the Spirit.

When you pray in tongues, you yield willingly and exercise faith in the beginning; but then you get to a point where, all of a sudden, the Spirit takes over.

Recently, our student body was praying together, and when we stopped the prayer, two of the students had gotten in that vein of prayer and couldn't come back! You can always come back, but it takes time. It's like running downhill. You run downhill, and then you want to stop. Your mind says, "Stop!"; you tell your body to stop; but it takes a few more steps before you finally stop. It is like that in the Spirit—it takes some time to come back.

Everyone else had stopped, but those two were still praying in the Spirit. When you initiate this kind of prayer, you are releasing your faith. As you keep praying, you get into that vein where it's rolling out of you. At that point, you can shift over into your natural language and declare the Word of the Lord. That's when you can shift over to an intelligible language and prophesy the Word of the God. You can do this because you are praying right out of the Spirit of God in your spirit!

People are trained not to do that. They say, *"The Bible says don't do that."* As a result, the majority of the people of God don't build their spirit man up the way they should. They don't understand the benefits that are available through praying in other tongues!

"Likewise the Spirit also helpeth our infirmities...." The word *infirmities* is the Greek word *astheneia*. It is the most commonly used word in the Greek language for *sickness*. The Spirit *helpeth* our sicknesses. The word *helpeth* has been translated *help* in English, but *helpeth* in the original language means "to take hold against together with." That means, *"Likewise the Spirit will take hold together with us against sicknesses."*

We don't know what to pray for as we should.

People are running around saying, *"Thy will be done."*

Oh, be quiet, and *pray in tongues*!

Likewise the Spirit will take hold together with us. Notice, He doesn't take hold *for* us. He can't. He's got to take hold *together with* us. He's got to have our cooperation! Likewise the Spirit will take hold together with us against sicknesses. When you pray in tongues, you get delivered. As a matter of fact, when you pray in tongues, you put the power of God to work in your life! You may have some symptoms occasionally, but they'll leave before they become dominant in your life. They will leave because you are cashing in on the power of God that is available to you!

Likewise the Spirit will take hold together with you against your sicknesses and make intercession for you with groanings, which cannot be uttered. When you are praying in tongues you are speaking mysteries to God.

Why are they mysteries? They are mysteries because you don't know them—you don't understand what you're saying! That's the only reason they're mysteries. They are not something that is extra-biblical. The Spirit of God is praying through you!

If there is a sickness attack on your life, and you get the Holy Ghost to start praying through you, you are probably saying in tongues to God, *"Christ has redeemed me from the curse of the law!"*

You're probably saying in tongues to God, *"The Blood was shed for my sins, but the Body was broken for my divine health!"* You're probably saying in tongues to God, *"By His stripes I was healed!"*

You may not know what you're saying! The Spirit knows that you don't know how to pray like you should, but if you yield your prayer language to Him by faith, He will take hold together with you against your sickness, and you will be set free.

CHAPTER 14

THE POWER OF HIS GLORY

If you would let the anointing in you loose, shafts of light would hit everybody around you! You would do more without trying than most people would do in their entire lifetime.

Arise, shine; for thy light is come, and the glory of the Lord is risen upon thee. For, behold, the darkness shall cover the earth, and gross darkness the people: but the Lord shall arise upon thee, and his glory shall be seen upon thee.

Isaiah 60:1-2 KJV

I want to teach you about walking in the power of His glory. The Church has lost sight of what New Testament Christianity is all about. By and large the Church world is not walking in power. It's not even walking in liberty! Many in the Church world today are walking after tradition and after religious bondage. Many are even shocked when they see God manifest His power.

People look at the power of God and shy away from it. There are churches beginning to relegate God to the back room. They don't want speaking in other tongues, and they don't want the power of God in demonstration. We have found that people don't understand the gifts of the Spirit or the anointing of God. Therefore, in the ministry's effort to please people, many have shied away from the power of God and the anointing of the Spirit.

On the other hand, the devil has been intelligent enough to present the occult as a scientific, viable alternative to narrow-minded religion. I want you to know that there is nothing scientific about the occult! It is a counterfeit, fraudulent display of effort by fallen demon spirits. It's an effort to copy God in power and in anointing.

True glory ought to be in the Church of Jesus Christ! A believer should know how to walk by faith, how to live by the Spirit, and how to live victoriously. A Christian should have his life put together by the Spirit of God.

In order for us to see that, we must be transformed in our thinking and delivered in our thought-life from that presumptuous, religious lie that would say, *"If God wants it done, it will be done."* That's the biggest lie Hell has ever come up with!

God does not do anything outside of the perimeters of His Word! He will do what His Word says, providing there is a believer at the other end of the Word who will lay claim to what the Word promises. It isn't by might, it isn't by power, but it is by the Spirit of the Lord. *"It's by My Spirit!"* says the Lord of Hosts. That Spirit is His anointing. It is His glory. It is His manifested presence.

The Church today is responsible for the lack of revival in the Earth. The Spirit of God has been injecting into my spirit things that are designed by Heaven to transform your life. I want to see God fulfill His destiny in your life!

We have to walk by the power of God. We cannot afford to allow the world to continue to mock the Church. We cannot allow the world to look at us as if we are an ignorant people who do not know what truth is all about. God has not left anything to chance! The Word of God is clear. If there is a lack of revival, it isn't God's doing. If there is a lack of the manifestation of power, it isn't because God has gotten old. It isn't because God has become weak. It is because *the Church* is distracted!

God is still raising up men and women who are not appointed by the "Board," who are not "voted in," who can't be "voted up." God is raising up ministry gifts to prepare the people to be used by the Spirit of God! *You* can walk by the power of God in your life! You can have that glory! You can have it every moment of your life! That glory is God's presence manifested to enforce and to perform His promises and His Word.

A City That Shines

Arise, shine; For your light has come! And the glory of the Lord is risen upon you.

Isaiah 16:1

This is a prophetic Word for the Church.

In the Hebrew language, the word for arise and shine is *zarach*, meaning, *to rise as the sun, to appear, to shoot forth beams, to radiate.* God said, *"Arise, and let your light shine."* We know what Jesus said about the Church: *"You are a city built on a hill! A city built on a hill cannot be hid—let your light so shine!"*

Why are you a city built on a hill? So that men will see your good works!

The world will see you opening the blind eyes! People will see you raising the dead! They will watch you cast out devils! They will see you standing in victory! They will give glory to your Father, which is in Heaven.

God prophesies, *"Arise and shine, because your light has come, and the glory—the splendor, the honor, the shekinah, the manifested presence of God—has risen upon thee!"* You can only rise if something has risen upon you. You can only arise if *Someone* has risen upon you! The good news is that Jesus has risen in order that He might shine on every believer! As a result, you can rise up and say, *"Hallelujah! I am here by the anointing of God! I am here by the power of the Spirit!"*

Then He goes on to say, *"Behold, darkness shall cover the earth."* The word *shall* is the future tense. Isaiah is talking prophetically. *"Darkness will cover the earth, gross darkness the people, but the Lord shall arise upon thee, and His glory shall be seen upon thee"* (Isaiah 60:2 KJV).

The Lord will arise upon thee!

Does this happen when we get to Heaven?

No! In Heaven there is no darkness! Right here, while there is gross darkness covering the Earth, the Lord will arise and shine on His people. His glory will be seen.

His glory will be seen while there's a guru speaking depression and deception. That glory will manifest even while the darkness is covering him, and the counsel of Hell is speaking through his lips. While there's an occultist, while there's a psychic, while there's a Satanist, while the people are deceived, there will still be a church, there will still be a believer, there will still be a Christian whom God has shined upon! The Bible said that the glory of the Lord will be seen upon you!

The Scripture tells us that the Sun of Righteousness will arise with healing in His wings, or in His beams—the shafts of light which come forth out of His being (Malachi 4:2). If you would let the anointing in you loose, shafts of light would hit everybody around you! You would do more without trying than most people would do in their entire lifetime.

The glory of God is radiating out of you!

Centers for Glory

God is building Churches. If we'll stick to the Word of God and not deviate from the truth, the day will come when churches will become a center for the glory! The corporate faith of the people will be too big for unbelievers to resist! There will be such a manifestation of God's glory that people will wake up in the morning all over the world and hear the Spirit of God and angels say, *"Go to that church!"*

It doesn't matter if someone doesn't believe it. *"But if our gospel be hid, it is hid to them that are lost: in whom the god of this world hath blinded the minds of them which believe not"* (2 Corinthians 4:3-4 KJV). We're not talking about someone who doesn't believe. We're talking about people who know how God operates! The Bible said that if two will agree as touching anything on Earth, it shall be done unto them! Angels and the Spirit of God will tell people all over the world to *"go to that church!"*

"I've been an alcoholic for twenty years."

"Go to that church!"

"I've been a drug addict for twenty years."

"Go to that church!"

"I've had five divorces already, and I'm 'shacking up' now."

"Go to that church!"

People will stay up all Saturday night, carousing and serving the devil, and come out of the bar on Sunday morning and hear the voice of the Lord say, *"Go to that church!"* They will walk into the building and the glory will be there! They'll fall out under the power and have an encounter with Heaven that will frustrate the drug dealer, embarrass the alcohol distributor, and defeat the demonic spirits that had them bound! The glory of the Lord is going to be seen on people!

I don't want to be a thirty-fold Christian. I don't want to be a sixty-fold Christian. Now don't misunderstand me. I thank God that I am where I am now. I'm not going to beat myself over the head because someone is ahead of me or pat myself on the back because someone is behind me. However, I'm not going to settle where I'm at either! I have the Word as my standard, and as long as the Word is my standard, I still have a long way to go. Sadly, in the Church world some people haven't even gotten started yet. You have to get started to get going!

Gross darkness will cover the people, but the Lord will rise on you and His glory will be seen on you. Ephesians 5:14 says, *"Wherefore he saith, Awake thou that sleepest, and arise from the dead, and Christ shall give thee light."*

What kind of light is it talking about?
What kind of resurrection is it talking about?

It's talking about the resurrection from spiritual death unto spiritual life called the new birth. God said, *"Now if you will arise from the dead, then Christ will give you light."*

This light is the light of the glory that is available to everyone who will believe. It is the light of the glory that makes the power of God—the anointing of God—resident and available to manifest in the believer's life. That's the reward of the believer! That belongs to the believer!

Knockdown Power

We were ministering in California one time, and the Spirit of the Lord had me teach on the mystery: *"Christ in you, the hope of glory"* (Colossians 1:27). As you've learned already, this is the mystery of God in man. It's the mystery of the power of God in the believer. Every service I would preach the mystery and minister to people. In that meeting there were seven or eight people with neck problems who were healed instantly. They testified that their pain was completely gone and that they were totally healed by the power of God!

Yet, I sensed in my spirit that we were begging. We were only getting little drips of God's power. God had so much more, but the people were not ready to receive it! So I kept preaching the mystery and sowing the seed of the Word every time we met. However, when I walked up to the pulpit during the final meeting, I couldn't even preach! I stepped out and began to minister, and the glory of God fell! The worship team got lost in the Spirit and began to sing prophetic songs. The gifts of the Spirit began to operate. People who had never experienced the power of God began to shake and act like they had known the power all their lives! It was the manifestation of the glory of God!

We had sown the seed, and some people got it. Others didn't get it, and some people got it and didn't know they had it! It was sown in their spirit man. When the Spirit of the Lord watered the seed that was sown, there was suddenly a visible manifestation of all of the sermons we had preached!

God hadn't been withholding His glory; He just wanted the Truth to be preached so that faith would be imparted and expectation would come. He wanted the people to glean and receive the benefit of His divine promises!

When the power of God began to fall, I called out a young lady to the altar. She had asthma, a neck problem, and a tumor in her body. I was standing in front of her, and the power of God began to move. I said, *"There it is!"* As it moved on her body, she began to shake and shout, *"Aaahhh!"* and fell out under the power! When she got up, she couldn't find the tumor. Not only was she free from pain, but she could breathe as normally as someone who didn't have asthma!

That's just a little manifestation of the glory of God. The glory of God will knock you out of bed! The glory of God will knock you down! God may not lay you on your back with sickness and disease, but God will lay you on your back with the glory! He will fill your life with visions and dreams and revelations of divine tomorrows in God! He's a good God!

There was a man in that meeting who told me later that he had been skeptical about the power of God. He didn't believe it, but was going to church anyway. As I was ministering that night, He sat there doubting. His friend (Steve) was sitting next to him. Steve started praying aloud, saying, *"Lord, please speak to me tonight through your servant!"* At that very moment I stopped and said, *"Is there anyone here named Steve?"* He started crying and came forward. The power of God hit him, and he fell down.

When the man saw what happened to his friend, he ran to the front and lifted his hands. I laid my hands on him, and it was as if a lightning bolt hit him. The glory of God knocked him down! He met me after the service and said, *"I want you to know that I will never doubt God again!"*

Well, there's a better way to become a believer! There's a way that says, *"I'm determined that when the Spirit of Truth reveals it to me, I will live my life pressing after it to apprehend it. I won't be someone who has to travel somewhere to find the glory; I'll be someone who's taking the glory with me wherever I go!"*

The glory of the Lord belongs to you!

Eyewitnesses of His Majesty

Isaiah said, *"God is going to shine upon you, and His glory is going to be seen by others."* The glory is light and the light is power. Out of Him comes shafts of light, which are the hiding places of His power. The Bible says that Jesus is the Word: *"...and the Word was with God, and the Word was God. ...In him was life; and the life was the light of men"* (John 1:1, 4). God's power is in His Word.

The Bible says," *The Word was made flesh...and we beheld his glory..."* (John 1:14).

When did we see the glory of the Word?

We saw the glory of the Word when the Word talked with the wisdom of God; not when the Word was silent; not when the Word was inactive; not in Nazareth where He could do no mighty works because of their unbelief. The glory was seen when the Word raised the dead! The glory was seen when the Word cast out devils! The glory was seen when the Word healed the sick! When the Word was in motion, His glory was seen: *"...the glory as of the only begotten of the Father, full of grace and truth."*

Lay hands on yourself and say,

> *I could live my whole life missing out on the purpose of Christianity. I could live my whole life missing out on the presence, the consciousness, the awareness, and the benefits of the glory. But I'm not going to! I'm going to learn about the glory of God!*

> **For we have not followed cunningly devised fables, when we made known unto you the power and the coming of our Lord Jesus Christ, but were eye witnesses of his majesty, for he received from God the Father, honor and glory when there came such a voice to him from the excellent glory, this is my beloved son in whom I am well pleased. And this voice which came from Heaven we heard, when we were with him in the holy mount.**

> **2 Peter 1:16-18 KJV**

Remember Peter on the Mount of Transfiguration?

Peter saw the glory and said, *"Let's build a house for the glory. In fact, let's build three houses for the glory."* Immediately after he said this, he had an encounter with the anointing of God that he would never forget. As a matter of fact, when the Holy Ghost came and directed him to write, Peter referred back to that encounter on the Mount of Transfiguration!

Let me remind you of the significance of that encounter.

Jesus said, *"Some of you standing here will not see death until you have seen the Kingdom of God come with power."* Then He took Peter, James, and John to a mountain apart by themselves to pray, and there Jesus began to be transfigured. They saw the invisible glory of God that was inside Him all along. They saw that glory manifest on the outside of His physical body.

The anointing overshadowed them in a cloud of glory, and a voice from Heaven came from the cloud saying, *"This is my beloved Son in whom I am well pleased."* Peter, James, and John fell down under the power and laid there in a manifestation of the glory of God until Jesus touched them saying, *"Don't fear."*

Peter is referring to this encounter when he said, *"We have not followed some cunningly devised story! We didn't believe some well put together 'con job' when we made known to you the power of the coming of the Lord. No! We were eye witnesses of His majesty and we heard the voice come from the excellent glory!"*

The glory of God enables royalty to operate in your life. The Bible says that you are a king and a priest, but without the anointing, you won't act like a king, and you won't live like a priest. You need the anointing! Without the anointing, you'll act like a beggar. I know preachers who act like beggars.

Why? It's because they don't have the anointing! The King of Kings, Christ, operates as a King because of the glory of God. Without the anointing, you can't act like a king!

The glory of God is the nature of God. God's nature is glory. Glory means "splendor." It means "the honor of God." That's His divine nature. When you notice God talking about the glory, you'll notice God talking about royalty, dignity, kingship, rulership, and dominion. These things go hand-in-hand. All of Heaven's power is in the glory of God.

God said, *"I am the Lord, I change not. My glory will I not give to another."* Yet Jesus said, *"Father, the glory you have given to me, I have given to them"* because we are not "another." We are His people who are called by His name! *"The glory you have given me—the glory that Peter saw on the mount of Transfiguration—I have given them!"*

More Than Enough Goodness

Moses asked God, *"Show me Thy glory."* God answered him and said, *"I will cause My goodness to pass before you"* (Exodus 33:18, 19). The glory of God is the goodness of God!

We all know that God is good, but how good is He in *your* life?

He is as good in your life as you allow the glory to be made known in your life! If you yield to the anointing, then the goodness of God will be more present in your life. The anointing, or the glory, is the goodness of God!

God said, *"I will cause my goodness to pass before you, and I will pronounce the name of the Lord."* In other words, *"I will speak the name of the Lord in front of you."* God said, *"I will put you in the cleft of the rock, and I'll pass by you. I'll cover you with My hand. And it will come to pass that when My glory passes by, I will take My hand away, and you'll get a glimpse from the back because you can't see My face. You can't see My presence and live."*

Why couldn't Moses look into the Glory?

Moses didn't have a heart of flesh. It was a heart of stone. No one under the Old Covenant had the right kind of heart. They couldn't see God's presence face-to-face. It would kill them because their heart had not been prepared. They needed a Redeemer, but the Redeemer had not yet come. In the meantime, even the blood of bulls and goats wasn't able to make them good enough.

God said I'm going to pronounce the name of the Lord.

The children of Israel wouldn't even say the name *Jehovah*. They didn't dare to carelessly speak the name because the name was a description of the Person. When God says about Himself, *"I am Jehovah-Rapha—I am the Lord that healeth thee; I am the Lord, the Compassionate One,"* those words are Spirit and life. Within the context of those words, the glory that is pertinent to that promise resides. The Word is Spirit and life.

The name *Jehovah* had the glory resident in it. They couldn't just speak that name with irreverence. They couldn't pronounce that name.

They had to meditate on that name and they had to believe that name. However, they could not articulate that name. Throughout the Old Testament, men and women had to avoid direct contact with the glory. If they didn't, it would kill them!

God said, *"No man will see My face and live, so I'm going to pass by you, Moses, and I'm going to pronounce the name of the Lord."*

What was that going to do?

That was going to bring into manifestation the power of the name—*The God Who is More Than Enough!* That name carries with it *all* of the anointing, *all* of the glory, *all* of the power that will make Him more than enough in your life!

Do you know what makes God more than enough in your life?

The anointing makes God more than enough in your life. It's not the bank! God can get the money out of a fish's mouth! He can get the fish out of the water and onto the grill without a net! He can multiply loaves and fishes, and if there are no loaves, He can rain manna down from Heaven!

God told Moses that He was going to pronounce the name: Jehovah-Rapha; Jehovah-Jireh; Jehovah-Nissi; Wonderful; Full of Glory.... That's the name of the Lord!

Do you know what is even better than that?

The Bible says, *"For thou hast magnified thy word above all thy name"* (Psalm 138:2). God has magnified His Word above all His name!

Some people take the name and say, *"He's Almighty God—He can do anything He wants to do."* No! He has magnified His Word above His name. Although He's Almighty God and can do anything He wants to do, He has taken His Word and magnified it above His sovereignty. Therefore, He will not do anything that He said in the Word He wouldn't do!

He's not the God who is going to make you sick just because He is sovereign! No! He has magnified His Word above all His name! As a result, when I get a hold of the Word, I can get a hold of the glory that is in the Word! I can get a hold of the anointing that is in the word! I can get a hold of the power that is in the Word, and things will happen in the natural realm. Most importantly, things will happen in me! On the inside of me, I will experience change!

Bright Morning Star

> We have also a more sure word of prophecy; whereunto ye do well that ye take heed, as unto a light that shineth in a dark place, until the day dawn, and the day star arise in your hearts; knowing this first, that no prophecy of the scripture is of any private interpretation. For the prophecy came not in old time by the will of man: but holy men of God spake as they were moved by the Holy Ghost.
>
> **2 Peter 1:19 KJV**

Peter said, *"We have not followed a lie. We have not followed a myth. We were eyewitnesses! We were on that mountain, and we saw the glory! We heard the voice from the excellent glory, but we have a more sure Word of prophecy. Don't settle for our experience! We have a more sure Word of prophecy, which you do well to heed as a light that shines in the dark place."*

What are you talking about Peter?

"I'm talking about Scripture! No prophecy of Scripture came at any time by the will of man. God is the one who brought Scripture! Holy men of God spoke as they were moved by the Holy Ghost. Don't settle for the fact that I had an encounter with God and saw Jesus transfigured and heard a voice from Heaven. Settle for the fact that Scripture is given by inspiration, and that the plan of God is in Scripture!"

What do we do with this more sure Word of prophecy, Peter?

"Adhere to it! Look at it! Make it your conviction! Be persuaded of it and driven to apprehend it! Go after it as you would go after a light that shines in a dark place!"

If you were driving in the desert, and your fuel gauge showed that you had only a quarter of a tank of gas left, would you start driving out into the darkness?

No! You would take heed unto a light that shines. If there were a light in any direction, that's the direction you would go! You don't have time to mess around and burn all of your fuel going in a direction that has no shining, radiant promise!

God says, *"The same way your common sense tells you to go toward a light when you're in a dark place, your common sense ought to tell you to take heed unto Scripture. If you do, you will keep on going in the right direction until the day dawns and the day star arises in your heart!"*

He's talking about a day for the believer. It's a day when the Lord is risen upon the believer. It's a day that's pertinent to *this* life.

To the Spirit-filled Ephesian church, Paul said, *"I'm praying that God will grant you, according to the riches of His glory, to be strengthened with might by His Holy Ghost (by His glory—His anointing) in your inner man, so that Christ may dwell and feel totally at home in your hearts through your faith. I'm praying that the eyes of your understanding would be enlightened so that you will know what is the hope of His calling."*

The Word has life in it, and the life has light in it. When the Word manifests, you can see the glory of the Father. You can see the manifestation of the Father!

God says, *"Meditate on the Word. Heed to the Word. Believe what the Word says about you!"*

Do you know what will happen when you do this?

You won't just be saved and on your way to Heaven. You won't just speak a couple of words in other tongues. No! There will come a day when the revelation of the resurrected Christ will rise up in your heart. Then, all of a sudden, *to live is Christ!* All of a sudden, you are crucified; nevertheless, you live! Yet, it's not Christ, but it's Christ who's living in you!

The Day Star is the phosphorous bright and morning star. Every other star we know gets its light from a higher light. The star that will rise in your heart doesn't get its light from anything else. God is the light! He doesn't get His light from any other source.

Knowing God, Knowing Power

God says, *"Take heed unto Scripture the same way you would take heed unto a light that shines in the dark place."*

How do you take heed?

When that theologian says, *"We're all sinners."* I take heed to the Word. I say, *"Wait a minute! I don't deny that I've sinned, but I deny that I'm a sinner. I was a sinner, and I needed a Savior. But I got a Savior! Now I am a Saint!"*

When someone says, *"God makes you sick;"* when a preacher says, *"We are empty vessels:"* when religion says, *"The power is not for today,"* I say, *"Wait! I'm going to take heed to the light that shines in a dark place!"* I look for it. I discover it. I get a hold of that light. I keep reminding myself about it. I quote it; I keep rehearsing it and I keep meditating on it. *"I'm the righteousness of God in Christ Jesus! I'm a new creature!"*

> When the world says, *"You're poor,"*
> I say, *"The Bible says I'm rich!"*
> When the devil says, *"You're sick,"*
> I say *"The Bible says I'm healed!"*
> When the devil says, *"You're confused,"*
> I say, *"The Bible says I have the mind of Christ!"*

I get a hold of it, and then the day dawns and the day star rises. Christ feels at home in my heart! He rises up, and I'm strengthened with might by His power in the inner man. Suddenly, the injection of His glory comes from the Holy Ghost into my spirit man, into my soul, and into my physical body. Resurrection life fills my being because the Scripture says, *"If the Spirit of Him that raised Christ up from the dead dwell in you, He will quicken and make alive your mortal body by His Spirit that dwells in you!"*

The Day Star is getting ready to rise upon those who know their God. It's not rising on those who know *about* their God, but on those who know their God personally through an experiential knowledge.

How?

It's through the Spirit of revelation! *"The eyes of your understanding being enlightened; that ye may know what is the hope of his calling"* (Ephesians 1:18).

What happens to people who know their God?

The Day Star rises in their hearts! They know their God, and they're strengthened with might in their inner man. They don't attend a church for two weeks and complain, *"I can't get anybody to go to dinner with me!"*

I've been to a lot of social events in the Church world, and they didn't help me. I'm not looking to get acquainted with man. Thank God for people. I love people, but I don't love people more than I love God or His Word!

The Day Star will arise in my heart and in your heart. The Bible says, *"The people that do know their God will be strong and do exploits"* (Daniel 11:32). It's not talking about when we get to Heaven! What kind of exploits are you going to do when you get to Heaven? It's talking about down here!

Why doesn't it say, *"Those whom God knows will do exploits"*? It is because it doesn't matter whether or not God knows you. *You have to know God!* Unless you know Him and the power of His resurrection, then His glory will not become yours *right now*. His power will not become visible in your life. You have to get a hold of the power!

At Large on Planet Earth

"Take heed, as unto a light that shineth in a dark place, until the day dawn...."

How does the day dawn?
How does the shining, the light, the glory, come?

The Bible says, *"The spirit of man is the candle* (or the lamp) *of the Lord, searching all the inward parts of the belly"* (Proverbs 20:27). That means the Holy Ghost brings it into your spirit.

The Bible tells us to guard our spirits with all diligence. Too many are robbed through the gates of the eyes, the gates of the ears, the billboards that are read, the commercials they see, and the religious statements that are heard. They are robbed of the benefits of the glory through the sense realm. You will have an abundance of whatever your mind is full of.

Guard your spirit with all diligence!

I hate religion! I cannot believe some of the stupid things that come in the guise of Christianity! If you're not on guard, those religious statements will creep in and rob you of the glory. Religious statements are designed to rob you of what belongs to you.

Every believer is a potential terror to the kingdom of darkness. The Bible says, *"Thou believest that there is one God; thou doest well: the devils also believe, and tremble"* (James 2:19).

Do you know why they're trembling?

Jesus already whipped them, but now they're trembling about *you* whipping them! They're trembling because they believe.

The Bible says,

> **But we speak the wisdom of God in a mystery… yet not the wisdom of this world, nor of the princes of this world, that come to nought; which none of the princes of this world knew: for had they known it, they would not have crucified the Lord of glory"**
>
> **1 Corinthians 2:6-8 KJV**

Let me paraphrase: *"Had they known what they were doing, they would have never done what they did!"*

What did they not know?

They didn't know that by killing Jesus, they would open the door for you to be filled with the glory! The devil knows he messed up. The devil knows he blew it! Now he has to work overtime to convince you that you're not who God said you are. The devil is saying, *"I wish I never killed Jesus!"*

The devil is afraid. He knows that Jesus said His earthly mission was finished. He knows that Jesus said, *"Go ye..."* He's not afraid of Jesus coming down to Earth and preaching another sermon, because he knows He won't. He knows that Jesus sat down and is waiting until His enemies are made His footstool.

The devil is terrified because the Word is still loose on Earth. There are copies of the Word of God all over the world, and the Holy Ghost is still at large on the planet. That terrifying thought is rippling throughout the kingdom of darkness! The devils know that one day someone is going to get a hold of the Word of God and stand up and fight the good fight of faith!

They know, they believe, and they tremble!

The Day Star is going to arise in those who know their God. If you could buy that with money, you would. If we could pay for even one revelation, we would sell everything we had to buy it. Thank God that Jesus paid for it in full! All we have to do is receive it by faith, and it will change our lives forever!

Immortality in the Glory

One of my good friends is a powerful businessman and a preacher. You'll never catch him without the Word in his mouth. He always talks the Word! I've never seen him depressed. When we get together, we preach the Word of God to each other. He laughs; he rejoices; he quotes the Word all of the time.

He's involved in a business and he's preaching. He's seventy years old, but he runs around with kindness, full of strength, prosperity, and joy! God is blessing him for the Kingdom of God. He looks young and he has the strength of a young man!

I know why he's strong. He keeps the Word in his mouth! He keeps the Word in his heart and the glory in that Word has slowed the aging process! We see that throughout the Bible. When Caleb was eighty-five years old he said, *"As my strength was then, even so is my strength now, for war, both to go out and to come in"* (Joshua 14:11).

Charles Camplejohn, scientist and former chief design engineer for the Apollo project, made the following observation, which is now common knowledge: If a person was launched from Earth in a rocket ship traveling at three fourths the speed of light and returned two months later, they would have aged only one month. Meanwhile, the rest of the Earth would be two months older.

If their space travel were accelerated to 99.999999 percent the speed of light, they would reach the center of our galaxy in twenty-seven days. Meanwhile, the Earth would have aged 27,000 years! A day with the Lord is as a thousand years, and a thousand years as one day!

He further said that if it were possible for man to reach the speed of light, he would live forever without aging. Science is discovering things that are available to us right now!

"In Him was life, and the life was the light of men" (John 1:4).

He has immortality dwelling in the light!

The Word of God is alive. When you get into the glory of the Word of God, you lose sight of the time! People say, *"Your services are so long!"* Not if you're in the Spirit! If you're in the Spirit, the time goes fast and you don't age!

A Glorious Image

> **Now the Lord is that Spirit; and where the Spirit of the Lord is, there is liberty. But we all, with open face beholding as in a [mirror] the glory of the Lord, are changed into the same image from glory to glory, even as by the Spirit of the Lord.**
>
> **2 Corinthians 3:17, 18 KJV**

The Spirit of God, the anointing of God, is the Lord. That anointing of God or the glory of God, will bring liberty. We no longer have to have our faces covered from the glory, but with an open face we behold the glory.

Why? It is because the presence of God is no longer alien or foreign to us!

Have you ever seen Christians get paranoid because of the presence of the glory? I have watched people come into the church and see the presence of God start moving and then just walk out of the church. I wonder, *"Aren't you saved? Don't you know what's available to you?"*

The Church hasn't been taught.

The glory belongs to you! When you look with an open face, when you behold without fear and without doubt, the glory is going to change you into the same image. The presence of God will change you. The anointing will change you into the same image.

What image?

He will change you into the image of His dear Son, which we have been predestined to be conformed into!

What does His dear Son look like?

The Bible said that He's the brightness of God's glory and the express image of His Person. The anointing will make you like Jesus! When you hold on to the promise of the anointing, when you meditate on the Scriptures regarding the anointing, then Jesus Himself—the Day Star—will rise up in you. His glory will be seen upon you, and He'll begin to be the one who conducts the transactions in your life.

Where you find the glory, you'll find the gold. Where you find the glory, you'll find the herds. Where you find the glory, you'll find the health. You'll find the benefits, and you'll find the blessings. These are not things that we're seeking. They are just benefits. They are added blessings.

We're pursuing the presence of God, but you can't find God and His presence without finding all the benefits that go along with His presence and His anointing!

Therefore seeing we have this ministry, as we have received mercy, we faint not.

2 Corinthians 4:1 KJV

What ministry is that?

The ministry is being conformed to His image by the anointing and teaching others how to be conformed as well. It's the ministry of beholding Him with an open face. It's the ministry where we don't have a veil blocking us from His presence. Since we have this ministry, we don't faint! We receive mercy. We have renounced the hidden things of dishonesty. We don't walk in craftiness and we don't handle the Word of God deceitfully.

Look at this:

> **...But by manifestation of the truth, commending ourselves to every man's conscience in the sight of God.**

2 Corinthians 4:2 KJV

What in the world is manifestation of the truth?

It is the Word manifested in motion! We beheld His glory by the manifestation of the Truth. The Truth said that they shall lay hands on the sick and they shall recover. We manifest that by laying hands on the sick and seeing them recover.

The Truth said that no weapon will prosper against us. We manifest that by demonstrating that we are not moved by what comes against us. We do that because we're being changed into His image, which means His victory belongs to us. People will see the same things that happened *in Him* are happening *in us!*

Are you ready for the anointing?

Lift your hands up and say:

> *God is getting my faith ready. He's preparing me for the anointing so that I know how to invite God to move without limits in my life."*

Chapter 15

Unleash the Power of Faith

It's not enough to have faith. You must have faith that talks, acts and lives.

It is not enough to have faith; you must have active faith. You cannot have dead faith because faith without works is dead. It cannot profit you, nor can it help you.

We are going to learn how to unleash the power of faith in our lives. In that process, we will learn how to unleash the power of God in our lives.

Do you want more of God's power in your life?
Do you want more of God's will active in your life?

"We having the same spirit of faith, according as it is written, I believed and therefore have I spoken; we also believe, and therefore speak" (2 Corinthians 4:13). It does not take any faith to speak what you're seeing, to speak what you're experiencing, or to speak what is in the natural. When you have the Spirit of faith, you speak what you believe, and you believe what you do not see. *"Now faith is the substance of things hoped for, the evidence of things not seen"* (Hebrews 11:1).

It's not enough to have faith. You must have faith that talks, acts and lives. When you have the same Spirit of faith that Jesus had—the one He gave to the disciples—you will not be satisfied only to believe God's Word. You will go beyond that and begin to act upon God's Word. You will begin to both confess and speak God's Word. I believe and that is why I have spoken.

You may have started to witness changes. Mighty testimonies may be coming to pass in your life, but it is just the beginning. You may wonder, *"Why won't God do more?"* You need to learn how to release the power of faith in your life in a bigger dimension. The problem is not God. The problem is at your end. God has more than enough power necessary to cause you to witness and experience victory in your life.

The Spirit Gives Life

Not that we are sufficient of ourselves to think any thing as of ourselves, but our sufficiency is of God; who also hath made us able ministers of the New Testament; not of the letter, but of the spirit; for the letter killeth, but the spirit giveth life.

2 Corinthians 3:5-6 KJV

The man of God is saying, *"We're not bragging on ourselves! We're not saying, 'It's us!' We're not saying, 'It's our ability!' No! We are saying, 'It's God Who has chosen us and made us able ministers of the New Testament!'"* In the Church today we ought to be hearing ministers who are able. They should be ministers of the New Testament, not of the Old Testament. Yet, there are people who preach the New Testament with an Old Testament edge.

You can't live by faith and be bound by religion. *Faith and religion never mix!* If you want to know why people have a hard time with faith, you'll find out that they're religious.

Faith is a New Testament gift given to people. It is a New Testament impartation given by the Author and the Finisher of our faith, the Lord Jesus Christ. Religion and faith are incompatible. You cannot have bondage from a religious standpoint and then live by faith. They don't mix, they don't cohabit, and they don't coexist. Religion was relegated to the Old Testament. It was a teacher that pointed to a relationship that a believer would be able to have with the Lord Jesus Christ.

Paul said, *"We are able ministers of the New Testament, not of the letter but of the Spirit."* People run around and debate, saying, *"I don't agree with this,"* and, *"I'm not in agreement with that."* Their opinions are useless if they are opinions of doctrine, or persuasion. The letter will kill. The letter will prove that you are incapable of doing what God has called you to do.

The Bible says that every jot and tittle of the Old Testament was perfect, but it was given to an imperfect people. It proved to those people that all of their righteousness was as filthy rags. They did not have the ability to do what the letter commanded them to do. The letter, in turn, killed them because it was God's witness to them that they needed another source of help! That source of help is the Holy Ghost!

Do you need another source of help? You should receive Him. You should allow Him. You should follow Him. *"We came to preach the New Testament, not the letter, but the Spirit. The letter kills, but the Spirit gives life."* That is the same Spirit of faith!

The Nature of Christ Is the Spirit of Faith

> **Now the Lord is that Spirit; and where the Spirit of the Lord is, there is liberty. But we all, with open face, beholding as in a glass the glory of the Lord, are changed into the same image from glory to glory, even as by the Spirit of the Lord.**
>
> **2 Corinthians 3:17-18 KJV**

We are New Testament creatures who preach the Spirit, not the letter. The Lord is that Spirit.

What spirit? It's the Spirit we preach. It's the Spirit we have. It's the same Spirit of faith.

The Word is nigh thee in your mouth and in your heart!

Who is the Word? Jesus Christ—the same Spirit! Where the Spirit of the Lord is, there is liberty. Liberty and religion don't mix. The Spirit is the anointing, and the anointing destroys the yoke! It annihilates, it destroys, and it shatters bondage. Bondage cannot coexist with the presence of the Spirit of God.

It says, *"The Lord is that Spirit, and where the Spirit of the Lord is, there is liberty—and we are beholding as in a mirror, God's glory."* The glory of the Lord is the Spirit of the Lord. We behold, as in a mirror, the glory, and we're being changed from glory to glory, even as by the Spirit of the Lord. In other words, the Spirit changes us! Religion couldn't change us. The letter couldn't change us, but the Spirit can.

People try to get faith through the letter, but it can't be done. Only the Spirit of faith can impact your life with the divine nature of God. He's a God of faith! The Bible said that He quickened the dead and called those things which are not as though they were. Then it said that He gave to us exceeding great and precious promises. It said that by these you might be partakers of the divine nature. That's God's nature of faith! He speaks what He believes!

He speaks what He believes because He is a Spirit of faith. His nature is a faith nature. He does not wait until you perform to call you a Saint. He does not wait until you succeed to call you more than a conqueror. God begins to call you that from the beginning. He speaks truth into your life. Some of us only had the report of the Lord to hold on to because the majority of public opinion was that we wouldn't amount to anything. *Aren't you glad that God knows?* He knows that the Spirit will give you life and enable you to become what He has called you to be!

Righteousness Speaks

Thank God that we don't have to conjure up some intellectual method of being like Jesus! He sends His Spirit and, from the inside-out we begin to change. His nature starts living on the inside of us, and we become believers. We begin to believe God's Word, and it begins to become a reality within our hearts and within our lives. We will be changed from glory to glory by the Spirit of the Lord!

Can you brag about your salvation?
Can you brag that you earned it?

"But that no man is justified by the law in the sight of God, it is evident" (Galatians 3:11).

There is no one who can say that their religion earned them access to God. *Nobody.* It doesn't matter how well they perform their religion. No one performs religion as well as some of the Scribes and the Pharisees did in Jesus' day. Yet, He said that unless your righteousness exceeds the righteousness of the Scribes and the Pharisees, you shall in no way enter into the Kingdom of God.

What kind of righteousness is He talking about? The Bible says that the righteousness which is of the law says, *"He which doeth those things shall live by them. But the righteousness which is of faith speaketh on this wise"* (Romans 10:5-6). Righteousness talks. It says, *"I don't have to go up to Heaven and bring the answer down. I don't have to go into the deep and resurrect it from the dead again. No! The answer is near me: it's in my heart and in my mouth! God is for me! Who can be against me? No weapon formed against me will prosper! I can do all things through Christ which strengthens me!"*

Religious people will get offended when you talk like that. They do not understand the righteousness of faith. Religion says, *"Be quiet,"* but righteousness talks! It speaks righteousness. It lives righteousness. It believes righteousness.

The Word says that no one is justified in the sight of God by the acts they perform. They can't be justified because of the works of the law or because of ritual or ceremonial observance. You're not justified because you go to church. You're not justified because you belong to a denomination. You're not justified because your friends like you. You're not justified because you do something. You're justified because of this: *the just shall live by faith.*

Somebody said, *"Let's not go overboard on faith."* I would counter, *"Then let's not go overboard on living!"* We don't want to go overboard, so let's not live. The Bible says *"The just shall live by faith!"* Are you alive when you're asleep? Are you alive when you're studying, talking and walking? If so, then you ought to be living that life by faith because the just shall *live* by faith!

New Testament Believers: Old Testament Edge

And the law is not of faith; but, the man that doeth them shall live in them.

Galatians 3:12 KJV

The law says, *"Do it, and after you've done it, you're justified."* The law is performance oriented. A lot of Christians are too, but they don't know it. They are New Testament people with an Old Testament edge. The law is legalistic. The law says, *"Do it, and you'll live in it."*

You can't be justified by the law. No one was able to keep its statutes. Everyone failed to do it the way it was supposed to be done. Only Jesus did it. *"There's none that doeth good, no, not one"* (Romans 3:12). No one could brag about how good they were!

The law is not of faith. The law says, *"When I see it, I'll believe it."* Some people think that's faith. They say, *"Well, I believe God can, but I'm not going to say He will. I just believe He can."*

Do you know what they're saying? They're saying, *"I'm not going to use an ounce of faith."* If you're waiting until He does it to believe, then you're living under the Old Covenant. In the Old Testament they looked forward to the Redeemer and said, *"When He comes, everything will be alright."* Now the Church is saying, *"When He comes again, everything will be alright."* We need to remember that He already came! He said, *"It is finished!"* The devil is under His feet! He paid it in full! It's been done!

Put your hands on your spirit and say this:

> *The answer is near me. It's in my mouth. It's in my heart. It's the Word of faith that I believe, and that is why I speak! I'm justified by faith in the sight of God. I live by faith. And I walk by faith, not by sight. I say what I believe, and I believe what God promised! I have that supernatural, God-given ability working in*

me because I live under the New Testament - the will and testament of the Lord Jesus Christ!

The Faith That Speaks

What's the best sermon ever preached?

Jesus said, *"Whosoever shall say to this mountain, 'Be thou removed, and be thou cast into the sea!' and shall not doubt in his heart, but shall believe that those things which he said shall come to pass, he shall have whatsoever he saith!"*

Jesus was faith talking.

He talked to the wind.
He talked to the waves.
He talked to the corpse.
He talked to the devil.
He talked to the fig tree.
He talked to a generation removed from Him.

He is the author and the finisher of faith. He exercised faith. By speaking faith, He triggered and unleashed the very power of God in His life.

Somebody may say, *"I don't believe that."* You can say that if you want to, but the Bible says that Jesus believed it! Jesus released God's faith, and those who watched Him said that His Words were filled with power. With authority and power He commanded the unclean spirits, and they obeyed! Somebody said, *"But that was Jesus!"* He sent seventy out and they came back rejoicing and saying, *"Even the devils are subject to us in Your name."* That means they went out and did some talking, too! They spoke faith!

I was in a Full Gospel meeting years ago when God began to anoint me for the ministry. As we were sitting there, a man came off the street, full of alcohol and completely bound up. The brothers were taking him off to the side because he was disrupting the order of the service. The Spirit of the Lord checked me, so I got up and walked over to them.

They were standing there talking to him, trying to counsel him. I said, *"Excuse me,"* and I moved everyone out of the way. I laid my hands on him, and he fell down under the power face forward. I grabbed him, flipped him over, and said, *"Look me in the eyes!"* Immediately, he did so. I said, *"Come out of him, in the name of Jesus!"* And he said, *"Aaaahhh!"* and was instantly set free!

Faith talks. Faith is what you believe when you will speak. Someone said, *"I just don't believe in that."* Maybe not, but you're going to be saying *something*, because out of the abundance of the heart, the mouth speaks. Now, if you fill your heart with faith, the Spirit of faith will talk through you. The words of faith will begin to live through you. You'll begin to see the power of God released in your life.

Performance Oriented Righteousness

The law is not of faith. Religion is not of faith. Legalism and tradition are not of faith. All of those things depend on performance. Like the law, they are performance-oriented. There are even people that are performance-oriented. They say, *"I can't say that I'm the righteousness of God in Christ Jesus because I still have problems!"*

If that's your conviction, then you'll *never* be able to confess your righteousness because you are always going to have problems. Somebody may say, *"I can't say I'm healed because I always get symptoms in my body."* Then the Scripture, *"By His stripes you were healed,"* doesn't apply to you! The Spirit of faith doesn't say what it *sees*. The Spirit of faith says what it *believes*.

I believe, and therefore have I spoken!

If a person wasn't having any symptoms, they wouldn't need to *believe* that they are healed! They would *know* that they are, and there wouldn't be any faith involved. A millionaire doesn't say, *"I believe I'm a millionaire."* No! It would take absolutely no faith to say that. In order to say what you believe, you need to yield to the Spirit of faith. You have to be moved by the unseen, by an internal conviction of faith. People, however, want to wait until it's done before they say it.

Some people are performance-oriented at God's end. They won't say what God is going to do, even when God said that He was going to do it! God said, *"I'm the God that healeth thee. I'm the God Who forgives all your iniquities and heals all your diseases!"* You can ask them, *"Do you believe God?"* and they'll answer, *"Oh, yes! Hallelujah!"* However, when you say, *"Then is He going to heal you?"* they'll answer, *"Well, I hope so."*

They are living under an Old Testament concept of God. They are performance-oriented. They're trying to get God to do it *before* they'll believe it. That letter will kill you. It will short circuit the very power of the Spirit of faith that came to help you.

You ask that person, *"Do you think God's going to heal you?"*
They reply, *"I certainly hope so."*
You go further, *"Did He say that He would heal you?"*
At that point they respond with, *"Well, I think He did."*
So you show them the promise in the Word. *"There it is, right there."* They see it and say, *"Yes, yes, it says it right there."*
Then you ask, *"Do you believe it?"*
They respond, *"Well, if it says it, I believe it."*
Satisfied with their progress, you finally ask, *"Then is He going to heal you?"* They still say, *"I don't know."*

They are performance-oriented! Something is wrong with this picture, and people make fun of *us* because we believe God! *Isn't it turned around?*

It's turned around, but we're going to set it right! We're going to teach people how to stand up! We're going to uncover the devil for the liar he really is! He's still running around acting like he's a big devil, but two thousand years ago he was defeated. He was reduced to nothing! We are going to tell people all over the world that he's defeated!

Don't be performance-oriented at either end. You are the righteousness of God in Christ Jesus, and because of that, you are a partaker of His nature! It will change you, and you'll continue to grow. God will do what He said He will do. As a matter of fact, God has *done* what He said He would do through Jesus Christ! It is done, and the Spirit of faith claims it, receives it, and acts upon it.

The Nature of the Curse

Christ hath redeemed us from the curse of the law.

Galatians 3:13 KJV

What curse was it?

In Romans, it talks about the kind of man that wants to do good but can't. He wants to obey the law of God, but he just can't do it. There are two laws in his members fighting against one another. The image given is of a person carrying a corpse that is decomposing on his or her body.

That was the curse of the law.

What did it mean? It meant you had a problem! You could not be justified until you fulfilled everything that God said you should do. The nature of the curse was that *you couldn't.* That was the curse. It was people carrying a corpse around, saying, *"I can't get rid of this corpse!"* The Bible, however, says, *"Christ has redeemed us from the curse."*

What did Jesus do?

"My child, you don't have to do it in order to be justified; you just have to believe it to be justified! If you will believe it, then I'll make a New Covenant with you. I'll take that old nature from you and put a new nature in you. I'll write my Word on the tablets of your heart and give you a new fleshly nature, a new character. It will be a new agreement between you and Me. I'll live on the inside of you, and I'll live through you. All you have to do now is believe it! For by grace are you saved through faith; and that not of yourselves; it is the gift of God. No one can boast about it!"

"And the law is not of faith; but, the man that doeth them shall live in them" (Galatians 3:12).

People want to live there. They say, *"I just don't want to say something and then find out that the Lord isn't going to do it."*

Do you know what they're saying?

"I'm just going to carry this corpse around, waiting until God does it so that I can believe it." You don't have to! He sent his Spirit to live on the inside of you, and that Spirit has the ability to help you to believe God and to speak what you believe!

That's why I refuse to stay where I am! Every year we grow in God! Every year we take more territory in Jesus! The anointing increases, the financial flow increases, and the outreach increases. Everything increases because our faith reaches out to next year and gets a hold of it! It says, *"Come here!"* We have something in God!

The Spirit of faith will help you live your life in New Testament proportion, rather than in Old Testament bondage. Christ has redeemed you from the curse. You don't have to carry that corpse on your back anymore! He was made a curse for you!

Embracing the Promise

> **Christ hath redeemed us from the curse of the law, being made a curse for us; for it is written, Cursed is every man that hangeth on a tree; that the blessing of Abraham might come on the Gentiles through Jesus Christ; that we might receive the promise of the Spirit through faith.**
>
> **Galatians 3:13-14 KJV**

One evening after Bible school, we said, *"Start praying in tongues. You are going to receive the baptism of the Holy Ghost. You're going to receive it by faith."* People who had never talked in tongues started praying in tongues just as fluently as everyone else.

We don't have to keep knocking and never see the door open. We are not called to keep asking and never get an answer. We don't have to die having not received the promise! Christ has redeemed us from the curse so that the blessings of Abraham would come upon us!

Now we can receive the promise
of the Spirit through faith!
What spirit is it? The same Spirit of faith.

How do I receive Him? Through faith!

First, I have to believe He's mine. Once I believe He's mine, I allow Him in. Now I can yield to His inspiration. He'll start letting the Word live to me. If I hear a lie, a tradition of man, and weigh it honestly and sincerely against the Word of God, I will get rid of it and hold on to Truth! I will grow in God and pursue after righteousness because I have the same Spirit that Jesus had.

Jesus died so that the blessings of Abraham would come upon us, that we might receive the promise of the Spirit though faith.

How did God bless Abraham? The Bible said that Abraham believed God, and it was accounted unto him for righteousness. Abraham lived before the law and before legalism. He was a type of the New Testament believer. He believed God, and he was called a friend of God. God blessed Abraham with everything He promised Him. God said, *"I'm going to increase you. I'm going to multiply you. I'm going to bless you."* Abraham was rich! People tried to give him money, and he said, *"No! I'm not taking your money because you might tell others you made Abraham rich."*

How did he get blessed? He believed God! Abraham didn't have the same Spirit of faith available to us under the New Covenant. The Author and Finisher of faith had not yet come. However, Abraham believed God. Based on Abrahams faith convictions, God did for him what He had promised. The Bible says that it is God who gives you the power to get wealth. It is God who gives you the power to do anything! *"It is not by might, not by power, but it is by My Spirit,"* said the Lord. The Spirit of God is the Person of power sent in to your life to aid you and help you do what He called you to do.

God said that you will receive the promise of the Spirit through faith. He was saying, *"Receive the Spirit of faith into your life. Invite Him in! Stop tarrying for the Holy Ghost—get the Holy Ghost! Receive the Holy Ghost. Start praying with other tongues. Start meditating on Scriptures through the Holy Ghost."* When you do that, the Spirit of God will expand faith in your heart. That faith will reach for every promise ever given by the Word.

The promise was made to Abraham. Jesus redeemed me from the curse of the law, being made a curse for me, that the blessings of Abraham would come upon me! All of a sudden, the Spirit of faith will give you the power to receive into your life the things that God has promised. All the things that God promised Abraham, Isaac, Jacob, Jesus, and anyone else are yours! The Spirit will give you the ability to receive it into your life before you see it!

Why don't you have to wait until you are rich to believe you're rich? The reason is simple. You're not living under the law! You don't have to perform before you believe. You can believe and therefore speak:

I'm rich now!
I'm healed now!
I'm holy now!
I'm anointed now!
I'm a Christian now!
I'm a conqueror now!
I'm happy now!
I'm the head and not the tail now!
I'm going over and not under now!
I'm making it all the way now!"

Somebody said, *"You are wild!"* What did they expect? There's a *Spirit* living in me! The Holy Ghost is living in the hearts of people in order to impact their lives with a characteristic that comes from God. That characteristic is faith. It talks before it ever believes!

Tutored by the Law

If you listen to how some Christians talk, you'll know they're not listening to the Holy Ghost! They'll look at someone and say, *"Look at them! If God ever saves them, it will be a miracle!"* People talk like that! They say, *"That man in driving me crazy!"*

Do you know anyone that talks like that? What are they doing? They're listening to the wrong spirit. They're living in the wrong realm. With their mouth they're choosing to believe what they see.

People complain, *"The preacher says all that stuff about giving. 'Give and it shall be given unto you.' But he doesn't know what I'm going through!"* What they're really saying is, *"I'm a baby! I can't believe that! I have to live under the law!"* The law is the babysitter. It's the schoolmaster that keeps them until they come to Christ. They are babies who don't have the ability to believe and say what God is saying until they see it!

The children of Israel were like that. They murmured, *"Taking us to the Promised Land? No way! You just brought us out here to kill us in the desert! You're not taking us to the Promised Land!"* When they got to the Promise Land, they complained, *"This is the Promised Land? I'm not going in there! There are giants in there! They'll kill us! We're grasshoppers in their sight! We can't handle the Promised Land!"*

The law was babysitting them! It was there as a schoolmaster, as a shadow of something that was to come.

Why is that? The Spirit of faith was not available to men and women during that day. Today faith is available, and the devil knows it! For two thousand years he's done his best to distort the message of the Gospel. He wants to get men and women to act religious so that they cannot benefit from the power available in the Gospel of Jesus Christ. The devil knows there is only one power on Earth that can defeat him. That power is God's Word mixed with a believer's faith.

Someone has to believe it!

Face It with Faith

If you have received the Spirit, then you can build yourself up on your most holy faith, praying in the Spirit. *Why?* He's the Spirit of faith! He's the Spirit that inspires confidence and absolute conviction in the Word of God. Through the Spirit, you can begin to see things God's way. By doing this you will begin to act like Him. As you act like Him, you will unleash the power of God's Word and the power of the faith in your life. Things will happen when you face life with faith!

Jesus said to the fig tree, *"No man will eat fruit from you now forever!"*

Do you know what happened? Those words went right to the core of that tree, and it withered. Peter marveled, saying, *"How quickly the tree that you cursed withered away!"* Jesus replied, *"Have the God kind of faith; whosoever shall say to this mountain be removed and be cast into the sea and will not doubt, they'll have what they said!"* He released the power of God, it went to work, and it brought change to a natural situation.

Someone bound up under the law would have said, *"Look at this fig tree! There is nothing on it. I can't stand fig trees with nothing on them!"* People like that live a life of reaction—they react to situations. They say, *"I don't understand why God allowed that fig tree not to have any figs on it! I give, but I don't get. I pray, but I don't receive. I don't understand; it just doesn't work!"* They keep saying it! Jesus didn't say to the fig tree, *"I can't stand you!"* No, Jesus said, *"No man will eat fruit from you now forever!"*

Jesus is saying, *"Listen! You face that fruitless thing in your life, that thing that does not line up with God's Word, and say to it, 'You're going to die! You're going to be separated out of my life! Spirit of poverty, conditions of lack, situations and obstacles, unbelieving thoughts, I'm not going to eat of your fruit! I'm going to starve you right out of my life! I'm not going to give you equal time!'"*

Do you know what will happen when you do this? The Word of God will go to work to bring about the will of God in your life! You, however, must be willing to believe the Word of God and to live by the Word of God!

Someone said, *"You just say all that because you're a preacher!"*

You could have asked my mother, and she would have told you that I was the *least likely* to write a book on this subject! I used to be a crack addict! When God got a hold of my life, He got a hold of somebody who was not impressed with the incense holder or the ash on the forehead. Later, I was not impressed with the banner or with the tambourine in the Charismatic church. I was not even impressed with the denomination. After I got a hold of the Holy Ghost, He changed my life! Where I am now is not where I was before. Faith brought me to this place. Where I am today is not where I'm going to be tomorrow. Faith fuels my tomorrows.

Before Faith Came

The Spirit wants to make the Word of God effective to our lives. The Bible said, *"By your traditions you make the Word of God of no effect."* Then it said, *"The Word of God did not benefit them because it wasn't mixed with faith in them that heard it."* God wants to make His Word relevant to you so that it can benefit you! It should be relevant to you that God has made you more than a conqueror. It should become so relevant you begin to experience it in your life.

You believe it, you speak it, and you exercise your faith for it.

"But before faith came, we were kept under the law, shut up (that means imprisoned, captive) *unto the faith which should afterward be revealed"* (Galatians 3:23). That means there was a day when the revelation of faith was not in the Earth. It was not available. There was a different testament, a testament of the letter. God didn't make us ministers of the letter.

God made us able ministers of the New Testament. We preach the Spirit, because the Spirit gives life! Before faith came, we were prisoners. We were shut up to the faith which was going to come afterward and be revealed. The law was our babysitter, sent to bring us unto Christ so that we might be justified by faith. Before faith came, we were shut up to the faith that was going to come afterward by revelation. We were kept under the law!

The law was our tutor. The law was our teacher. The law said, *"Do it"* and people had to do it. However, they didn't understand. They had a veil over their faces. They didn't know because they were children. God said, *"Do it"* and when they asked, *"Why?"* He said, *"Because I said so."* Now, being born again, we can look back to the rituals, the sacrifices, and the ceremonies they performed. We have a revelation of why they did them. We understand because we now have a real relationship with Jesus Christ!

The law said, *"Do it. And after you've performed it, then you will be righteous."* That schoolmaster, however, was only there to bring us to the real Author, the real Promise, and the real Champion.

The Bible says, *"Before faith came...."*

Do you know when faith came? Faith came when the Word became flesh. Faith came in the form of revelation. The Old Testament talks about courage and boldness and uses other words to describe *trusting* and putting *confidence* in God. The Spirit of faith was not yet available. When Jesus came, faith came!

Faith in the Blood

Why did faith come? Faith came so that we would be justified by faith, just as if we had never sinned. Do you believe that you could ever live with the boldness and confidence towards God that causes you to know that it is *just as if you'd never sinned?* When you get to that place, you'll never have a *"No!"* answer to a prayer. *Never.*

We may not be there yet, but when we get there, we will have a *"Yes!"* answer to every prayer! The Bible says that if our heart does not condemn us, then we have confidence towards God. If we have confidence towards God, then we know that we have the petitions that we ask of Him. Jesus walked at that level because He never sinned. Now, it's just as if *you* never sinned.

How do you get to the place where you believe it? You must have faith in the Blood!

How clean does the Blood make you? Does it purge you, completely and totally? Yes! It cleanses you thoroughly. *Every part of you* becomes new because of the Blood. He cleanses you from all unrighteousness, and He gives you the confidence and ability to approach God's throne with boldness. You are a prime candidate for a miracle because you know that you are the handiwork of God! The Bible said that Jesus Christ came, so that we would be justified by faith.

You can be a Christian and walk in guilt. You can be a Spirit-filled, tongue-talking Christian and walk in unbelief. You must go beyond the fact that you've received the Spirit of God. You must allow Him to impress you and lead you so that you can put confidence in what Jesus did for you on Calvary. You're justified by faith!

Someone may say, *"It's just the grace of God."* No! It's the grace of God mixed with your faith. The grace of God brought salvation. Remember, where sin abounds, grace does much more abound. However, it does not help those who are not placing any faith in that grace. We are saved by grace through faith, and we're justified by faith.

Joined to the Lord

"But after that faith is come, we are no longer under a schoolmaster, for ye are all the children of God by faith in Christ Jesus. For as many of you as have been baptized into Christ have put on Christ" (Galatians 3:25-27). The original Greek says *introduced into union with* Christ. Now the Lord is that Spirit, and we receive the promise of the Spirit through faith. The Bible said, *"He who is joined unto a harlot is one body, for He said two will be made one. But he that is joined to the Lord is one Spirit."* Now the Lord is that spirit, but when you're joined to the Lord, your spirit and His Spirit become *One* together.

One with God.

The Spirit of God begins to impregnate your spirit with a divine nature. As this happens, you begin to grow in God. You don't even want to do the things you used to do. Your life is different! You don't act the way you used to act. You've been changed! People notice, *"You're so positive now!"* The Spirit of faith living in you has united Himself with your spirit. Now you are one Spirit with the Lord! That does not make you the Lord, but it makes you *one with the Lord.*

Do you know that husbands and wives become "one flesh"? Although they are one, the husband does not become the wife, and the wife does not become the husband. They become one with each other because there is a joining together.

When you come together with the Lord, you are one with the Lord. You're in agreement with the Lord. You would have to work overtime to fall out of agreement with the Holy Ghost! When you hear the truth, the Spirit of God will touch your heart and give you a witness to that truth. As many as were baptized into Christ have put on Christ. They have come into union with Christ.

Power to Become Sons

> **And because you are sons, God has sent forth the Spirit of his Son into your hearts, crying, Abba, Father. Wherefore thou art no more a servant, but a son, and if a son, then a heir of God through Christ.**
>
> **Galatians 4:6-7 KJV**

He was saying, *"Faith came! You don't have to let the letter kill you anymore! Through faith you can be justified with God. Through faith you've been baptized into Jesus, you've put on Jesus!"*

A child can be an heir. Although a child, they can be destined to inherit everything. While they are under age, they will be given tutors. They will be given babysitters. They will be given a chaperone that will watch them in all their ways. When they come of age, however, they will step into their inheritance. They will run the estate.

> **Now I say, that the heir, as long as he is a child, differeth nothing from a servant, though he be Lord of all.**
>
> **Galatians 4:1 KJV**

To as many as believed, Jesus gave them the power to become Sons of God (John 1:12).

What is that power? It is the Holy Ghost! He causes the Word of God to live, and the Word of God causes you to grow! A born again child desires the sincere milk of the Word. They start out as a baby, but the Holy Ghost and the Word of God will grow them up as a son. When you grow up to be a son, you're no longer under tutors. You're no longer subject to things that guard you and keep you. You are no longer subject to religion and tradition. You've become free! You have grown in the Lord and the Word of God has become the standard in

your life. The nature and the character of Christ lives on the inside of you. In the midst of that Christ nature, there is a union and a harmony between you and the rest of the family of God.

If you are a son, then you are an heir of God through Christ. He sent the Spirit of His son into your heart crying, *"Abba, Father."* Jesus is Spirit and the Spirit of the Son of God is the Spirit of faith. He said, *"I'm going to destroy this temple, and I'm going to raise it up again. After three days I'll raise it up."* No one had ever done that before! He said, *"I have raised other people from the dead, but this time, I'm going to lay it down, and I'm going to take it up again."*

How do you know that, Jesus?

Before He overcame the prince of this world, He said, *"Be of good cheer! I have overcome the world."* How do you know that? You haven't even been to the cross yet! You haven't even shed your life's blood yet! You haven't stripped principalities and powers yet! *"I have a Spirit of faith! I believed, and therefore have I spoken!"* The Bible says that God has given you the Spirit of His Son so that you can cry, *"Abba, Father,"* and say, *"Thank you, Lord, that You never lie! Your Word is the Truth, and I believe it! I have the Spirit of Jesus!"*

The Father's Estate

"Wherefore thou art no more a servant, but a son, and if a son, then a heir of God through Christ." I want you to see an analogy. A multimillionaire has a child, and that child is the designated heir of his entire estate. The child, however, is just seven years old, so the father has hired people to take care of him. He has hired one to feed him, another to drive him, and another to teach, or tutor, him. One day this seven year old rises up and tells his teacher, *"Listen to me! All of this is mine! I don't want to do any schoolwork today!"* The teacher says, *"No! You listen to me. This is my job. I get paid to teach you. Now, you are going to sit down right here and do your schoolwork."* The teacher knows he's still a child!

Positionally, that child has access to all of his father's estate, but he doesn't yet have the authority to claim the inheritance he has. As long as you're still operating in a law mentality, a legalism mentality, a performance mentality, you'll short-circuit the power to claim what belongs to you! *Why?* Your mentality is, *"When I have it, I'll have it."* However, the power to claim what belongs to you is the faith that Jesus gave you by the Spirit of God! You receive from Him through faith.

The moment you allow the Spirit of God to cause faith to live in your heart, you've broken the power of the law off your life. You are no more a servant. You're not a child anymore. A child cannot fend for himself. A child cannot run the estate.

The moment you know and believe the Word of God, you've graduated! You're living in the Spirit, and you are no more a servant. You're a son and an heir of God though Christ. Who then, is Christ? The Lord is that Spirit.

That means you're now inheriting in life.

Somebody said, *"I have a problem with my temper."*

You've inherited the character of the Lord!

Somebody said, *"I'm confused."*

You've inherited the mind of Christ!

Somebody said, *"I'm weak."*

You've inherited strength!

How have you inherited it? You have inherited it through faith. You've inherited it through the Spirit of faith. You've inherited it through putting your confidence in what God said. Through Jesus you can receive everything that God has promised! God promised it to you, and it comes to you through Jesus. You are no more a child, but a grown up because you're free from unbelief! Christ has redeemed you from the curse of the law and has exposed you to a revelation of the living faith that He has for you.

Getting in Position

Get ready! Part of triggering, releasing, and unleashing the power of God in your life has to do with what you know about your position in Christ.

> **For if the blood of bulls and of goats, and the ashes of a heifer sprinkling the unclean, sanctifieth to the purifying of the flesh; how much more shall the blood of Christ, who through the eternal spirit offered himself without spot to God, purge your conscience from dead works to serve the Living God? ... Which was a figure of the time then present, in which were offered both gifts and sacrifices, that could not make him that did the service perfect, as pertaining to the conscience.**
>
> Hebrews 9:13, 9 KJV

God is saying, *"Listen! Faith was reserved. Men did not have the revelation of it. People could not live by it; it was not living in people. So I gave them a schoolmaster, a teacher, a babysitter, to teach them and lead them to the time when I would do something about their heart."* God could not do anything about the heart of man under the Old Covenant dispensation. The blood of bulls and blood of goats could not make the one doing the service perfect, as pertaining to conscience.

That means the bulls died. The goats died. The rams died. The turtledoves died. The types were sacrificed, and the blood was sprinkled. The blood of those sacrifices was just a shadow of the Blood of Christ. All it did was to cover the sinner so that God could ignore the sin and their sinful nature for another year. It would cover them for a period of time because there was a promise that a Redeemer was going to come. When the Final Sacrifice would give His life, God would be able to give man a new heart.

Man was conscious—he knew he was a sinner! He knew he was a failure. He knew he had lost the kingdoms and the dominions of the Earth's realm. He knew he had given them to the devil. There was nothing that could save him from the awareness of failure on the inside of him. The blood sacrifices would relieve him for a while, but

it couldn't produce a change of heart. All of Israel looked forward to their Redeemer!

Faith Works

"... The blood of bulls and of goats, and the ashes of a heifer sprinkling the unclean, sanctifieth to the purifying of the flesh." These sacrifices provided an exterior cleaning for man. Remember, Jesus did not deny that the Pharisees cleansed the outside of the cup. He didn't say that they *tried* to clean the outside of the cup. He said, *"You cleaned it well, but your problem is the inside of the cup!"*

The law provided an exterior cleansing.

Do you know churches where, on the outside, everyone looks good? You can operate under the law and have a certain amount of God-likeness on the outside. The sacrifices made before Jesus came had a certain amount of power. When man put his faith in them, his flesh was cleansed exteriorly. The Bible said, *"If the blood of bulls and if the blood of goats and the ashes of a heifer could sanctify the unclean and purify the flesh, how much more shall the blood of Christ purge your conscience from dead works to serve the Living God?"*

The sacrifice of bulls, the sacrifice of Old Testament blood, could not make man's conscience perfect. The Word of God says, *"How much more shall the blood of Christ purge your conscience from dead works to serve the Living God?"* We are delivered from the dead works of the law by the Blood of Jesus. The Blood of Jesus will cleanse our conscience from the performance mentality that says, *"When He heals me, I'm healed. When He blesses me, I'm blessed. When He does it, I'll believe it. If I just act holy for another year, then I'll say I'm a saint."* No! That is a conscience problem that man cannot do anything about. He needs the Blood! The Blood will cleanse your conscience from dead works and give you faith works!

Faith works say this:

I am, so I say I am! I believe, so I am! God is near me; His word is in my mouth. I'm the redeemed of the Lord, and I'm going to say so! I was bought with a price, so I'm rich! He pays my bills! He provides all of my needs! He'll never leave me nor forsake me! He's with me always! Goodness and mercy follow me all the days of my life! There is no where I can go that God doesn't go with me! Every place the soles of my feet tread, God has given it to me! My conscious has been purged by the blood of Christ, and I know that God and I are walking hand in hand. I've been freed from dead works, and I've been called to faith works!

Faith without works is dead.

What is faith? Faith is the title deed of things hoped for.

What are faith works? Faith works are acting, talking, and living in agreement with something you don't have!

Someone said, *"You don't have it."* Oh, but I have the title deed! Someone said, *"Then where is it?"* It's in the mail! I have the title deed. Someone bought it for me!

The Living Work of Calvary

"How much more shall the blood of Christ, who through the eternal spirit offered himself without spot to God, purge your conscience from dead works to serve the Living God?" It was through the eternal Spirit that Christ offered Himself—the same Spirit of faith. Calvary would be irrelevant today had Jesus not exercised faith in it. He offered Himself without spot to God.

The Bible says that God looked down upon some and said, *"Your worship is like a stench in my nostrils!"* To others He said, *"Your worship is like a sweet smelling savor in my mouth."* That means it's not the act; it's the attitude God is looking for. God is looking for the Spirit by which the act is performed.

Jesus was not performing a dead work called *Calvary*. It was a living work. It was a work of faith. The Bible said that through faith He offered Himself. No one knew it. No one believed it. He said, *"I lay my life down; I take it up again!"* The Spirit of faith living in Him reached back and got a hold of people from previous generations and then reached forward to get a hold of people all the way to the end of the age. He hung on the cross two thousand years ago, isolated in one geographic location. In His faith He reached out to America, and to South America, and to Africa, and to the far corners of the globe.

Through the Spirit of Faith He said, *"I know that everyone thinks that I'm the underdog. But I'm the King of Kings, and I'm the Lord of Lords! The Blood that I'm shedding right now is going to touch everyone who will ever believe, and they will become a recipient of that same Spirit of faith!"*

God looked down and was pleased with Calvary. Jesus not only died on His own, but the Spirit of faith in Him said, *"I am dying with everyone who will ever believe, so that they will die with Me and be buried with Me. And I'm going to rise again with everyone who will believe, so that they will rise up with Me and live with Me!"* That's faith!

How much more shall the Blood of Christ, who through the eternal Spirit, offered Himself without spot unto God, purge your conscience from dead works to serve the Living God?

I'm no longer a sinner! I'm the righteousness of God in Christ Jesus! My conscience does not condemn me! The Blood of the Lamb has washed me! I'm a new creation! Everything that God has promised me, belongs to me, in Jesus' mighty name!

Is this for you, too?

Say this out loud:

> *Father, I'm sorry for the weak, beggarly things I allow to dominate and to hinder me from being a new creature, in active and living form. I'm sorry for allowing my conscience to condemn me and my awareness of sin to be bigger than my awareness of righteousness. I'm sorry for short-circuiting the power of God in my life and thinking that there's something more that You could do than You've already done. You've given me all things that pertain to life and godliness, and I'm sorry that sometimes I don't put to use what You've given me.*
>
> *Spirit of God, today and from today forward, You're*

welcome to remind me. You're welcome to stir me up. You're welcome to speak to my heart, so that when I cry, "Abba, Father," there will be an absolute conviction and awareness of the presence of my Master and my King and His ever present willingness to perform everything that He's promised. I'm going to live and not die! I'm going to declare the goodness of the Lord! I'm going to see the goodness of the Lord in the land of the living! I'm going to magnify the Lord and give God glory because faith lives in me by the Holy Ghost. Spirit of God, move in me today, in the mighty name of Jesus.

CHAPTER 16

RELEASE YOUR FAITH

———◆———

It's not enough for Jesus to bring resurrection to your gift. He wants to loose your gift. He wants to release your gift.

Now the Spirit speaketh expressly, that in the [last days] some shall depart from the faith, giving heed to seducing spirits, and doctrines of devils.

1 Timothy 4:1 KJV

This know also, that in the last days perilous times shall come.

2 Timothy 3:1 KJV

Say this out loud:

This is the Word of God! It is not man's opinion. It is not subject to religious tradition. It is not a suggestion! It is not a truth—it is the Truth! Let God be true and every man a liar! If I see it in God's Word, it will be the Truth that I choose to believe and choose to obey. Speak to me, Lord. Reveal it in your Word, and I will change by the power of it. In Jesus name! Glory to God!

I want to teach you about the resurrection and release of your faith. I don't know if you've noticed or not, but you're living in perilous times. You're not living in a time of ease and comfort. You're living in a challenging hour. You're living in the day and in the hour that God has reserved for those who will be strong in Him and in the power of

His might.

These are difficult times. These are dangerous times. These are fierce times. These are times that demand men and women to hold on to the Truth of the Word of God. People will no longer be able to say, *"I thought that was the way it should be,"* or, *"I had good intentions,"* because only the strong in the Lord will be able to stand firm in perilous times.

Contending for the Faith

I preach the Word of God, by the inspiration of the Spirit, to cause you to understand that it is *urgent* for you to hold on to the pure faith. Your grandmother can't give it to you. Your mother in law can't help you with it. Faith cometh by hearing, and hearing by the Word of God!

Notice what the Bible said, *"The Spirit is speaking expressly."* That means He is outspokenly declaring it and distinctly telling it. The Holy Ghost is not whispering in some isolated insignificant corner on planet Earth! He is shouting from the mountain top! He is declaring, *"In the last days perilous times will come!"*

Why is He doing this?

Men will depart from the faith. They're going to give heed to seducing spirits and doctrines of devils. They're going to heap unto themselves teachers having itching ears. They're going to run to a place where they can hear a comfortable message of compromise. Seducing spirits are at work in this day to distort the purity of the message of the Gospel.

The good news is that faith can come to your heart by the Word of God! There's a generation that is not going to depart from the faith! They are going to be a mountain moving generation. They are going to embarrass the devil on every avenue of life! We haven't come to bow the knee to religious tradition or denominational preferences! We've come with a mandate from God!

He didn't send us to everybody. He sent us to those who have an ear to hear what the Spirit will say to the Church. He sent us to raise up an army of men and women who are committed to the purposes of

God. They are going to say, *"Bless God! I'm not departing from the faith! I'm going to hold on to the faith!"*

The Bible admonishes believers to contend for the faith that was once delivered unto the Saints' safekeeping. The Word further says that in these perilous times, seducing spirits are going to work on people in order to get them to doubt what God is saying in His Word.

God is not a man that He should lie, nor the son of man that He should repent.

> If He promised to do it, *He's going to do it!*
> If He said He would heal you, *He will heal you!*
> If he said He would deliver you, *He will deliver you!*
> If He said He would direct you, *He will direct you!*
> If He said He would protect you, *He will protect you!*
> If He said that He's on your side, then *He will see to it that you win the battle!*

We're going to preach the truth! Men and women who have an ear to hear are going to get hooked on the Truth. I do not want to raise up casual participants in Christ. I want to raise up addicts for Jesus! They're going to get up in the morning, and the first thought on their mind will be to get a hold of God. They will get a hold of Heaven and get a hold of the Word of God. I want to raise up fanatics! Not fanatics in the sense that they're foolishly extreme, but fanatics who are so committed to the Word of God that they don't care what others say or believe. They're going to stand on the Word of God and believe in "Thus saith the Lord."

When Faith Dies

Faith dies. The Bible says, *"As the body without the spirit is dead, so is faith without works dead also."* Your faith can die. I have had a lot of opportunities to let my faith die, but I refuse to allow it to die! I know I *don't* have the scars to prove it, but you don't have to keep the scars. There is a balm in Gilead! There's a Healer in the house! It doesn't matter if you go through the fire—you don't have to be burned! You can still come out on the other side shouting, *"Glory!"* and testifying of the victory!

I refuse to take works out of my faith. I'm going to act on what the Word of God says! The moment a person stops responding to the Word, their faith dies. It becomes stagnant. It becomes unimpressive. It doesn't impress the sinner and it doesn't impress God. It becomes non-relevant. It doesn't apply to their life anymore.

Why does faith die?

The works, the flow, the life, the release of the faith of God—which He put in you—was knocked out of your life through a disappointment that you experienced. I've heard many preachers say, *"I used to believe like that. But I prayed and didn't see an answer, and I quit believing."*

Do you know what happened?

Their faith died! The Bible says, *"Don't cast away your confidence! It has a great recompense of reward!"* It also says, *"Be not weary in well doing!"*

If you're weary in well doing, you'll stop doing well! If you stop doing well, your faith will die! There are many in the Church world today with dead faith. Some of them are in the pulpit! That's why there are dead churches. Religion is dead faith going nowhere. The life of God is not in it. It's like a riverbed that has become dry.

They lost their testimony. Instead of having a river, or a flow, that is always expressing the goodness and the faith of God, they have become stagnant. They lost their enthusiasm in the Spirit because of disappointment. When they lost their enthusiasm, they took the works out of their faith.

They may say, *"I believe that,"* but their faith is dead. Their faith died, and it cannot help them now. Just like the body dies when the spirit leaves it, faith dies when the believer stops acting on it.

Say this out loud:

It's not enough for me to have faith! I must have living faith!

Faith had died in the Pharisees and Sadducees. Jesus said that they cleansed the outside of the cup, but the inside was filled with dead men's bones. Their faith was dead! Instead of their faith being a by-product of a living relationship with God, it was the by-product of religious tradition and rituals. They were serving God only to make men to see them and appreciate them. God said that this was a stench in His nostrils. He didn't like it!

Many in the Church world today are not in church, but in the bar, on the street, or dealing drugs. Enticed by sin, they left the church and wandered back into the world. At one time the call of God was on their life. At one time God Himself said, *"I'm calling you to preach!"* At one time they were tongue talkers. At one time they read the Word of God. At one time the Lord Himself felt at home in their spirit man. However, somewhere along the way a disappointment hit their life. A seducing spirit came and caused them to depart from the faith by stopping their corresponding action to what the Word of God said. Their faith died, and, as a result, you can see the dead works of the enemy operating in their lives.

Diagnose Your Faith

When Jesus heard that, he said, this sickness is not unto death, but for the glory of God, that the son of God might be glorified thereby,

John 11:4 KJV

The moment disappointment hits your life your faith gets sick. Your faith wanes. Some Christians have sick faith, and it is threatening to die any minute!

God is going to help your faith today. The devil may have told you that you won't be healed, but you're going to have a resurrection in your faith. You're going to receive your miracle! You will never be the same again. God is going to heal you today!

This Scripture is about Lazarus, whose name means *whom God helps*, but he's from Bethany, which means *house of sorrow*. Your life becomes a life of sorrow when your faith is sick and dying. You go through unnecessary pain, disappointment, and despair, when your faith is not where it should to be in God.

The Bible says, *"Now faith is the substance of things hoped for, the evidence of things not seen"* (Hebrews 11:1 KJV). If the faith you have is not giving you an assurance twenty-four hours a day that things are alright with you, that the devil is under your feet, that your situation is taken care of, that God has won the battle, that Jesus is faithful, that the Word works, *examine it!* It might be sick!

Here is the good news: if your faith is sick, *this sickness is not unto death*! God is going to get a hold of your faith and bring your faith to life again! The devil has told some of you that you'll never amount to anything, and he's caused your faith to become sick.

I don't care if it dies! The Word of God said, *"This sickness is not unto death!"* God has an eternal investment in your faith! He will not leave your faith in the grave. He's going to call your faith to life again and bring it into motion!

You're going to heal the sick! You're going to cast out devils! You're going to travel around the world! You're going to bring a visitation to others! Your relatives are going to be saved! Your husband is going to come to Jesus! This sickness is not unto death!

The Word of God will apply to every part of your life!

How do you know if your faith is sick?

When you go to the doctor and tell him what you're feeling, he diagnoses your symptoms. I'm going to teach you how to diagnose your symptoms. If the Word of God doesn't move you any more because you have more important priorities, your faith is sick and threatening to kick the bucket any minute! If you think that the Word of God is not relevant to what you need, your faith is sick. If you think, *"I'm alright where I am,"* your faith is sick. If you think, *"I'm alright with God. I do what I can,"* your faith is sick!

Take Your Medicine

The Bible says that a happy heart does good like medicine. If you need medicine for your faith, *get your heart happy!*

> Be filled with the Spirit, speaking to yourselves in psalms and hymns and spiritual songs.
>
> ### Ephesians 5:18-19 KJV

> The Lord is my shepherd I shall not want, he maketh me to lie down in green pastures; He leadeth me beside the still waters, he restoreth my soul.
>
> ### Psalm 23:1-3 KJV

Speak to *yourself* in Psalms, hymns, and spiritual songs!

> Bless the Lord, oh my soul and all that's within me, bless his holy name. Bless the Lord, oh my soul, and forget not all his benefits, who forgiveth all thine iniquities; who healeth all thine diseases"
>
> ### Psalm 103:1-3 KJV

If you talk to yourself like that, medicine will flow to your faith. Your faith will receive an injection of healing and rise up. It will say, *"Where's the devil?! Did he get out from under my feet again? Get back down where you belong! You're the footstool of the believer!"*

Disappointments will cause your heart to become unimpressed, unmoved and unchallenged. It won't rejoice anymore in the things of God. When that happens, your faith gets sick. Some people know exactly what they need to do to heal their faith, but they still stand by and let it die. They say, *"I thought the Lord was going to do it, but I guess it wasn't His time. I don't want to have high hopes. I don't want to be presumptuous and believe that God is going to keep His Word."*

They let their faith die.

It's a sorry situation when faith has left the house. People run frantically around trying to save themselves from a storm. *What happened to faith?* It dove overboard! It drowned! It died! That's when people argue with one another and blame shift. When people are blame shifting and fighting each other, their faith is either sick or dead.

Jesus came to do something about the condition of people's lives. God wants to change your house from a house of misery to a house of rejoicing. The only way He can do that is to call the gift of God in you to life again. He has to call the gift of faith to life again. He has to resurrect your hopes and dreams.

Do you know what you're going to find out when you question God about His plan for you now?

You're going to find out that He didn't change what He had intended in the first place! He didn't change His plan. He didn't change His mind. If He had a good plan for you when you heard Him the first time, it hasn't changed.

You're not good enough to mess up God's plan! No matter how bad you blew it, He hasn't changed His mind. His plan is still the same. You were not good enough at failure to talk Him out of His plan of success for your life. He'll take you right back!

Where Did You Bury Your Faith?

Jesus came to Bethany *"And said, Where have ye laid him? They said unto him, Lord, come and see"* (John 11:34 KJV). When your faith dies, the best thing you can do is to take the Word of God to the place of your faith's burial. Jesus asks you, *"Where did you bury you faith?"*

Guess where you'll find your faith buried? You'll find it right at the point where you cast away your confidence! You'll find it right where you stopped acting on it! Right at the place in your life where you became disappointed, when you departed from the faith, when you talked yourself out of God's plan, when you believed the lies of the devil regarding you.

You go to church and say, *"I need a Word from God!"* You consult the Word of God, and He comes on the scene and asks you, *"Where did you bury your faith?"* God says, *"Let's go back and find out where you left it because you need it for the journey."*

Where have you laid it?
Where did you put it?

Today the Holy Ghost is going to show you where you left it. Some have left it in a church.

"The preacher fell into sin. He fell into homosexuality," they reason.

"I was involved in a ministry, and there was financial abuse and misappropriation of funds."

"I gave into the ministry of a national evangelist, and he fell into sin. I was disappointed, so I don't trust anyone anymore. It's just me and God."

The Word says, *"Take me back to the burial point where you left your faith because I still have need for that faith in your life."* There's no excuse to bury your faith! There is no one who is worthy enough for you to bury your faith because of their failure or mistake. Some of you buried your faith when your husband left or when your wife left. A relative of mine buried their faith when their father died of cancer. They blamed God for it.

The Word of God says, *"Where have ye laid him?"*

Where's your faith?

If you have faith that you're not using, *it's buried!* Let's break it down a little more. If you know to do good, and you're not doing it; if you're living in unbelief rather than in faith; chances are there's a grave somewhere within the realm of your influence. You will find your faith buried there.

This is why I don't like counseling very often. Praise God for godly counsel. Praise God for being anointed by the Holy Ghost and being able to minister to people. We want to minister to people, but most of the time we're dealing with someone who has buried their faith. When we try to give them the Word of God, *"The Lord is going to supply...,"* they interrupt saying, *"...all my needs according to His riches in glory. I know that."*

They know the Word, but they're not acting on it. Why? The faith that came by that Word was buried. It's dead. It got sick because they didn't act on it. Then it died, and they buried it.

Where did you bury your faith?

Someone may think, *"I don't have to listen to this! I'll just go to a dead church."* It doesn't matter where you go. You can go to the other side of the world, and twenty years from now, when you consult the Word of God, Jesus will say, *"Where did you bury your faith?"* and you'll have to go back to that place. It doesn't matter how far you run, God is going to demand of you a reckoning, a report of the faith that He put in your life.

When my God puts a mountain moving deposit in you, it is not supposed to be locked away in the recesses of your spirit! God has put all things that pertain to life and godliness in you.

Before we are through with this generation, we're going to resurrect faith out of the graveyards of lives and bring it forth to be used by God. We're going to send it out to the hospitals to heal the sick and the terminally ill! We're going to send it to the prisons to lead people to Christ! We're going to send it to the streets to break the bondage of the devil. We're going to send it to the insane asylum to cast out the demonic spirits! We're going to put faith to work!

Where did you lay it?

The Word of God wants to locate your faith. The Word of God will help you go there if you'll be honest with Him and say, *"Lord, here's where I blew it. Here's where I quit."*

Only those who make a decision to backslide will backslide. You won't compromise until you make the decision to compromise. You won't stop doing what you've been doing unless you become weary in what you've been doing.

The Word says, *"Take me back to where you became weary."*

"Why, Lord?" *"Because I have plans. I have plans for the thing you became weary of. Take me back to where you become weary in well-doing."*

"Why, Lord?" *"Because that's where you buried well-doing, and I have plans for that same well-doing you buried."*

Take Away the Stone

Jesus said, take ye away the stone. Martha, the sister of him that was dead, saith unto him, Lord, by this time he stinketh; for he hath been dead four days. Jesus saith unto her, said I not unto thee, that, if thou wouldest believe, thou shouldest see the glory of God?

John 11:39-40 KJV

Look at what Jesus said: *"Take ye away the stone."* When you bury your faith, you cover it with an excuse. You *always* cover it.

"They're to blame."
"They did it."
"You did it."
"You all *did it!"*

People get mad at God: *"He did it!"* That's their excuse.
People get mad at their brother: *"He did it!"*

They always cover their dead faith with the stone of excuse. When they take Jesus to where they buried it, they say, *"It's in there, but it stinks because it's been dead, motionless, and lifeless for so long."* Some Christians know that it stinks, but they're more comfortable with the smell.

Jesus says, *"Take away the stone."*

Don't mess with God! When you get around the Resurrection and the Life, He's not going to allow you to have a tombstone over your faith! He's going to meddle in your affairs! The Word is not here to tell you what you *want* to hear. The Word of God is here to tell you what you *need* to hear! He's going to meddle in your life. He's going to step on your toes. He's going to move in your life. He's going to move in your spirit. He's going to move in your affairs until He lines things up. He's God!

He is the Resurrection and the Life, and He comes to bring resurrection life. The Word of God is not dead. The Word of God is alive! The Word of God is a miracle worker! The Word of God is a creative force! The Word of God will never allow you to put up with excuses that keep your faith buried and unused.

"I guess I should invite people to church, but I'm too busy."
Take away the stone.
"I guess I should pray for the sick, but I've got my own needs."
Take away the stone.
"I guess I should be rejoicing in the Lord, but I've got problems."
Take away the stone.
"I would pray, but I don't have time."
Take away the stone.
"I would read the Word of God, but I'm too busy with the kids."
Take away the stone.
"My husband is the problem."
Take away the stone.

Do you know what the Word of God is saying?

Stop stalling! Let's get on with it!

"Dr. Harfouche is just too intense! Even the Lord took six days to create the world!" Yes, but He's been working on you for *a whole lot longer than that* telling you the same thing that I'm telling you. Take away the stone!

The moment you deal with the dead forgotten things of your faith, the power of God will invade your life, and you'll never be the same again! The moment you put motion to the Word of God, the moment you begin to obey what the Word says, you'll embark on a journey full of challenge and fulfillment. It's not a bed of roses, but every enemy that comes your way will be embarrassed! If you will obey, God will have His way in your life.

I plan to build a church of men and women who are so far *right* that they are *right on* with the Word of God! We're not going to bomb abortion clinics, we're going to bomb the kingdom of darkness with prayer! We're going to embarrass the devil! There won't be a school in this area without born again, Spirit-filled kids, anointed by God and sent out from here to lay hands on their friends and get them delivered! They will walk into school, and when the drug dealer says, *"Do you want a joint?"* they'll say, *"Come out of him, you foul spirit!"* and the power of God will knock the pusher down!

The day will come when people will have to look down both sides of the road to make sure the coast is clear—to make sure that there is not a Christian around, praying with other tongues, quoting the Word of God, and believing for their eternal soul! *We will be ready!*

People will say, *"I guess I will come to church when I am ready to."*

We'll answer, *"I am with you. I'll help you take away the stone. I'll help you get rid of it."*

"But I don't have a car."
"I'll drive you!"
"I don't have time."
"I'll wait for you."
"I can't wake up early."
"I'll call you!"

Take away the stone!

God says, *"I haven't changed My plans for you. You have a call on your life. Where did you bury your faith?"*

You can show God the burial place of your faith. *"It's over here."*

Take away the stone!

"But God, it's been so many years. You can't do anything with that gift. It stinks."

Take away the stone!

God has the element you need to experience a faith resurrection in your life.

Gift of God, Come Forth!

Then they took away the stone from the place where the dead was laid. And Jesus lifted up his eyes, and said, Father I thank thee that thou

> hast heard me. And I knew that thou hearest me always; but because of the people which stand by I said it, that they may believe that thou hast sent me. And when he thus had spoken, he cried with a loud voice, Lazarus, come forth.
>
> John 11:41-43

If you will only invite the Word of God…
If you will only consult the Word of God…
If you will only bring the Word of God to the point of burial in your life…
If you will only obey the Word of God and take away the excuse, the barrier, the thing that keeps your gift locked in and dead; then the Word of God will shout! It won't be a suggestion; it will be a *command!*

> The Word of God will say, *"Faith! COME FORTH!*
> *"Gift of God! COME FORTH!*
> *"Dead, forgotten, shattered dream! COME FORTH!*
> *"Vision that has been buried away in the tomb of tradition and covered with the stone of excuse,*
> *COME FORTH!*
> *"Gift of God that men have isolated and buried away with the lying deceptions that say,*
> *'It won't work. God doesn't keep His Word. You may have heard God wrong,'"*
> *COME FORTH!*

Let the gift of God come forth! God has a shout of resurrection in your life. You don't have to start all over again. You can pick up right where you left off!

"But I disappointed Him!"

You can pick up where you left off! You don't have to start all over again. He will get you flowing right now!

Loose Your Gift, and Let It Go!

And he that was dead came forth, bound hand and foot with grave clothes; and his face was bound about with a napkin. Jesus said unto them, loose him and let him go.

John 11:44 KJV

Before you can bury your faith, you have to mummify your faith. Your faith is not easily buried. You have to wrap it up with the grave clothes of tradition. You have to wrap it up with the grave clothes of unbelief. You have to wrap it up with the report of the world. You have to wrap it up with the report of the situation. It told you that your faith won't work. It said that it's impossible to believe God. You allowed those lying, ugly grave clothes to wrap up the gift of God that He put in your life; and you buried it.

It's not enough for Jesus to bring resurrection to your gift. He wants to loose your gift. He wants to release your gift. He doesn't want it walking around, bound up in the grave clothes of tradition. He wants it completely free from the bondage that you and others have put on it. He's not going to leave you with mummified faith. He's not going to leave you to walking around with grave clothes on. He wants your faith loosed! However, *first you have to find where you laid it.*

Say this to the Lord:

Father, help me find the place where I've compromised my potential in You. I don't want a buried gift. I don't want my faith mummified and buried. Help me take the Word of God to that place of burial.

The Lord will take the stone away when you lead Him to the burial place. God will not only roll away the stone, He will heal you from the stone. He will touch that place that produced the excuse. He will heal that place of hurt and disappointment. He will heal you from the reason for that condition, and He will bring resurrection to your faith.

Your faith will rise again!

There are times when I am ministering that I lay my hands on someone and say, *"I bind unbelief in the name of Jesus! Loose their faith!"* They may get upset with me at first and think, *"How dare you?!"* A lady once told me, *"After you said that to me I went home, and something was totally different about me. All of a sudden, I could believe God!"*

God doesn't only want to bring a resurrection to your faith; He wants to bring your faith forth. God wants to release your faith from the things that bound it. Once you locate the place where you laid it down, you must begin to utilize it the right way. If you cannot release your faith, your faith won't work for you! Jesus said, *"Loose him, and let him go."*

Assault on a Miracle

> **Much people of the Jews therefore knew that he was there; and they came, not for Jesus' sake only, but that they might see Lazarus also, whom he had raised from the dead. But the chief priests consulted that they might put Lazarus also to death; because that by reason of him many of the Jews went away, and believed on Jesus.**
>
> **John 12:9-11 KJV**

God will get you to roll away the stone if you're willing. The Word of God, the Resurrection and the Life, will call forth your faith out of the grave. God will give you the necessary equipment to loose your faith and let it go.

Once your faith is working, people will know that there has been a faith resurrection in your life. They will say, *"What's going on with you? You look different. You look better! What's going on in your life?"*

You'll say, *"I found Him! I'm walking with God! Faith is resurrected in my life!"* People will be drawn to you because they knew you when your faith was in the grave, and they can see that faith has been loosed and released in your life.

However, demonic spirits will immediately dispatch religious rulers to kill your miracle. Immediately the hypocrites in the religious world will be mobilized by demon spirits.

Why?

There are two things demons want to kill: the Word of God and the resurrection of faith! They want to kill the Word and the influence of the Word in the life of people. If they can't, the Word will produce a resurrection and a release of faith. They'll go after your faith to kill it.

Demons will not only use people but also situations to kill it. Did you ever have a faith resurrection in your life, and, suddenly, all hell broke loose? The devil said, *"I want to kill that Lazarus! I want to kill that faith in their life because through that faith others are believing!"* He's trying to rob you of your testimony. The only way he can do that is to kill your faith.

Here's the good news: once your faith is out of the grave, once your faith is out of those grave clothes, once your faith is loose and running about, then your faith cannot fail! It will always produce on behalf of God! I don't care who rages—I'm going to be as stable as a rock! It doesn't matter if the devil brings out the big guns and shoots. No weapon formed against me shall prosper! My faith is alive!

You may have experienced living faith in your life but have become the target of spiritual assassins. These assassins have attempted to put your faith to death for the results it was getting in the spirit realm.

Lift your hands to God and say,

> *Thank you, Jesus, for my faith! Because I believe Your Word, people are believing in Jesus. People are coming to see my Lazarus!*

They're coming to see your living faith! They are wondering, *"Why do they laugh in the Spirit? Why do they prophesy in the Holy Ghost? Why do they run around the Church? I don't know, but it looks like they're having fun!"*

The Resurrected Miracle

The Lord says:
Many of you have experienced a resurrection of Lazarus in your life.
I visited the tomb that once was.
I've taken away the excuse that used to be.
I've brought forth the gift that used to lie.
I broke the power of the grave clothes that used to bind.
And because of that, you have been attacked and targeted.
Some of you have been attacked by physical instruments…
…men and women influenced by demonic spirits.
Others have been attacked by situations and circumstances.
And you said, *"What's going on?"*
I'm speaking to you prophetically today to let you know
that they did it to Me 2000 years ago
to kill the miracle that testified of Me.
They'll do it to you to try to kill the miracle in your life
that testifies of Me also.
My good news for you is that the enemy will come one way
but flee seven ways.
My testimony for you is that nothing that he shoots against you…
…will penetrate the shield of resurrected faith in your life.
My good news for you is that, as you hold on in faith and in patience,
YOU WILL RECEIVE THE PROMISE.
I will not fail to cause the resurrected miracle in your life…
…to become a magnet that draws others to Me.
And when you rise up and testify…

"God saved my house! Yes, I almost lost my house, but God saved it!"
When you rise up and testify…
"I was physically healed from an incurable disease! God healed me!"
When you get up and testify…
"God provided for me a home when I didn't have one!"
When you rise up and testify…
"I didn't have enough money, and now I have more than enough!"
When you rise up and testify…
"My lost loved ones came to the Lord!"
then people will be drawn
by the power of the testimony of your faith,
and they'll come to see
and they'll believe on Me.
So do not allow the world to kill what I resurrected in your life,
but rather keep it loose, and keep it mobile…
…and it will produce in your life what I desire for it to produce.

ABOUT THE AUTHOR

Dr. Christian Harfouche is both an apostle and a prophet to the nations. Having received a divine mandate to mobilize the army of God, Dr. Harfouche has invested over 25 years in training a generation of miracle workers. Through the Word of God and the move of the Spirit, Dr. Harfouche is launching everyday believers into prophetic destiny. As a team, Drs. Christian and Robin Harfouche have ignited hearts and blazed a trail of revival across America and throughout the world. Their sincerity, genuine love and fervent commitment to global revival has inspired multitudes to answer the call of God.

Drs. Christian and Robin Harfouche are committed to training New Testament disciples at The World Center in Pensacola, Florida. The World Center is home to both the International Miracle Institute Bible Training Center and a vibrant, multi-cultural, cross-denominational church. People from around the world move to Pensacola for training and impartation from a major miracle ministry. Drs. Christian and Robin Harfouche continue to travel worldwide, conducting Miracle Soul-Winning Crusades and imparting their lives to the Body of Christ. Their influence and the miracle testimonies of their disciples can be seen daily on the highly acclaimed television program, *Miracles Today*.

Year One of IMI powerfully equips those called to walk on the cutting edge in the Word of God. This foundation enables you as a believer to live and operate in the supernatural and fulfill the call of God on your life. **Year One is an accredited year of bible college, containing over 100 hours of teaching on 96 CD's.**

Your Authority:
Become all that you can be by knowing, understanding, and exercising your authority in Jesus Christ.

Heavenly Identity:
Understand your identity in Christ.

The God Man:
Learn all about the unlimited abilities invested in you.

Great Faith:
Find out how you can grow to be a wonder worker by building your faith in God.

The Anointing:
Find out about the Anointing in you and how you can cooperate with this unction.

Miracles:
Step into a place in the Lord where nothing is impossible.

IMI offers two training options!

IMI In-Residence Training (Pensacola, Florida)
IMI Correspondence Program (home study program)

IMI Training At A Glance

- Receive training by Drs. Christian and Robin Harfouche.
- Grow in a practical revelatory understanding of the Word of God.
- Learn how to have continual supernatural results in God.
- Impact the world with signs, wonders and miracles following.
- Fully accredited to confer both undergraduate and graduate degrees.

For More Information:
Visit: www.globalrevival.com
Email: IMI@globalrevival.com
Phone: 850-439-6225

International Miracle Institute
Correspondence Program Year One Training Curriculum

Year One of IMI powerfully equips those called to walk on the cutting edge in the Word of God. This foundation enables you as a believer to live and operate in the supernatural and fulfill the call of God on your life. **Year One is an accredited year of bible college, containing over 100 hours of teaching on 96 CD's.**

Your Authority:
Become all that you can be by knowing, understanding, and exercising your authority in Jesus Christ.

Heavenly Identity:
Understand your identity in Christ.

The God Man:
Learn all about the unlimited abilities invested in you.

Great Faith:
Find out how you can grow to be a wonder worker by building your faith in God.

The Anointing:
Find out about the Anointing in you and how you can cooperate with this unction.

Miracles:
Step into a place in the Lord where nothing is impossible.

International Miracle Institute
Correspondence Program Training Curriculum
Year Two

Year Two of IMI continues where Year One left off, helping you unlock the deep truths and revelation in the Word of God. Building on the foundation of Year One, **Year Two further enables you as a believer to live and operate in the supernatural** and fulfill the call of God on your life. **Year Two is an accredited year of bible college, also containing over 100 hours of teaching on 96 CD's.**

Advanced Studies in Faith:
A study to build your faith from level to level.

Understanding the Supernatural:
Learn to operate in the highest dimension of life in the spirit.

Healing in the Atonement:
Understand your divine right to the provision and benefits of healing in the atonement.

Ministry Gifts:
"And God gave gifts unto men…" A study of the Call-The Office.

Prophets and Prophecy:
A study of Old and New Testament Prophets; recognize the spirit of error, develop the spirit of pioneer, study the predictive future Word, and learn to cooperate with the Anointing.

Demons & Demonology:
Understand the origin, operation, strategies, and the believers' dominion over the powers of darkness.

IMI

Remember, miracles don't just happen. By the Word of God and the power of the Spirit, the IMI Correspondence Program will train and equip you to be a miracle worker for this end-time harvest of souls.

"Study to show yourself approved unto God, a workman that needs not to be ashamed, rightly dividing the Word of Truth." 2 Timothy 2:15

For More Information:
Visit: www.globalrevival.com
Email: IMI@globalrevival.com
Phone: 850–439–6225

For additional teaching resources
by Dr. Christian Harfouche
please visit us on the web at www.globalrevival.com

or contact:

Global Revival Distribution
421 North Palafox St., Pensacola, Florida 32501
Email: info@globalrevival.com
Order Line: 850–439–9750

MIRACLES | TODAY

Televised five days a week to a potential viewing audience of over five billion people, "Miracles Today" captures the passion and purpose of a global generation finding divine inspiration. Unscripted victories and real-life miracle testimonies... this is Reality Christian Television.

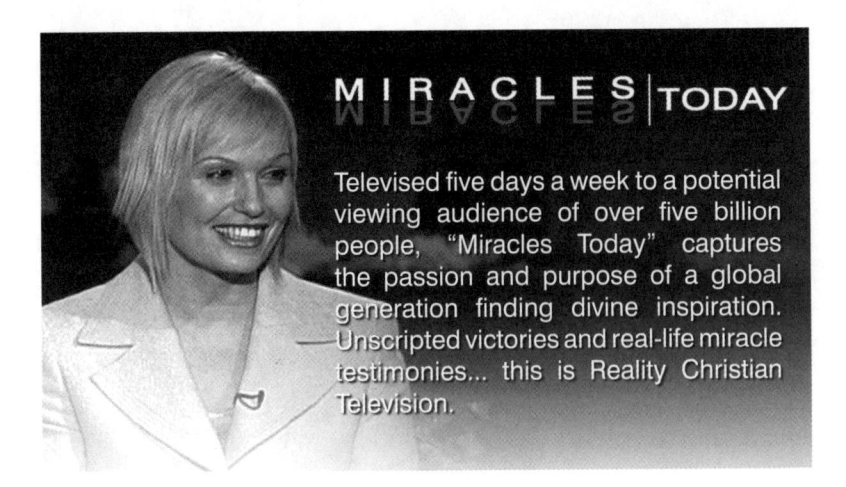

Real people living extraordinary lives – Miracle's Today celebrates the voice of the disciple. Televised daily around the world, Miracles Today captures the passion and purpose of a generation with a divine mandate. Embracing the promises of God and the triumphant walk of faith, Miracle's Today is the celebration of unscripted victories and real life miracle testimonies. Trained and mentored by Drs. Christian and Robin Harfouche, these disciples have answered a global call to broadcast the creative expression of God throughout the Earth. Miracle's Today is God's method of stirring a generation into destiny.

For broadcast times and stations, please visit:

www.globalrevival.com

For further information:
Christian Harfouche Ministries
421 N. Palafox St. • Pensacola, FL 32501

Office: 850–439–6225

Website: www.globalrevival.com
Email: info@globalrevival.com

For prayer: 1–86–Miracle–4
prayer@globalrevival.com